Advanced Raspberry Pi

Raspbian Linux and GPIO Integration

Second Edition

Warren Gay

Apress®

Advanced Raspberry Pi: Raspbian Linux and GPIO Integration

Warren Gay
St. Catharine's, Ontario, Canada

ISBN-13 (pbk): 978-1-4842-3947-6   ISBN-13 (electronic): 978-1-4842-3948-3
https://doi.org/10.1007/978-1-4842-3948-3

Library of Congress Control Number: 2018960398

Managing Director, Apress Media LLC: Welmoed Spahr
Acquisitions Editor: Aaron Black
Development Editor: James Markham
Coordinating Editor: Jessica Vakili

Cover image designed by Freepik (www.freepik.com)

Distributed to the book trade worldwide by Springer Science+Business Media New York, 233 Spring Street, 6th Floor, New York, NY 10013. Phone 1-800-SPRINGER, fax (201) 348-4505, e-mail orders-ny@springer-sbm.com, or visit www.springeronline.com. Apress Media, LLC is a California LLC and the sole member (owner) is Springer Science + Business Media Finance Inc (SSBM Finance Inc). SSBM Finance Inc is a **Delaware** corporation.

For information on translations, please e-mail rights@apress.com, or visit http://www.apress.com/rights-permissions.

Apress titles may be purchased in bulk for academic, corporate, or promotional use. eBook versions and licenses are also available for most titles. For more information, reference our Print and eBook Bulk Sales web page at http://www.apress.com/bulk-sales.

Any source code or other supplementary material referenced by the author in this book is available to readers on GitHub via the book's product page, located at www.apress.com/978-1-4842-3947-6. For more detailed information, please visit http://www.apress.com/source-code.

Printed on acid-free paper

For Jackie.

Table of Contents

About the Author

Warren Gay started out in electronics at an early age, dragging discarded TVs and radios on his way home from public school. In high school he developed a fascination for programming the IBM 1130 computer, which resulted in a career plan change to software development. After attending Ryerson Polytechnic Institute, he has enjoyed a software developer career for over 35 years, programming mainly in C/C++. Warren has been programming Linux since 1994 as an open source contributor and professionally on various Unix platforms since 1987.

Before attending Ryerson, Warren built an Intel 8008 system from scratch before there were CP/M systems and before computers got personal. In later years, Warren earned an advanced amateur radio license (call sign VE3WWG) and worked the amateur radio satellites. A high point of his ham radio hobby was making digital contact with the Mir space station (U2MIR) in 1991.

Warren works at Datablocks.net, an enterprise-class ad serving software services company. There he programs C++ server solutions on Linux back-end systems.

About the Technical Reviewer

Martin Rothwell has followed his interest in computers from an early
age, fascinated by the magic of computers and digital electronics in
general. Self-described as too curious for his own good, he would spend
many of his early years tinkering with the building of computers and the
programming of software. This led naturally to undertaking a degree
in computer science, which was completed in 2007. Since then Martin
has pursued a career in education and is currently employed as a senior
lecturer at The University of Central Lancashire. His thirst for knowledge
and need to satisfy his curious nature have led to a healthy obsession with
maintaining active self-development.

Martin would like to thank the Raspberry Pi Foundation in general for
their efforts and their Pi Academy program for helping to inspire digital
making in schools and hopefully helping more of the current generation of
younger makers to become fascinated, also, by the magic of computing.

CHAPTER 1

The Raspberry Pi

The Raspberry Pi is amazing at two levels—the advanced functionality that you get in a credit card-sized SBC (Single Board Computer) and its price. Even with today's Pi competitors, the Raspberry Pi reigns supreme because few can beat its price. Further, it enjoys great software and community support.

Price is an important advantage of the Pi that competitors don't always appreciate. Hobbyists and makers are applying the Pi in new and sometimes risky ways. Someone starting out doesn't want to lose their SBC because of a rookie mistake. At the low Pi price point, the loss can be absorbed without losing heart. Imagine a student buying an Intel Joule[1] (when it was offered) for $349 USD and toasting it by accident. That would be enough to make most people give up right there! Price allows everyone to proceed fearlessly in their learning.

SBC Inventory

Before considering the details about the resources within the Raspberry Pi, it is useful to take a high-level inventory. In this chapter, let's list what you get when you purchase a Pi.

Within this book, you'll be examining each resource from two perspectives:

- The hardware itself—what it is and how it works

- The driving software and API behind it

© Warren Gay 2018
W. Gay, *Advanced Raspberry Pi*, https://doi.org/10.1007/978-1-4842-3948-3_1

In some cases, the hardware will have one or more kernel modules behind it, forming the device driver layer. They expose a software API that interfaces between the application and the hardware device. For example, applications communicate with the driver by using ioctl(2) calls, while the driver communicates with the I2C devices on the bus. The /sys/class file system is another way that device drivers expose themselves to applications. You'll see this when GPIO (general purpose input/output) is examined in Chapter 12.

There are some cases where drivers don't exist in Raspbian Linux, requiring you to use a "bare metal" approach. An example of this is creating PWM signals using software. By mapping the GPIO registers into the application memory space, the desired result can be obtained directly from the application program. Both direct access and driver access have their advantages and disadvantages.

So while the summary inventory simply lists the hardware devices, you'll be examining each resource in greater detail in the chapters ahead.

Models

The hardware inventory is directly affected by the model of the unit being examined. Several models have been produced over the years, starting with the Model B, followed by the Model A. Since then, several other units have become available and these are summarized in Table 1-1. Much more detail can be seen online.[2]

Table 1-1. *Summary of the Raspberry Pi Models*

Model	Introduced	Price	CPU	SoC	Misc
Model A	Feb 2013	$25	ARMv6Z	BCM2835	32-bit
Model A	Nov 2014	$20	ARMv6Z	BCM2835	32-bit
Model B	April 2012	$35	ARMv6Z	BCM2835	32-bit
	July 2014	$25	ARMv6Z	BCM2835	32-bit
Model B 2	Feb 2015	$35	ARMv7-A	BCM2836	Quad 32-bit
Model B 2 (1.2)	Oct 2016	$35	ARMv8-A	BCM2837	Quad 32/64-bit
Model B 3	Feb 2016	$35	ARMv8-A	BCM2837	Quad 32/64-bit
Model B 3+	Mar 2018	$35	ARMv8-A	BCM2837B0	Quad 32/64-bit
Compute Module 1	Jan 2016	$30	ARMv6Z	BCM2835	32-bit
Compute Module 3	Jan 2017	$30	ARMv8-A	BCM2837	Quad 64-bit
Compute Module 3 Lite	Jan 2017	$25	ARMv8-A	BCM2837	Quad 64-bit
Zero (1.2)	Nov 2015	$5	ARMv6Z	BCM2834	32-bit
Zero (1.3)	May 2016	$5	ARMv6Z	BCM2834	32-bit
Zero W	Feb 2017	$10	ARMv6Z	BCM2834	Wireless 32-bit

Raspberry Pi Model B

Figure 1-1 illustrates a Raspberry Pi Model B, generation 1. This board was released around April 2012 for $35 USD. Notice that it used the large SDHC (secure digital high capacity) card, shown at left in the photo. The socket underneath is illustrated in Figure 1-2. The GPIO strip was a 26-pin header at the time, the same as the Model A that followed. There was also a 4x2 header labeled P5, which had power, ground, and four more GPIO pins.

Figure 1-1. Raspberry Pi Model B (top side), generation 1

The ARM architecture used is ARMv6Z. The single 32-bit core ran at 700 MHz, using 256 MB of SDRAM. In May 2016 this was increased to 512 MB. The board includes 2 USB ports, a 15-pin MIPI camera interface, a LCD MIPI interface, HDMI and RCA composite video outputs, 3.5 mm audio jack, and GPIOs. The network interface consists of a 10/100 Mbit/s Ethernet adapter.

Figure 1-2. *Raspberry Pi Model B (bottom), generation 1*

The power rating was approximately 700 mA (3.5 W) taken from the Micro-USB connector or header strip.

Raspberry Pi 2 Model B

The Raspberry Pi 2 Model B came out February 2015 for $35 USD. This model uses the ARMv7A 32-bit architecture. The main improvement was the support of four CPU (central processing unit) cores, running at 900 MHz. Another improvement was the 1 GB of SDRAM, allowing for larger application mixes. Figure 1-3 illustrates the top side of the pcb, while Figure 1-4 shows the bottom.

Other notable changes included the Raspberry Pi standardized 40-pin header strip for GPIO. Four USB ports were provided and the mounting holes were moved on the pcb (printed circuit board).

Figure 1-3. *The top side of the Raspberry Pi 2 Model B*

The board also uses the Micro-SDHC slot for file storage. Figure 1-3 shows it sticking out from under the pcb at the middle left. Power consumption drops to 220 mA when idle (1.1 W) but jumps up to 820 mA (4.1 W) under stress. This required a larger power adapter to properly feed the unit.

Figure 1-4. *The bottom side of the Raspberry Pi 2 Model B*

Raspberry Pi 3 Model B

February 2016 brought with it the arrival of the Raspberry Pi 3 Model B, again for $35 USD. This offered the ARMv8-A 64/32-bit architecture. The quad cores ran at a brisk 1.2 GHz with the provided 1 GB of SDRAM. Another gift was the addition of IEEE 802.11n-2009 wireless support and Bluetooth 4.1. Figure 1-5 illustrates the top side of the pcb while Figure 1-6 shows the bottom.

Power consumption is 300 mA (1.5 W) when idle but increases to 1.34 A (6.7 W) under stress. The figures show a heat sink added to the CPU, which is not included. Adding the heat sink prevents the core from reducing the clock speed to regulate the temperature.

Figure 1-5. Top side of Raspberry Pi 3 Model B

Figure 1-6. Bottom side of Raspberry Pi 3 Model B

Raspberry Pi 3 Model B+

This model arrived in March 2018, again for the great price of $35 USD. It is a *64-bit*, 1.4 GHz quad core, with 1 GB of SDRAM. The network port supports 10/100/1000 Mbits/s Ethernet, although the top speed is limited to about 300 Mbit/s because of its internal use of the USB hub. The wireless support now included 802.11ac for dual band 2.4/5 GHz operation. Bluetooth was upgraded to Bluetooth 4.2 LS BLE.

Power consumption is 459 mA (2.295 W) at idle and increases to 1.13 A (5.661 W) under full stress. Notice the metal cap on the CPU chip in Figure 1-7. This helps to dissipate the heat without requiring a heat sink (although it may still be beneficial to use one). The underside of the pcb is shown in Figure 1-8.

Figure 1-7. *Top side of Raspberry Pi 3 Model B+*

Figure 1-8. Bottom side of Raspberry Pi 3 Model B+

Raspberry Pi Zero

Not every maker project requires the full resources of a 64-bit quad core and 1 GB of SDRAM. The first Raspberry Pi Zero came out in November 2015 and later upgraded in May 2016. At a unit price of $5 USD, it makes an ideal SBC for many small projects.

The Zero is an ARMv6Z architecture (32-bit) device and runs the single core at 1 GHz. SDRAM is limited at 512 MB, which is still very sufficient for most projects. The first Zeros lacked the MIPI camera interface, which was added in the 2016 revision.

To save on cost, there is no soldered header strip or connector. There are also marked points on the pcb for the composite video, should the end user need it. The HDMI output is provided through a Mini-HDMI connector and the stereo audio is provided via PWM (Pulse Width

Modulation) GPIO. There is also no wired Ethernet port on the Zero. It can be provided by using the one Micro-USB port and an Ethernet adapter.

The power is provided through the other Micro-USB connecter, and the consumption at idle is 100 mA (0.5 W), and 350 mA (1.75 W) under stress. Figures 1-9 and 1-10 illustrate the Raspberry Pi Zero and the Raspberry Pi Zero W.

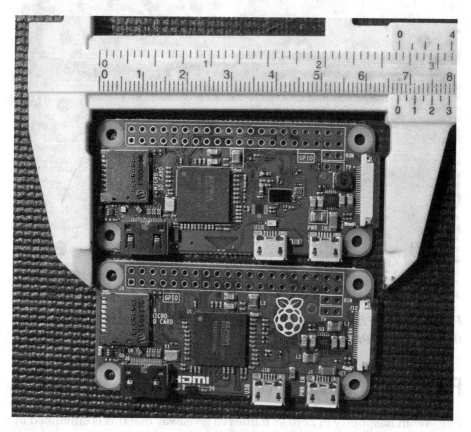

Figure 1-9. *The top side of the Raspberry Pi Zero (at bottom) and the Raspberry Pi Zero W (at top)*

11

Figure 1-10. *The bottom side of the Raspberry Pi Zero (bottom) and the Raspberry Pi Zero W (at top)*

Raspberry Pi Zero W

The "W" in Raspberry Pi Zero W name is a giveaway that this is enhanced by the wireless capability, over the Zero. It is priced at $10 USD. The wireless standards supported are 802.11n and Bluetooth 4.1. Like the Zero, the Zero W has no wired Ethernet connector and only one Micro-USB port (the other is used for power only). Having the WIFI (WIFI is a trademark of the Wi-Fi Alliance) access greatly increases the device's communication versatility.

Which Model?

The question that naturally arises is "which model to buy?" The answer is much like buying a car—it depends. If you are looking for a cheap computer that you can attach keyboard, mouse, and monitor to, then buy the most powerful device, like the Raspberry Pi 3 Model B+. Another class of project involving AI (artificial intelligence) or video recognition is another case for powerful hardware.

For building something that must weather outside and take photos of birds in a nest, then the Raspberry Pi Zero W with WIFI connectivity seems appropriate. There are perhaps other projects that don't require network access at all, where the lowest price like the Zero applies. The best news is that you have a wide range of choices at low prices.

CHAPTER 2

Preparation

While it is assumed that you've already started with the Raspberry Pi, there may be a few more things that you want to do before working through the rest of this book. For example, if you normally use a laptop or desktop computer, you may prefer to access your Pi from there.

If you plan to do most or all of the projects in this book, I highly recommend using something like the Adafruit Pi T-Cobbler (covered later in this chapter). This hardware breaks out the GPIO lines in a way that you can access on a breadboard.

Static IP Address

The standard Raspbian image provides a capable Linux system, which when plugged into a network, uses DHCP (dynamic host configuration protocol) to automatically assign an IP address to it. If you'd like to connect to it remotely from a desktop or laptop, then the dynamic IP address that DHCP assigns is problematic.

There are downloadable Windows programs for scanning the network. If you are using a Linux or Mac host, you can use nmap to scan for it. The following is an example session from a Devuan Linux, using the nmap command. Here a range of IP addresses are scanned from 1–250:

```
root@devuan:~# nmap -sP 192.168.1.1-250
```

© Warren Gay 2018
W. Gay, *Advanced Raspberry Pi*, https://doi.org/10.1007/978-1-4842-3948-3_2

```
Starting Nmap 6.47 ( http://nmap.org ) at 2018-06-01 19:59 EDT
Nmap scan report for 192.168.1.1
Host is up (0.00026s latency).
MAC Address: C0:FF:D4:95:80:04 (Unknown)
Nmap scan report for 192.168.1.2
Host is up (0.044s latency).
MAC Address: 00:1B:A9:BD:79:02 (Brother Industries)
Nmap scan report for 192.168.1.77
Host is up (0.15s latency).
MAC Address: B8:27:EB:ED:48:B1 (Raspberry Pi Foundation)
Nmap scan report for 192.168.1.121
Host is up (0.00027s latency).
MAC Address: 40:6C:8F:11:B8:AE (Apple)
Nmap scan report for 192.168.1.80
Host is up.
Nmap done: 250 IP addresses (4 hosts up) scanned in 7.54
seconds
root@devuan:~#
```

In this example, the Raspberry Pi is identified on 192.168.1.77, complete with its MAC address (these appear above the line where "Raspberry Pi Foundation" is reported). While this discovery approach works, it does takes time and is inconvenient.

If you'd prefer to change your Raspberry Pi to use a static IP address, see the "Wired Ethernet" section in Chapter 8 for instructions.

Using SSH

If you know the IP address of your Raspberry Pi, discovered it with nmap, or have the name registered in your hosts file, you can log into it using SSH. In this example, we log in as user pi on a host 192.168.1.77 from a Devuan Linux box:

```
$ ssh pi@192.168.1.77
pi@192.168.1.77's password:
Linux raspberrypi 4.14.34-v7+ #1110 SMP Mon Apr 16 15:18:51 BST
2018 armv7l
```

The programs included with the Debian GNU/Linux system are free software;
the exact distribution terms for each program are described in the individual files in /usr/share/doc/*/copyright.

Debian GNU/Linux comes with ABSOLUTELY NO WARRANTY, to the extent permitted by applicable law.
Last login: Fri Jun 1 20:07:24 2018 from 192.168.1.80
$

Files can also be copied to and from the Raspberry Pi, using the scp command. Do a man scp on the Raspberry Pi for usage information.

It is also possible to display X Window System (X-Window) graphics on your laptop/desktop, if there is an X-Window server running on it. (Windows users can use Cygwin for this, available from www.cygwin.com.) Using Linux as an example, first configure the security of your X-Window server to allow requests. Here I'll take the lazy approach of allowing all hosts by using the xhost command (on a Linux box that is not a Pi, or is another Pi):

```
$ xhost +
access control disabled, clients can connect from any host
$
```

Now log into the remote Pi using ssh with the -Y option:

```
$ ssh pi@192.168.1.77 -Y
pi@192.168.1.77's password:
Warning: No xauth data; using fake authentication data for X11
forwarding.
Linux raspberrypi 4.14.34-v7+ #1110 SMP Mon Apr 16 15:18:51 BST
2018 armv7l

The programs included with the Debian GNU/Linux system are free
software;
the exact distribution terms for each program are described in
the individual files in /usr/share/doc/*/copyright.

Debian GNU/Linux comes with ABSOLUTELY NO WARRANTY, to the
extent permitted by applicable law.
Last login: Fri Jun  1 20:14:40 2018 from 192.168.1.80
$
```

From the Raspberry Pi session, we can launch xpdf so that it opens a window on the local Linux box:

```
$ xpdf &
```

If that fails, try exporting a DISPLAY variable on the remote (pi) to inform the software where the X-Window server and screen exist:

```
$ export DISPLAY=192.168.1.80:0
```

Here, I've specified the Devuan Linux address (alternatively, an /etc/ hosts name could be used) and pointed the Raspberry Pi to use Linux's display number :0. We run the xpdf command in the background so that we can continue to issue commands in the current SSH session. In the meantime, the xpdf window will open on the Linux screen, while the xpdf program runs on the Raspberry Pi.

This doesn't give you graphical access to the Pi's *desktop*, but for developers, SSH is often adequate. If you want remote graphical access to the Raspberry's desktop, one option is to use VNC.

VNC

If you're already using a laptop or your favorite desktop computer, you can conveniently access your Raspberry Pi's graphical desktop over the network. Once the Raspberry Pi's VNC server is configured, all you need is a VNC client on your accessing computer. This eliminates the need for a keyboard, mouse, and HDMI display device connected to the Raspberry Pi. In other words, you can run the Pi "headless."

Getting VNC working requires a bit of setup. Raspbian Linux has taken measures to make it easy. If not set up correctly, the VNC viewer will just provide a black screen when you try to log in.

To use VNC, you must have the desktop software installed (GUI). This will also make it easier for you to get it configured. If you have a Raspbian *Lite* distribution installed, it will *not* include the necessary desktop server software.

Start up the graphical desktop, then from the Raspberry icon (at top left), pull down the menu and select "Preferences," and choose "Raspberry Pi Configuration." That should bring up a dialog box like the one in shown in Figure 2-1.

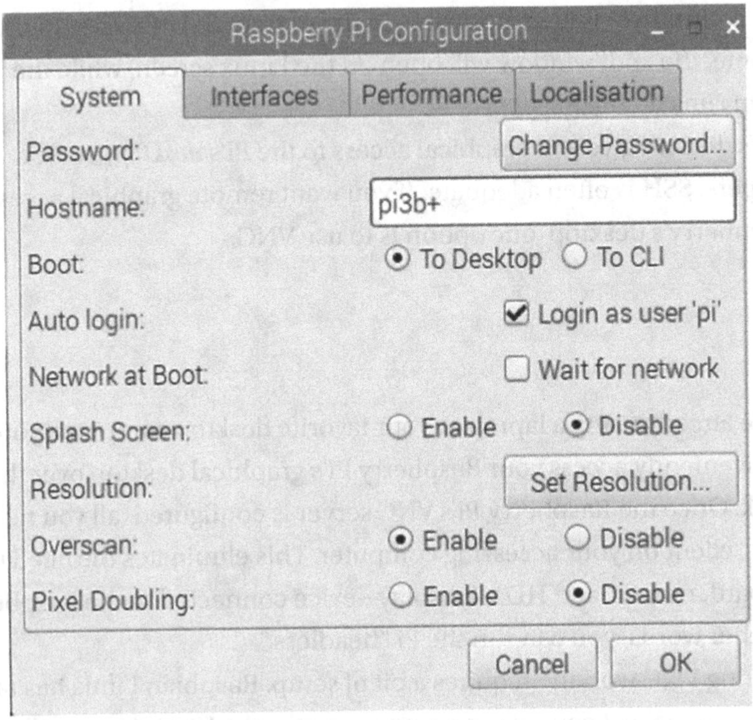

Figure 2-1. Raspberry Pi Configuration dialog. Note how the Boot: selection has the radio button "To Desktop" checked.

You may already have the "Boot" option set to "To Desktop" but otherwise click that now. This will cause the desktop software to start after a boot so that you can connect to it through VNC.

After you have configured the desktop to start after a reboot, you also need to enable the VNC server as shown in Figure 2-2, by clicking on the "Interfaces" tab.

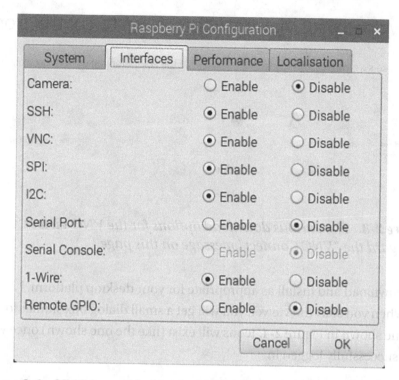

Figure 2-2. *VNC is enabled in the Interfaces tab of the dialog box*

In the Interfaces dialog, click the VNC radio button labeled "Enable." Click OK at the bottom right to save your settings. Then reboot your Pi. Allow time for a reboot and for the graphic desktop to start.

VNC Viewers

To access the VNC server, a corresponding VNC *viewer* is needed on the client side. One solution is to use the free realvnc viewer from:

```
https://www.realvnc.com/en/connect/download/viewer/
```

From that website, you'll find download links for your favorite desktop, as depicted in Figure 2-3. Ignore the site's reference to "VNC Connect."

Download VNC Viewer to the device to control from

Make sure you've downloaded VNC Connect to the computer you want to control.

Figure 2-3. *The various download options for the VNC Viewer. Disregard the "VNC Connect" message on this page.*

Download and install as appropriate for your desktop platform.

When you start the viewer, you will get a small dialog box similar to the one shown in Figure 2-4. Icons will exist (like the one shown) once you have successfully logged in.

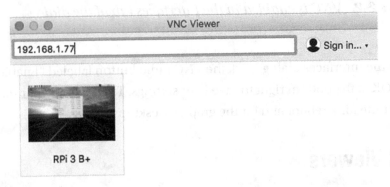

Figure 2-4. *The inital VNC Viewer dialog and one previously used icon for login*

Once you have successfully connected and logged in, you should have your Pi desktop displayed for you. Figure 2-5 illustrates a desktop window (on a Mac).

Figure 2-5. *A connected Raspberry Pi VNC session on a Mac*

If your VNC viewer connects and seems to hang, be patient. The rate of your VNC screen updates will depend upon the ability of your network to transfer that graphic data. I found that I was able to use VNC with the Pi 3 B+ using a WIFI connection, without too much delay.

While the VNC facility is great for providing remote graphical desktop access, it probably goes without saying that the performance won't be suitable for viewing video or fast action games.

Black VNC Screen

If you change the configuration of the Pi to boot to command-line mode (see Figure 2-1 button "To CLI") instead of the desktop, you will experience a black screen when you use VNC Viewer (see Figure 2-6). Selecting command-line mode causes the desktop software not to run, even though you may have VNC enabled (Figure 2-2 "Enable").

Figure 2-6. *A black VNC Viewer screen indicates that the desktop software is not running*

To regain VNC desktop access, you must change the configuration to "To Desktop" (Figure 2-1), and reboot. The alternative is to go to the command line (console or ssh) and start the X server manually. From the console login, simply do:

```
$ startx
```

From an ssh session, you'll need to be root (using sudo):

```
$ sudo -i
root@pi3bplus:~# startx
```

After giving the server software time to start up, the VNC Viewer should be able to attach to your desktop. Of course, if you log that ssh session out, the server will also exit and terminate desktop access.

Breadboard Setup

It is possible to work without a breadboard and Pi T-Cobbler adapter, but you will find that experiments are much more fun with a quality breadboard and adapter. A recommended T-Cobbler can be purchased from Adafruit ® and is illustrated in Figure 2-7 alongside a cheap copy.

https://www.adafruit.com/product/2028

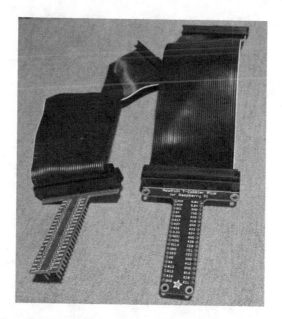

Figure 2-7. *Two Pi T-Cobbler breadboard adapters. Notice how the unit from China (left) requires a cable twist. The Adafruit unit (right) is recommended.*

Summary

With these details out of the way, the remainder of the book can focus on the various resources that the Raspberry Pi has to offer. The Pi has much to offer, so let's get started.

CHAPTER 3

Power

One of the most frequently neglected parts of a system tends to be the power supply—at least when everything is working. Only when things go wrong does the power supply begin to get some scrutiny.

The Raspberry Pi owner needs to give the power supply extra respect. Unlike many AVR class boards, where the raw input voltage is followed by an onboard 5 V regulator, the Pi expects its power to be regulated at the input. The Pi does include onboard regulators, but these regulate to lower voltages (3.3 V and lower).

Figure 3-1 illustrates the rather fragile Micro-USB power input connector. The original model B has a large round capacitor directly behind the connector that is often grabbed for leverage. Avoid doing that, since many have reported "popping it off" by accident.

Figure 3-1. *Micro-USB power input*

© Warren Gay 2018
W. Gay, *Advanced Raspberry Pi*, https://doi.org/10.1007/978-1-4842-3948-3_3

Over the years since the original Model B, other models have been produced without the large capacitor. But they all use the fragile Micro-USB power input like the one in shown in Figure 3-1. Use care and be gentle when inserting the power connector.

Calculating Power

Sometimes power supplies are specified in terms of voltage and power handling capability in watts. The Pi's input voltage of 5 V must support varying input currents according to the model being used. Table 3-1 summarizes the model power requirement minimums.

Table 3-1. Summary of Raspberry Pi Minimum Power Requirements

Model	Minimum Current	Power
Pi Model B	700 mA	3.5 W
Pi 2 Model B	820 mA	4.1 W
Pi 3 Model B	1.34 A	6.7 W
Pi 3 Model B+	1.13 A	5.65 W
Pi Zero and W	350 mA	1.75 W

Let's verify a power supply figure for the Raspberry Pi 3 Model B+ in watts (this does not include any added peripherals):

$$P = V \times I$$
$$= 5 \times 1.13$$
$$= 5.65W$$

The 5.65 W represents a minimum requirement, so we should overprovision this by an additional 50%:

$$P = 5.65 \times 1.50$$
$$= 8.475W$$

The additional 50% yields a power requirement of approximately 8.5 W.

Tip   Allow 50% extra capacity for your power supply. A power supply gone bad may cause damage or several other problems. One common power-related problem for the Pi is loss of data on the SD card.

Current Requirement

Since the power supply being sought produces one output voltage (5 V), you might see power adapters with advertised *current* ratings instead of power. In this case, you can simply factor a 50% additional current instead (for the Pi 3 Model B+):

$$I_{supply} = I_{pi} \times 1.50$$
$$= 1.13 \times 1.50$$
$$= 1.695A$$

To double-check our work, let's see whether this agrees with the power rating we computed earlier:

$$P = V \times I$$
$$= 5 \times 1.695$$
$$= 8.475W$$

The result agrees. From this evaluation, you can conclude that you *minimally* need a 5 V supply that produces one of the following:

- 8.475 W or more

- 1.695 A or more (ignoring peripherals)

Supplies that can meet either requirement should be sufficient. However, you should be aware that not all advertised ratings are what they seem. Cheap supplies often fail to meet their own claims, so an additional margin must always be factored in.

Peripheral Power

Each additional circuit that draws power, especially USB peripherals, must be considered in a power budget. Depending on its type, a given USB peripheral plugged into a USB 2 port can expect up to 500 mA of current, assuming it can obtain it.

Wireless adapters are known to be power hungry. Don't forget about the keyboard and mouse when used, since they also add to power consumption. If you've attached an RS-232 level shifter circuit (perhaps using MAX232CPE), you should budget for that small amount also in the 3.3 V supply budget. This will indirectly add to your +5 V budget, since the 3.3 V regulator is powered from it. (The USB ports use the +5 V supply.) Anything that draws power from your Raspberry Pi should be tallied.

3.3 Volt Power

The input to the Raspberry Pi is a regulated 5 volts. But the Pi itself depends upon a 3.3 V supply, which is provided by an onboard regulator. The onboard regulators may provide additional lower voltages for other support ICs, depending upon the model. Because the 3.3 V supply is indirectly derived from the input 5 V supply, the maximum excess current for the original Model B that can be drawn from it is 50 mA; the Pi uses up the remaining capacity of the regulator.

When planning a design, you need to budget this 3.3 V supply carefully. Each GPIO output pin draws from this power source an additional 3 to 16 mA, depending on how it is used. Projects that have higher current budgets may need to include their own 3.3 V regulator, fed from the input 5 V input instead.

Powered USB Hubs

If your power budget is stretched by USB peripherals, you may want to consider the use of a *powered* USB hub. In this way, the *hub* rather than your Raspberry Pi provides the necessary power to the downstream peripherals.

Not all USB hubs work with (Raspbian) Linux. The kernel needs to cooperate with connected USB hubs, so software support is critical. The following web page lists known working USB hubs:

```
http://elinux.org/RPi_Powered_USB_Hubs
```

Power Adapters

For the high current quad core models of the Raspberry Pi, you'll simply want to purchase a proper adapter. Don't mess around with cheap or inferior supplies for your high-performance gear.

For the low power Pi's, like old Model B, the Zero, or Zero W, you might be tempted to try some cheaper solutions. Let's examine some of the options.

An Unsuitable Supply

The example shown in Figure 3-2 was purchased on eBay for $1.18 with free shipping (see the upcoming warning about fakes). For this reason, it is tempting to use it.

31

Figure 3-2. *Model A1265 Apple adapter*

This is an adapter/charger with the following ratings:

- *Model*: A1265

- *Input*: 100–240 VAC

- *Output*: 5 V, 1 A

When plugged in, the Raspberry Pi's power LED immediately lights up, which is a good sign for an adapter (vs. a charger). A fast rise time on the power leads to successful power-on resets. When the voltage was measured, the reading was +4.88 V on the +5 V supply. While not ideal, it is within the range of acceptable voltages. (The voltage should be within 10% of +5 V — 4.75 and 5.25 V.)

The Apple unit seemed to work fairly well when HDMI graphics were *not* being utilized (using serial console, SSH, or VNC). However, I found that when HDMI was used and the GPU had work to do (move a window across the desktop, for example), the system would tend to seize up. This clearly indicates that the adapter does not fully deliver or regulate well enough.

Caution   Be very careful of counterfeit Apple chargers/adapters. The Raspberry Pi Foundation has seen returned units damaged by these. For a video and further information, see www.raspberrypi.org/ archives/2151.

E-book Adapters

Some people have reported success using e-book power adapters. I have also successfully used a 2 A Kobo charger.

Power Source Quality

While it is possible to buy USB power adapters at low prices, it is wiser to spend more on a high-quality unit. It is not worth trashing your Raspberry Pi or experience random failures for the sake of saving a few dollars.

If you lack an oscilloscope, you won't be able to check how clean or dirty your supply current is. A better power adapter is cheaper than an oscilloscope. A shaky/noisy power supply can lead to all kinds of obscure and intermittent problems.

A good place to start is to simply Google "recommended power supply Raspberry Pi." Do your research and include your USB peripherals in the power budget. Remember that wireless USB adapters consume a lot of current—up to 500 mA.

Note   A random Internet survey reveals a range of 330 mA to 480 mA for wireless USB adapter current consumption.

Voltage Test

If you have a DMM (digital multimeter), it is worthwhile to perform a test after powering up the Pi. This is probably the very first thing you should do if you are experiencing problems.

Follow these steps to perform a voltage test (the now standardized 40-pin header strip is assumed for pin numbering):

1. Plug the Raspberry Pi's Micro-USB port into the power adapter's USB port.

2. Plug in the power adapter.

3. Measure the voltage between P1-02 (+5 V) and P1-39 or P1-06 (Ground): expect +4.75 to +5.25 V.

4. Measure the voltage between P1-01 (+3.3 V) and P1-39 or P1-06 (Ground): expect +3.135 to +3.465 V.

Caution   Be very careful with your multimeter probes around the pins of P1. *Be especially careful not to short the +5 V to the +3.3 V pin*, even for a fraction of a second. Doing so will zap your Pi! Use Dupont wires for safety.

Figure 3-3 illustrates the testing of the +5 V supply on the Raspberry Pi 3 Model B+. Notice the use of a red Dupont wire on the header strip for the +5V supply (pin P1-02). A blue Dupont wire attaches to the ground connection.

Figure 3-3. *Testing the +5V supply for the Raspberry Pi 3 Model B+*

Figure 3-4 likewise illustrates the measuring of the regulated 3.3 V supply from the onboard regulator of the Pi. The red Dupont wire in this figure is attached to P1-01 where the regulated output appears.

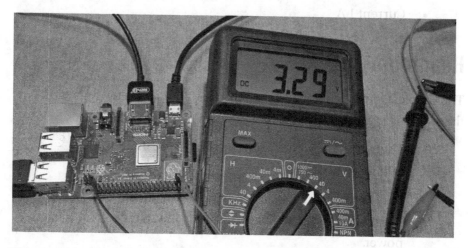

Figure 3-4. *Testing the +3.3 V supply for the Raspberry Pi 3 B+*

Appendix B lists the ATX power supply standard voltage levels, which include +5 ± 0.25 V and +3.3 ± 0.165 V as a comparison guide.

Battery Power

Because of the small size of the Raspberry Pi, it may be desirable to run it from battery power (especially for the Zero or Zero W). Doing so requires a regulator and some careful planning. To meet the Raspberry Pi requirements, you must form a power budget. Once you know your maximum current requirement, you can flesh out the rest. The following example assumes that 1 A is required.

Requirements

For clarity, let's list the power requirements that the battery supply must somehow meet:

- Voltage 5 V, within ± 0.25 V
- Current 1 A

Headroom

The simplest approach is to use the linear LM7805 as the 5 V regulator. But there are disadvantages to this approach:

- There must be some headroom above the input voltage (about 2 V).
- Allowing too much headroom increases the power dissipation in the regulator, resulting in *wasted* battery power.
- A lower maximum output current might also result.

Your batteries should provide a minimum input of 5+2 V (7 V). Any lower input voltage to the regulator will result in the regulator "dropping out" and dipping below 5 V. Clearly, a 6 V battery input will not do.

LM7805 Regulation

Figure 3-5 shows a very simple battery circuit using the LM7805 linear regulator. The battery supply goes into V_{IN} with the regulated output of +5 V coming out of pin 1 at the right.

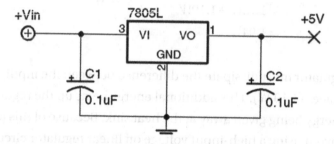

Figure 3-5. *Battery regulator circuit using the LM7805 regulator chip*

An 8.4 V battery supply can be formed from seven NiCad cells in series, each producing 1.2 V. The 8.4 V input allows the battery to drop to a low of 7 V before the minimum headroom of 2 V is violated.

Depending on the exact 7805 regulator part chosen, a typical heat-sinked parameter set might be as follows:

- *Input voltage*: 7–25 V

- *Output voltage*: 1.5 A (heat-sinked)

- *Operating temperature*: 125°C

Be sure to use a heat sink on the regulator so that it can dissipate heat energy to the surrounding air. Without one, the regulator can enter a thermal shutdown state, reducing current flow to prevent damage. When this happens, the output voltage will drop below +5 V.

Keep in mind that the amount of power dissipated by the battery is more than that received by the load. If we assume that the Raspberry Pi Zero is consuming 350 mA, a minimum of 350 mA is also drawn from the battery through the regulator (and this could be slightly more). Realize that the regulator is dissipating additional energy because of its higher input voltage. The total power dissipated by the regulator (P_R) and the load (P_L) is as follows:

$$P_d = P_L \times P_R$$
$$= 5V \times 0.350A + (8.4V - 5V) \times 0.350A$$
$$= 1.75W + 1.19W$$
$$= 1.94W$$

The regulator must dissipate the difference between the input and the output voltages (1.19 W). This additional energy heats up the regulator with the energy being given away at the heat sink. Because of this problem, designers avoid using a high-input voltage on linear regulator circuits.

If the regulator is rated at a maximum of 1.5 A at 7 V (input), the power maximum for the regulator is about 10.5 W. If we apply an input voltage of 8.4 V instead of 7, we can derive what our 5 V maximum current will be:

$$I_{max} = \frac{P_{max}}{V_{in}}$$
$$= \frac{10.5W}{8.4V}$$
$$= 1.25A$$

From this, we find that the 8.4 V battery regulator circuit can provide a maximum of 1.25 A at the output, without exceeding the regulator's power rating. Multiply 8.4 V by 1.25 A to convince yourself that this equals 10.5 W.

DC-DC Buck Converter

If the application is designed for data acquisition, for example, it is desirable to have it run as long as possible on a given set of batteries or charge cycle. A switching regulator may be more suitable than the linear regulator because of its greater efficiency.

Figure 3-6 shows a very small pcb that is about 1.5 SD cards in length. This unit was purchased from eBay for $1.40, with free shipping. At these prices, why would you build one?

Figure 3-6. *DC-DC buck converter*

They are also simple to use. The converter provides + and – input connections and + and – output connections. Feed power in at one voltage and get power out at another voltage.

But don't immediately wire it up to your Raspberry Pi, until you have calibrated the output voltage. While it *might* come precalibrated for 5 V, it is best not to count on it. If the unit produces a higher voltage, you might fry the Pi.

The regulated output voltage is easily adjusted by a multiturn trim pot on the pcb. Adjust the pot while you read your DMM.

The specifications for the unit I purchased are provided in Table 3-2 for your general amusement. Notice the wide range of input voltages and the fact that it operates at a temperature as low as –40°C. The wide range of input voltages and current up to 3 A clearly makes this a great device to attach to solar panels that might vary widely in voltage.

Table 3-2.   *DC-DC Buck Converter Specifications*

Parameter	Min	Max	Units	Parameter	Min	Max	Units
Input voltage	4.00	35.0	Volts	Output ripple		30.9	mA
Input current		3.0	Amps	Load regulation	±0.5	%	
Output voltage	1.23	30.0	Volts	Voltage regulation	±2.5	%	
Conversion efficiency		92	%	Working temperature	–40	+85	°C
Switching frequency		150	kHz	PCB size		45×20×12	mm
				Net weight		10	g

The specification claims up to a 92% conversion efficiency. Using 15 V on the input, I performed my own little experiment with measurements. With the unit adjusted to produce 5.1 V at the output, the readings shown in Table 3-3 were taken.

Table 3-3.   *Readings Taken from Experiment*

Parameter	Input	Output	Units
Voltage	15.13	5.10	Volts
Current	0.190	0.410	Amps
Power	2.87	2.09	Watts

From the table we expected to see more power used on the input side (2.87 W). The power used on the output side was 2.09 W. The efficiency then becomes a matter of division:

$$\frac{2.09}{2.87} = 0.728$$

From this we can conclude that the measured conversion efficiency was about 72.8%.

How well could we have done if we used the LM7805 regulator? The following is a best case estimate, since I don't have an actual current reading for that scenario. But we do know that at least as much current that flows out of the regulator must flow into it (likely more). So what is the absolute best that the LM7805 regulator could theoretically do? Let's apply the same current draw of 410 mA for the Raspberry Pi at 5.10 V, as shown in Table 3-4. (This was operating without HDMI output in use.)

Table 3-4. *Hypothetical LM7805 Power Use*

Parameter	Input	Output	Units
Voltage	7.1	5.10	Volts
Current	0.410	0.410	Amps
Power	2.91	2.09	Watts

The power efficiency for this best case scenario amounts to this:

$$\frac{2.09}{2.91} = 0.718$$

The absolute best case efficiency for the LM7805 regulator is 71.8%. But this is achieved at its *optimal input* voltage. Increasing the input voltage to 12 V causes the power dissipation to rise considerably, resulting in a 42.5% efficiency (this calculation is left to the reader as an exercise). Attempting to operate the LM7805 regulator at 15.13 V, as we did with the buck converter, would cause the efficiency to drop to less than 33.7%. Clearly, the buck converter is much more efficient at converting power from a higher voltage source.

Signs of Insufficient Power

In the forums, it has been reported that ping sometimes doesn't work from the desktop (with HDMI), yet works OK in console mode. Additionally, I have seen that desktop windows can freeze if you move them (HDMI). As you start to move the terminal window, for example, the motion would freeze part way through, as if the mouse stopped working.

These are signs of the Raspberry Pi being power starved. The GPU consumes more power when it is active, performing accelerated graphics. Either the desktop freezes (GPU starvation) or the network interface fails (ping). There may be other symptoms related to HDMI activity.

Another problem that has been reported is resetting of the Raspberry Pi shortly after starting to boot. The board starts to consume more power as the kernel boots up, which can result in the Pi being starved.[3]

If you lose your Ethernet connection when you plug in a USB device, this too may be a sign of insufficient power.[4]

While it may seem that a 1 A power supply should be enough to supply a 700 mA Raspberry Pi, you will be better off using a 2 A supply instead. Many power supplies simply don't deliver their full advertised ratings.

The Micro-USB cable is something else to suspect. Some are manufactured with thin conductors that can result in a significant voltage drop. Measuring the voltage as shown previously in the "Voltage Test" section may help diagnose that. Try a higher-quality cable to see whether there is an improvement.

Summary

This chapter has been a brief introduction to some of the power issues that you may encounter in your work with the Raspberry Pi. You should now be prepared to make informed choices about power adapters or battery supply options.

CHAPTER 4

LEDs and Header Strips

This chapter introduces the Raspberry Pi LEDs and header strips. These are important interfaces from the Pi to the outside world. You may want to use a bookmark for Table 4-5, which outlines the GPIO (general purpose input/output) pins on the modern header strip P1.

Status LEDs

The Raspberry Pi has different sets of LED indicators, depending upon the model. Table 4-1 provides an overall reference chart.[5] The Raspberry Pi Zero and Zero W have been lumped together.

Table 4-1. *Table of Raspberry Pi LED Indicators*

LED	Color	A	A+	B	B+	Pi 2	Pi 3	Zero/W
OK/ACT	Green	Yes	Yes	Yes	Yes	Yes	Yes	Yes
PWR	Red	Yes	Yes	Yes	Yes	Yes	Yes	No
FDX	Green	No	No	Yes	Yes	Jack	Jack	No
LINK	Green	No	No	Yes	Jack	Jack	Jack	No
10M/100	Yellow	No	No	Yes	No	No	No	No

© Warren Gay 2018
W. Gay, *Advanced Raspberry Pi*, https://doi.org/10.1007/978-1-4842-3948-3_4

OK/ACT LED

This is the SD (secure digital) card activity indicator.

PWR LED

On the original Model B and the following Model A, this LED was wired to the 3.3 V regulator and indicated that the regulator had power. In later models, this LED will flash when the input power falls below 4.63 V.

FDX LED

This indicates that the network is full duplex connected.

LINK LED

The LINK LED indicates if there is network activity on the LAN (local area network).

10M/100 LED

This yellow LED indicates when the network is operating at 100 Mbit/s.

Original Header P1

The original Raspberry Pi models A and B used a 13 x 2 header strip identified as P1, which exposes the GPIO pins. This includes the I2C, SPI, and UART peripherals as well as power connections. Table 4-2 lists the connections for this older header strip.

Table 4-2. Original Pi GPIO Header Connector P1 (Top View)

Lower Left	Pins		Upper Left
3.3 V power	P1-01	P1-02	5 V power
GPIO 0 (I2C0 SDA)+*R1=1.8k*	P1-03	P1-04	5 V power
GPIO 1 (I2C0 SCL)+*R2=1.8k*	P1-05	P1-06	Ground
GPIO 4 (GPCLK 0/1-Wire)	P1-07	P1-08	GPIO 14 (TXD)
Ground	P1-09	P1-10	GPIO 15 (RXD)
GPIO 17	P1-11	P1-12	GPIO 18 (PCM_CLK)
GPIO 21 (PCM_DOUT)	P1-13	P1-14	Ground
GPIO 22	P1-15	P1-16	GPIO 23
3.3 V power	P1-17	P1-18	GPIO 24
GPIO 10 (MOSI)	P1-19	P1-20	Ground
GPIO 9 (MISO)	P1-21	P1-22	GPIO 25
GPIO 11 (SCKL)	P1-23	P1-24	GPIO 8 (CE0)
Ground	P1-25	P1-26	GPIO 7 (CE1)

Revised GPIO Header P1

Table 4-3 illustrates the revisions made to the original a 13 x 2 header strip P1. Notice that the I2C peripheral changed from I2C0 to I2C1.

47

Table 4-3. *Revised Original Pi GPIO Header Connector P1 (Top View)*

Lower Left	Pins		Upper Left
3.3 V power, 50 mA max	P1-01	P1-02	5 V power
GPIO 2 (I2C1 SDA1)+R1=1.8k	P1-03	P1-04	*5 V power*
GPIO 3 (I2C1 SCL1)+R2=1.8k	P1-05	P1-06	Ground
GPIO 4 (GPCLK 0/1-Wire)	P1-07	P1-08	GPIO 14 (TXD0)
Ground	P1-09	P1-10	GPIO 15 (RXD0)
GPIO 17 (GEN0)	P1-11	P1-12	GPIO 18 (PCM_CLK/GEN1)
GPIO 27 (GEN2)	P1-13	P1-14	*Ground*
GPIO 22 (GEN3)	P1-15	P1-16	GPIO 23 (GEN4)
3.3 V power, 50 mA max	P1-17	P1-18	GPIO 24 (GEN5)
GPIO 10 (SPI_MOSI)	P1-19	P1-20	*Ground*
GPIO 9 (SPI_MISO)	P1-21	P1-22	GPIO 25 (GEN6))
GPIO 11 (SPI_SCKL)	P1-23	P1-24	GPIO 8 (CE0_N)
Ground	P1-25	P1-26	GPIO 7 (CE1_N)

Older models that had the P1 connector in Table 4-3 also had the P5 header shown vin Table 4-4.

Table 4-4. *Rev 2.0 P5 Header (Top View)*

Lower Left	Pins		Upper Left
(Square) 5 V	P5-01	P5-02	3.3 V, 50 mA
GPIO 28	P5-03	P5-04	GPIO 29
GPIO 30	P5-05	P5-06	GPIO 31
Ground	P5-07	P5-08	Ground

Revision 2.0 GPIO Header P1

Starting with the Model B+ and A+, the GPIO header was standardized to use a 40-pin (20 x 2) header. GPIO pins ID_SD (GPIO0, P1-27) and ID_SC (GPIO1, P1-28) are reserved for board (HAT) detection/identification. These pins are used to read the 24Cxx type 3.3 V 16-bit addressable I2C EEPROM in the HAT.

Table 4-5. *The Standardized 40-Pin Raspberry Pi GPIO Header (All Modern Units)*

Lower Left	Pins		Upper Left
3.3 V power, 50 mA max	P1-01	P1-02	5 V power
GPIO 2 (I2C1 SDA1)+R1=1.8k	P1-03	P1-04	*5 V power*
GPIO 3 (I2C1 SCL1)+R2=1.8k	P1-05	P1-06	Ground
GPIO 4 (GPCLK 0/1-Wire)	P1-07	P1-08	GPIO 14 (TXD0)
Ground	P1-09	P1-10	GPIO 15 (RXD0)
GPIO 17 (GEN0)	P1-11	P1-12	GPIO 18 (PCM_CLK/GEN1)
GPIO 27 (GEN2)	P1-13	P1-14	Ground
GPIO 22 (GEN3)	P1-15	P1-16	GPIO 23 (GEN4)
3.3 V power	P1-17	P1-18	GPIO 24 (GEN5)
GPIO 10 (SPI_MOSI)	P1-19	P1-20	*Ground*
GPIO 9 (SPI_MISO)	P1-21	P1-22	GPIO 25 (GEN6))
GPIO 11 (SPI_SCKL)	P1-23	P1-24	GPIO 8 (CE0_N)
Ground	P1-25	P1-26	GPIO 7 (CE1_N)
GPIO0 (ID_SD)	P1-27	P1-28	GPIO1 (ID_SC)

(continued)

Table 4-5. (*continued*)

Lower Left	Pins		Upper Left
GPIO5	P1-29	P1-30	Ground
GPIO6	P1-31	P1-32	GPIO12 (PWM0)
GPIO13 (PWM1)	P1-33	P1-34	Ground
GPIO19 (MISO)	P1-35	P1-36	GPIO16
GPIO26	P1-37	P1-38	GPIO20 (MOSI)
Ground	P1-39	P1-40	GPIO21 (SCLK)

Safe Mode

Raspbian Linux used to support a *safe mode*, but it has been removed as of March 2014. However, NOOBS may still support it.[6]

Pin P1-05, GPIO3 is special to the boot sequence. Grounding this pin or jumpering this to P1-06 (ground) causes the boot sequence to use a safe mode boot procedure. If the pin is used for some other purpose, you can prevent this with a configuration parameter:

```
avoid_safe_mode=1
```

Be very careful that you don't accidentally ground a power pin (like P1-01 or P1-02) when you do use it. If your Pi fails to respond to safe mode, it may be due to a manufacturing error or lack of firmware support. See this message:

```
www.raspberrypi.org/phpBB3/viewtopic.php?f=29&t=12007
```

When safe mode is invoked by the jumper, the `config.txt` file is ignored except for the `avoid_safe_mode` parameter. Additionally, this mode overrides the kernel command line, and `kernel_emergency.img` is loaded. If this file is unavailable, `kernel.img` is used instead.

The intent of this feature is to permit the user to overcome configuration problems without having to edit the SD card on another machine in order to make a correction. The booted emergency kernel is a BusyBox image with /boot mounted so that adjustments can be made. Additionally, the /dev/mmcblk0p2 root file system partition can be fixed up or mounted if necessary.

Logic Levels

The logic level used for GPIO pins is 3.3 V and is *not* tolerant of 5 V TTL logic levels. The Raspberry Pi pcb is designed to be plugged into pcb extension cards (HATs) or otherwise carefully interfaced to 3.3 V logic. Input voltage parameters V_{IL} and V_{IH} are described in more detail in Chapter 11.

GPIO Configuration at Reset

The Raspberry Pi GPIO pins can be configured by software control to be input or output, to have pull-up or pull-down resistors, or to assume some specialized peripheral function. After reset, only GPIO14 and 15 are assigned a special function (UART). After boot up, however, software can even reconfigure the UART pins as required.

When a GPIO pin is configured for output, there is a limited amount of current that it can drive (source or sink). By default, each P1 GPIO is configured to use an 8 mA driver, when the pin is configured as an output. Chapter 11 has more information about this.

Note   Raspbian default 1-Wire bus is GPIO 4 (GPCLK0) Pin P1-07.

1-Wire Driver

The default GPIO pin for the 1-Wire driver used to be hard-coded to use GPIO4. This can now be configured.

Summary

This chapter provided an introduction to the LED indicators and header strips found on your Raspberry Pi. While all new Pi's now use the 20 x 2 GPIO header strip, the original headers were described for reference purposes. A Pi is never too old to be put to work!

CHAPTER 5

SDRAM

The original Model B Rev 2.0 Raspberry Pi had 512 MB of SDRAM (synchronous dynamic random access memory), while the older revisions and the Model A had 256 MB. Modern Pi's now come equipped with 1 GB of RAM except for the Raspberry Pi Zero, which has 512 MB. Contrast this to the AVR class ATmega328P, which has 2 KB of static RAM!

There isn't much about the memory hardware that concerns the average Pi developer because the operating system provides a rich facility for managing program use. However, let's examine some useful Raspbian Linux interfaces that inform us how that memory is utilized. You'll also examine how to access the memory-mapped ARM peripherals directly from your Linux application.

/proc/meminfo

The pseudo file /proc/meminfo provides us with information about memory utilization. This information varies somewhat by architecture and the compile options used for that kernel. Let's study an example that was produced by a Raspberry Pi 3 Model B+ running Raspbian Linux:

```
$ cat /proc/meminfo
MemTotal:          949452 kB
MemFree:           631676 kB
```

© Warren Gay 2018
W. Gay, *Advanced Raspberry Pi*, https://doi.org/10.1007/978-1-4842-3948-3_5

```
MemAvailable:       756320 kB
Buffers:             20532 kB
Cached:             158004 kB
SwapCached:              0 kB
Active:             170108 kB
Inactive:           107020 kB
Active(anon):        99576 kB
Inactive(anon):      13172 kB
Active(file):        70532 kB
Inactive(file):      93848 kB
Unevictable:             0 kB
Mlocked:                 0 kB
SwapTotal:          102396 kB
SwapFree:           102396 kB
Dirty:                  40 kB
Writeback:               0 kB
AnonPages:           98596 kB
Mapped:              79016 kB
Shmem:               14152 kB
Slab:                22444 kB
SReclaimable:        10640 kB
SUnreclaim:          11804 kB
KernelStack:          1768 kB
PageTables:           3376 kB
NFS_Unstable:            0 kB
Bounce:                  0 kB
WritebackTmp:            0 kB
CommitLimit:        577120 kB
Committed_AS:       809528 kB
VmallocTotal:      1114112 kB
VmallocUsed:             0 kB
```

```
VmallocChunk:            0 kB
CmaTotal:             8192 kB
CmaFree:              6796 kB
```

All of the memory values shown have the units *KB* to the right of them, indicating kilo (1,024) bytes. These reported values are described in great detail online.[7] But let's summarize some values of interest.

MemTotal

The MemTotal line indicates the total amount of memory available, minus a few reserved binary regions. Note that memory allocated to the GPU is not factored into MemTotal. Some owners may choose to allocate the minimum of 16 MB to the GPU to make more memory available when not using the graphical desktop. The default is to assign 64 MB.

If this is broken down a bit further, accounting for memory allocated to the GPU, we find that there is about 32 MB of memory that is unaccounted for, outlined in Table 5-1. This will vary with the Pi model and the GPU memory assigned because of the way the GPU addresses memory.

Table 5-1. *GPU and Main Memory Breakdown*

Memory	Model B	Comments
SDRAM	1,048,576 KB	Hardware-equipped memory
MemTotal	949,452 KB	/proc/meminfo
Difference	99,124 KB	Remaining memory
gpu_mem	65,536 KB	/boot/config.txt (gpu_mem=64 by default)
Difference	33,588 KB	Unaccounted for

MemFree

MemFree normally represents the sum of LowFree + HighFree memory in kilobytes on the Intel x86 platform. For ARM, this simply represents the amount of memory available to user space programs.

Buffers

This value represents temporary buffers used within the kernel for raw disk blocks, and so forth. This value should not get much larger than about 20 MB or so.[8]

Cached

This value represents the read file content that has been cached (page cache). This does not include the content reported for SwapCached.

SwapCached

The value shown for SwapCached represents memory that was swapped out and is now swapped back in. For efficiency, these memory pages are still represented by swap disk space, should they be needed again. The fact that the value is reported as zero is a happy sign that no swapping has occurred or is no longer pertinent.

Active

The Active memory value represents recently used memory that is not reclaimed, unless absolutely necessary.

Inactive

This value represents memory that is not active and is likely to be reclaimed when memory is needed.

Active(anon)

This value represents memory that is not backed up by a file and is active. Active memory is not reclaimed unless absolutely necessary.

Inactive(anon)

This value represents memory that is not backed up by a file and is not active. Inactive memory is eligible to be reclaimed if memory is required.

Active(file)

This value represents file-backed memory, which is active. Active memory is reclaimed only if absolutely required.

Inactive(file)

This value represents inactive memory that is backed by a file. Inactive memory is eligible for reclamation, when memory is required.

Unevictable

This amount reflects the total amount of memory that cannot be reclaimed. Memory that is locked, for example, cannot be reclaimed.

Mlocked

This value reports the amount of locked memory.

SwapTotal

This value reports the total amount of swap space available in kilobytes.

SwapFree

This value reports the remaining amount of swap space available in kilobytes.

Dirty

This value represents the kilobytes of memory that have been modified and are waiting to be written to disk.

Writeback

This value reports the amount of memory in kilobytes being written back to disk.

AnonPages

This represents the non-file-backed pages of memory mapped into user space.

Mapped

This value reports the files that have been mapped into memory. This may include library code.

Shmem

This parameter does not appear to be documented well. However, it represents the amount of shared memory in kilobytes.

Slab

This parameter is described as "in-kernel data structures cache."

SReclaimable

This parameter is described as "Part of Slab that might be reclaimed, such as caches."

SUnreclaim

This parameter is described as "Part of Slab that cannot be reclaimed [under] memory pressure."

KernelStack

This value reports the memory used by the kernel stack(s).

PageTables

This value reports the amount of memory required by the page tables used in the kernel. Clearly, with more memory to manage, there is more memory dedicated to page tables.

NFS_Unstable

This value represents "NFS pages sent to the server, but not yet committed to stable storage." This example data suggests that NFS is not being used.

Bounce

This reports the memory used for "block device bounce buffers."

WritebackTmp

This parameter reports the memory used by FUSE for "temporary writeback buffers."

CommitLimit

The documentation states:

> Based on the overcommit ratio (vm.overcommit_ratio), this is the total amount of memory currently available to be allocated on the system. This limit is only adhered to if strict overcommit accounting is enabled (mode 2 in vm.overcommit_memory). The CommitLimit is calculated with the following formula:

$$CommitLimit = (vm.overcommit\_ratio \times PhysicalRAM) + swap$$

For example, a system with 1 GB of physical RAM and 7 GB of swap with a vm.overcommit_ratio of 30 would yield a CommitLimit of 7.3 GB. For more details, see the memory overcommit documentation in vm/overcommitaccounting.

The formula can be written as follows:

$$C = (R \times r) + S$$

The elements of this formula are described here:

- C is the overcommit limit.

- R is the physical RAM available (MemTotal).

- S is the swap space available (SwapTotal).

- r is the overcommit ratio percent (expressed as a fraction).

The overcommit ratio, r, is not reported in the /proc/meminfo data. To obtain that ratio, we consult another pseudo file. This example was taken from a Rev 2.0 Model B, but it appears to be a value common to all Pi's:

```
$ cat /proc/sys/vm/overcommit_ratio
50
```

The value 50 is to be interpreted as r = 0.50 (50%).

Using the overcommit formula, the value for S can be computed for the swap space available:

$$S = C - (R \times r)$$
$$= 577120 - (949452 \times 0.50)$$
$$= 82394 \, KB$$

The overcommit ratio is configurable by the user, by writing a value into the pseudo file. This example changes the ratio to 35%:

```
$ sudo -i
# echo 35 >/proc/sys/vm/overcommit_ratio
# cat /proc/sys/vm/overcommit_ratio
35
```

Committed_AS

This parameter is described as follows:

> The amount of memory presently allocated on the system. The committed memory is a sum of all of the memory which has been allocated by processes, even if it has not been "used" by them as of yet.

A process which *malloc()*'s 1 GB of memory, but only touches 300 MB of it will only show up as using 300 MB of memory even if it has the address space allocated for the entire 1 GB. This 1 GB is memory which has been "committed" to by the VM and can be used at any time by the allocating application. With strict overcommit enabled on the system (mode 2 in *vm.overcommit_memory*), allocations which would exceed the *CommitLimit* (detailed above) will not be permitted. This is useful if one needs to guarantee that processes will not fail due to lack of memory once that memory has been successfully allocated.

VmallocTotal

This represents the total amount of allocated virtual memory address space.

VmallocUsed

This is the amount of virtual memory that is in use, reported in kilobytes.

VmallocChunk

This value reports the largest size of a vmalloc area, in kilobytes.

Physical Memory

Normally, physical memory isn't a concern to application programmers because the operating system and its drivers provide an abstract and often portable way to access it. However, when this support is absent, direct access to a peripheral like the PWM controller is necessary.

Figure 5-1 illustrates the physical addressing used on the Raspberry Pi for the original Pi Model B (for simplicity). The SDRAM starts at physical address zero and works up to the ARM/GPU split point (Chapter 17 defines the split point). The ARM peripherals are mapped to physical memory starting at the address of 0x20000000, on the Pi Model B. This starting address is of keen interest to programmers.

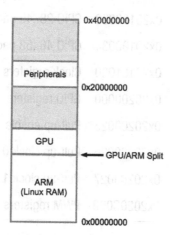

Figure 5-1.   *Physical memory layout*

With modern Pi models, we cannot assume a constant for the starting peripheral address. Later in the book, a way to determine this value at runtime will be shown.

In the region labeled Peripherals, the offsets and addresses indicated in Table 5-2 are of interest to us.

Table 5-2.   *Peripheral Offsets for the Raspberry Pi Model B*

Peripheral	Offset	Address	Description	C Offset Macro
Base	0x00000000	0x20000000	Starting address	BCM2708_PERI_BASE
PADS_GPIO	0x00100000	0x20100000	PADS base	PADS_GPIO_BASE
GPIO 00..27	0x0010002C	0x2010002C	GPIO 00..27 pads	PADS_GPIO_00_27
GPIO 28..45	0x00100030	0x20100030	GPIO 28..45 pads	PADS_GPIO_28_45
GPIO 46..53	0x00100034	0x20100034	GPIO 46..53 pads	PADS_GPIO_46_53
Clock	0x00101000	0x20101000	Clock registers	CLK_BASE
GPIO	0x00200000	0x20200000	GPIO registers	GPIO_BASE
GPPUD	0x00200025	0x20200025	Pull-up enable	
GPPUDCLK0	0x00200026	0x20200026	Pull-up clock 0	
GPPUDCLK1	0x00200027	0x20200027	Pull-up clock 1	
PWM	0x0020C000	0x2020C000	PWM registers	PWM_BASE

Memory Mapping

To gain access to physical memory under Linux, you use the /dev/mem character device and the mmap(2) system call. The /dev/mem node is shown here:

```
$ ls -l /dev/mem
crw-r----- 1 root kmem 1, 1 Jun  5 20:24 /dev/mem
```

From the ownership information shown, it is evident that you'll need root privileges to access it. This is sensible given that a process can cause havoc with direct access to the physical memory. Exercise caution in what the applications do with this memory access.

The mmap(2) system call API is shown here:

```
#include <sys/mman.h>

void *mmap(
    void     *addr,     /*Address to use */
    size_t    length,   /*Number of bytes to access */
    int       prot,     /*Memory protection */
    int       flags,    /*Option flags */
    int       fd,       /*Opened file descriptor */
    off_t     offset    /*Starting off set */
) ;
```

Rather than look at all the options and flags available to this somewhat complicated system call, let's look at the ones that we use in the following code:

```
static char *map = 0;

static void
gpio_init() {
    int fd;
    char *map;

    fd = open("/dev/mem",O_RDWR|O_SYNC) ;    /*Needs root
    access */
    if ( fd < 0 ) {
        perror("Opening /dev/mem") ;
        exit(1) ;
    }
```

```
map = (char *) mmap(
    NULL,                        /* Any address */
    BLOCK_SIZE,                  /* # of bytes */
    PROT_READ|PROT_WRITE,
    MAP_SHARED,                  /*Shared */
    fd,                          /* /dev/mem */
    GPIO_BASE                    /* Offset to GPIO */
) ;

if ( (long)map == -1L ) {
    perror("mmap(/dev/mem)");
    exit(1) ;
}

close(fd);
ugpio = (volatile unsigned *)map;
}
```

The first thing performed in this code is to open the device driver node /dev/mem. It is opened for reading and writing (O_RDWR), and the option flag O_SYNC requests that any write(2) call to this file descriptor results in blocking the execution of the caller until it has completed.

Address

Next, the mmap(2) call is invoked. The address argument is provided with NULL (zero) so that the kernel can choose where to map it into the caller's address space. If the application were to specify a starting address to use and the kernel was not able use it, the system call would fail. The starting address is returned and assigned to the character pointer map in the preceding listing.

Length

Argument 2 is supplied with the macro BLOCK_SIZE in this example. This
is the number of bytes you would like to map into your address space. This
was defined earlier in the program as 4 KB:

```
#define BLOCK_SIZE (4*1024)
```

While the application may not need the full 4 KB of physical memory
mapped, mmap(2) may insist on using a multiple of the page size. This can
be verified on the command line as follows:

```
$ getconf PAGE_SIZE
4096
```

A program can determine this directly by using the sysconf(2) system
call:

```
#include <unistd.h>

    ...
    long sz = sysconf(_SC_PAGESIZE);
```

Protection

The third mmap(2) argument is supplied with the flags PROT_READ and
PROT_WRITE. This indicates that the application wants both read and write
access to the memory-mapped region.

Flags

The flags argument is supplied with the value MAP_SHARED. This permits
nonexclusive access to the underlying mapping.

File Descriptor

This argument supplies the underlying opened file to be mapped into memory. In this case, we map a region of physical ARM memory into our application by using the opened device driver node /dev/mem.

Offset

This last argument specifies the location in physical memory where we want to start our access. For the GPIO registers, it is the address 0x20200000 on the original Pi Model B.

Return Value

The return value, when successful, will be an application address that points to the physical memory region we asked for. The application programmer need not be concerned with what this address is, except to save and use it for access.

The return value is also used for indicating failure, so this should be checked and handled:

```
if ( (long) map == -1L ) {
    perror("mmap(/dev/mem)");
    exit(1);
}
```

The returned address (pointer) map is cast to a long integer and compared to -1L. This is the magic value that indicates that an error occurred. The error code is found in errno.

Volatile

The last section of this initialization code for GPIO assigns the address map to another variable, ugpio, as follows:

```
ugpio = (volatile unsigned *)map;
```

The value ugpio was defined earlier in the program:

```
static volatile unsigned *ugpio = 0;
```

There are two things noteworthy about this:

- The data type is an unsigned int (32 bits on the Pi).

- The pointed-to data is marked as *volatile*.

Since the Pi registers are 32 bits in size, it is often more convenient to access them as 32-bit words. The unsigned data type is perfect for this. But be careful with *offsets* in conjunction with this pointer, since they will be *word* rather than byte offsets.

The volatile keyword tells the compiler not to optimize access to memory through the pointer variable. Imagine code that reads a peripheral register and reads the same register again later, to see whether an event has occurred. An optimizing compiler might say to itself, "I already have this value in CPU register *R*, so I'll just use that because it's faster." But the effect of this code is that it will never see a bit change in the peripheral's register because that data was not fetched back into the register. The volatile keyword forces the compiler to retrieve the value even though it would be faster to use the value still found in the register.

Virtual Memory

In the previous section, you looked at how to access physical memory in an application, provided that you had the access (root or setuid). The Broadcom Corporation PDF manual "BCM2835 ARM Peripherals," page 5, also shows a *virtual* memory layout on the right. This should not be confused with the *physical* memory layout that was examined earlier. Virtual memory can be accessed through /dev/kmem driver node using mmap(2).

Summary

Some parameters such as Buffers impact the performance of Raspbian Linux on the Pi. How much memory is allocated to file data that has been read from disk, for example? Other configuration parameters determine how much SDRAM is dedicated to GPU use.

Probably the most important aspect of memory allocation is how much memory is available to developer application programs. The value of MemFree is therefore a useful metric. When exceeding physical memory limits, the swapping parameters then become measurements of interest.

Finally, access to the Raspberry Pi peripherals directly using mmap(2) was introduced. Until Raspbian Linux gains device drivers for peripherals such as PWM, the direct access technique will be necessary. Even with driver support, there are sometimes good reasons to access the peripheral registers directly.

CHAPTER 6

CPU

Several models of the Raspberry Pi have emerged since the first Model B and Model A successor. In this chapter, the ARM architecture is introduced along with CPU features supported by your Pi. Then the Linux API (application programming interface) for managing CPU in your application will be covered (threads).

/proc/cpuinfo

Raspbian Linux provides a nice character device at /proc/cpuinfo, to list information about your CPU. A sample was provided in Listing 6-1 taken from a Raspberry Pi 3 Model B+. You don't need root access to read this information.

Listing 6-1. Session output listing /proc/cpuinfo on a Raspberry Pi 3 model B+

```
$ cat /proc/cpuinfo
processor       : 0
model name      : ARMv7 Processor rev 4 (v7l)
BogoMIPS        : 38.40
Features        : half thumb fastmult vfp edsp neon vfpv3 tls
                  vfpv4 \ idiva idivt vfpd32 lpae evtstrm crc32
CPU implementer : 0x41
```

© Warren Gay 2018
W. Gay, *Advanced Raspberry Pi*, https://doi.org/10.1007/978-1-4842-3948-3_6

```
CPU architecture : 7
CPU variant      : 0x0
CPU part         : 0xd03
CPU revision     : 4
...
Hardware         : BCM2835
Revision         : a020d3
Serial           : 00000000d4b81de4
```

There are four groups with processors identified as 0 through 3 (only the first was shown in the figure). At the bottom of the file is listed Hardware, Revision, and a Serial number.

In the processor group is a line labeled "model name." In this example, we see "ARMv7 Processor rev 4 (v7l)" listed. Also at the bottom, there is "Hardware" listed with the value "BCM2835". Let's take a moment to discuss what the architecture name implies.

ARM Architecture

An architecture is a *design*. In this case it defines the ARM programmer's model, including registers, addressing, memory, exceptions, and all aspects of operation. In the Raspberry Pi context, different ARM architectures have been used, listed in Table 6-1.

Table 6-1. *Raspberry Pi ARM Architectures and Implementations*

Architecture Name	Bus Size	Instruction Sets	SoC
ARMv6Z	32-bit	ARM and Thumb (16-bit)	BCM2835
ARMv7-A	32-bit	ARM and Thumb (16-bit)	BCM2836
ARMv8-A	32/64-bit	AArch32 (compatible with ARMv7-A) and AArch64 execution states.	BCM2837

The design and general capabilities are summarized in the columns Bus Size and Instruction Sets. Each new architecture added new features to the instruction set and other processor features.

The column SoC (system on chip) identifies the *implementation* of the architecture by Broadcom.

The new ARMv8-A architecture has two possible run states:

- AArch32, with ARMv7-A architecture compatibility.

- AArch64, with a new ARM 64-bit instruction set.

The execution state must be chosen at system startup, which is why Raspbian Linux reports the following on a Raspberry Pi 3 model B+:

```
$ uname -m
armv7l
```

It is running the AArch32 execution state, for compatibility with the 32-bit Raspbian Linux code. Someday hopefully, we will see a true 64-bit Raspbian Linux.

Architecture Suffix

Newer architectures have a suffix to identify the Cortex family:

- "A" for the Cortex-A family of *application* processors.

- "R" for the Cortex-R family of *real-time* processors.

- "M" for the Cortex-M family of low power, *microcontroller* processors.

In the architecture names ARMv7-A or ARMv8-A, we see that these belong to the application processor family. These are fully capable members, while the Cortex-R and Cortex-M families are often subsets or specialize in a few areas.

Features

Looking again at the /proc/cpuinfo output, notice the line labeled "Features."
It has a list of names identifying features, which are unique to the CPU
(central processing unit). Table 6-2 lists some ARM features that you
might see.

Table 6-2. *ARM Features That May Be Listed in /proc/cpuinfo*

Feature Name	Description
half	Half-word loads and stores
thumb	16-bit Thumb instruction set support
fastmult	32x32 producing 64-bit multiplication support
vfp	Early SIMD vector floating-point instructions
edsp	DSP extensions
neon	Advanced SIMD/NEON support
vfpv3	VFP version 3 support
tls	TLS register
vfpv4	VFP version 4 with fast context switching
idiva	SDIV and UDIV hardware division in ARM mode
idivt	SDIV and UDIV hardware division in Thumb mode
vfpd32	VFP with 32 D-registers
lpae	Large physical address extension (>4 GB physical memory on 32-bit architecture)
evtstrm	Kernel event stream using generic architected timer
crc32	CRC-32 hardware accelerated support

Execution Environment

Connected with the idea of the CPU is program execution itself. Before you look at program execution, take the high-level view of the execution context. Figure 6-1 shows the operating environment of an executing program.

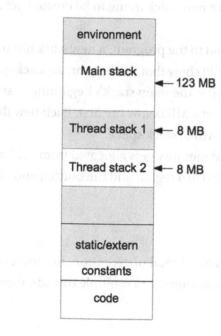

Figure 6-1. *Program execution context*

At the lowest end of the address space is the "text" region containing the program code. This region of virtual memory is read-only, holding read-only program constants in addition to executable code.

The next region (in increasing address) contains blocks of uninitialized arrays, buffers, static C variables, and extern storage.

At the high end of memory are environment variables for the program, like PATH. You can easily check this yourself by using getenv("PATH") and printing the returned address for it. Its address will likely be the highest address in your Raspberry Pi application, except possibly for another environment variable.

Below that, your main program's stack begins and grows downward. Each function call causes a new stack frame to be created below the current one.

If you now add a thread to the program, a new stack has to be allocated for it. Experiments on the Pi show that the first thread stack gets created approximately 123 MB below the main stack's beginning. A second thread has its stack allocated about 8 MB below the first. Each new thread's stack (by default) is allocated 8 MB of stack space.

Dynamically allocated memory gets allocated from the *heap*, which sits between the static/extern region and the bottom end of the stack.

Threads

Every program gets one main thread of execution. But sometimes there is a need for the performance advantage of multiple threads, especially on a Pi with four cores.

pthread Headers

All pthread functions require the following header file:

```
#include <pthread.h>
```

When linking programs using pthreads, add the linker option:

```
-lpthread
```

to link with the pthread library.

pthread Error Handling

The pthread routines return zero when they succeed and *return an error code when they fail*. The value errno is *not* used for these calls.

The reason behind this is likely that it was thought that the traditional Unix errno approach would be phased out in the near future (at the time POSIX threads were being standardized). The original use of errno was as follows:

```
extern int errno;
```

However, this approach doesn't work for threaded programs. Imagine two threads concurrently opening files with open(2), which set the errno value upon failure. Both threads cannot share the same int value for errno.

Rather than change a vast body of code already using errno in this manner, other approaches were implemented to provide each thread with its own private copy of errno. This is one reason that programs today using errno must include the header file errno.h. The header file takes care of defining the thread specific reference to errno.

Because the pthread standard was developing before the errno solution generally emerged, the pthread library returns the error code directly and returns zero when successful. If Unix were to be rewritten from scratch today, all system calls would probably work this way.

pthread_create(3)

The function pthread_create(3) is used to create a new thread of execution. The function call looks more daunting than it really is:

```
int pthread_create(
  pthread_t *thread,
  const pthread_attr_t *attr,
  void *(*start_routine)(void *),
  void *arg
);
```

The call to pthread_create(3) creates a new stack, sets up registers, and performs other housekeeping. Let's describe the arguments:

> thread: This first argument is simply a pointer to a pthread_t variable to receive the created thread's ID value. The ID value allows you to query and control the created thread. If the call succeeds, the thread ID is returned to the calling program.

> attr: This is a pointer to a pthread_attr_t attribute object that supplies various options and parameters. If you can accept the defaults, simply supply zero or NULL.

> start_routine: As shown in the following code, this is simply the name of a start routine that accepts a void pointer and returns a void pointer.

> arg: This generic pointer is passed to start_routine. It may point to anything of interest to the thread function (start_routine). Often this is a structure containing values, or in a C++ program, it can be the pointer to an object. If you don't need an argument value, supply zero (or NULL).

> returns: Zero is returned if the function is successful; otherwise, an error number is returned (not in errno).

Error	Description
EAGAIN	Insufficient resources to create another thread, or a system-imposed limit on the number of threads was encountered.
EINVAL	Invalid settings in attr.
EPERM	No permission to set the scheduling policy and parameters specified in attr.

The C language syntax of argument 3 is a bit nasty for beginning C programmers. Let's just show what the function for argument 3 looks like:

```
void *
start_routine(void *arg) {
    ...
    return some_ptr;
}
```

The following is perhaps the simplest example of thread creation possible:

```
static void *
my_thread(void *arg) {
    ...                                        // thread execution
    return 0;
}

int
main(int argc, char **argv) {
    pthread_t tid;                             // Thread    ID
    int rc;

    rc = pthread_create(&tid,0,my_thread,0);
    assert(!rc);
```

This example does not use thread attributes (argument 2 is zero). We also don't care about the value passed into my_thread(), so argument 4 is provided a zero. Argument 3 simply needs to tell the system call what function to execute. The value of rc will be zero if the thread is successfully created (tested by the assert(3) macro).

At this point, the main thread and the function my_thread() execute in parallel. Since there is only one CPU on the Raspberry Pi, only one executes at any instant of time. But they both execute concurrently, trading blocks of execution time in a preemptive manner. Each, of course, runs using its own stack.

Thread my_thread() terminates gracefully, by returning.

pthread_attr_t

There are several thread attributes that can be fetched and set. You'll look
only at perhaps the most important attribute (stack size) to keep this crash
course brief. For the full list of attributes and functions, you can view the
man pages for it:

```
$ man pthread_attr_init
```

To initialize a new attribute, or to release a previously initialized
pthread attribute, use this pair of routines:

```
int pthread_attr_init(pthread_attr_t *attr);
int pthread_attr_destroy(pthread_attr_t *attr);
```

> attr: Address of the pthread_attr_t variable to
> initialize/destroy
>
> returns: Zero upon success, or an error code when
> it fails (not in errno)

Error	Description
ENOMEM	Insufficient resources (memory)

The Linux implementation of pthread_attr_init(3) may never
return the ENOMEM error, but other Unix platforms might.

The following is a simple example of creating and destroying an
attribute object:

```
pthread_attr_t attr;

pthread_attr_init(&attr);     // Initialize attr
...
pthread_attr_destroy(&attr); // Destroy attr
```

Perhaps one of the most important attributes of a thread is the stack size attribute:

```
int pthread_attr_setstacksize(pthread_attr_t *attr, size_t
stacksize);
int pthread_attr_getstacksize(pthread_attr_t *attr, size_t
*stacksize);
```

> attr: The pointer to the attribute to fetch a value from, or to establish an attribute in.
>
> stacksize: This is a stack size value when setting the attribute, and a pointer to the receiving size_t variable when fetching the stack size.
>
> returns: Returns zero if the call is successful; otherwise, returns an error number (not in errno).

The following error is possible for pthread_attr_setstacksize(3):

Error	Description
EINVAL	The stack size is less than PTHREAD_STACK_MIN (16,384) bytes.

The Linux man page further states:

> *On some systems, pthread_attr_setstacksize() can fail with the error EINVAL if stack size is not a multiple of the system page size.*

The following simple example obtains the system default stack size and increases it by 8 MB:

```
pthread_attr_t  attr;
size_t          stksiz;
```

```
pthread_attr_init(&attr);                        // Initialize attr
pthread_attr_getstacksize (&attr,&stksiz);       // Get stack size
stksiz  += 8 * 1024 * 1024;                       // Add 8 MB
pthread_attr_setstacksize(&attr,stksiz);          // Set stack size
```

The system default is provided by the initialization of attr. Then it is a matter of "getting" a value out of the attr object, and then putting in a new stack size in the call to pthread_attr_setstacksize().

Note that this set of operations has simply prepared the attributes object attr for use in a pthread_create() call. The attribute takes effect in the new thread, when the thread is actually created:

```
pthread_attr_t attr;

...

rc = pthread_create(&tid,&attr,my_thread,0);
```

pthread_join(3)

In the earlier pthread_create() example, the main program creates my_thread() and starts it executing. At some point, the main program is going to finish and want to exit (or return). If the main program exits before my_thread() completes, the entire process and the threads in it are destroyed, even if they have not completed.

To cause the main program to wait until the thread completes, the function pthread_join(3) is used:

```
int pthread_join(pthread_t thread, void **retval);
```

> thread: Thread ID of the thread to be joined with.

> retval: Pointer to the void * variable to receive the returned value. If you are uninterested in a return value, this argument can be supplied with zero (or NULL).

> returns: The function returns zero when successful; otherwise, an error number is returned (not in errno).

The following example has added pthread_join(3), so that the main program does not exit until my_thread() exits.

```
int
main(int argc,char **argv) {
    pthread_t tid;                          // Thread ID
    void *retval = 0;                       // Returned
                                            // value pointer
    int rc;

    rc = pthread_create(&tid,0,my_thread,0);
    assert(!rc);
    rc = pthread_join(tid,&retval);         // Wait for
                                            // my_thread()
    assert(!rc);
    return 0;
}
```

pthread_detach(3)

The function pthread_join(3) causes the caller to wait until the indicated thread returns. Sometimes, however, a thread is created and never checked again. When that thread exits, some of its resources are retained to allow for a join operation on it. If there is never going to be a join, it is better for that thread to be forgotten when it exits and have its resources immediately released.

The pthread_detach(3) function is used to indicate that no join will be performed on the named thread. This way, the named thread becomes configured to release itself automatically, when it exits.

```
int pthread_detach(pthread_t thread);
```

The argument and return values are as follows:

> thread: The thread ID of the thread to be altered, so that it will not wait for a join when it completes. Its resources will be immediately released upon the named thread's termination.

> returns: Zero if the call was successful; otherwise, an error code is returned (not in errno).

Error	Description
EINVAL	Thread is not a joinable thread.
ESRCH	No thread with the ID thread could be found.

The pthread_detach function simply requires the thread ID value as its argument:

```
pthread_t tid;              // Thread ID
int rc;

rc = pthread_create(&tid,0,my_thread,0);
assert(!rc);
pthread_detach(tid);        // No joining with this thread
```

pthread_self(3)

Sometimes it is convenient in a piece of code to find out what the *current* thread ID is. The pthread_self(3) function is the right tool for the job:

```
pthread_t pthread_self(void);
```

An example of its use is shown here:

```
pthread_t tid;

tid = pthread_self();
```

pthread_kill(3)

The pthread_kill(3) function allows the caller to send a signal to another thread. The handling of thread signals is beyond the scope of this text. But there is one very useful application of this function, which you'll examine shortly:

```
#include <signal.h>

int pthread_kill(pthread_t thread, int sig);
```

Notice that the header file for signal.h is needed for the function prototype and the signal definitions.

> thread: This is the thread ID that you want to signal (or test).
>
> sig: This is the signal that you wish to send. Alternatively, supply zero to test whether the thread exists.
>
> returns: Returns zero if the call is successful, or an error code (not in errno).

Error	Description
EINVAL	An invalid signal was specified.
ESRCH	No thread with the ID thread could be found.

One useful application of the pthread_kill(3) function is to test whether another thread exists. If the sig argument is supplied with zero, no actual signal is delivered, but the error checking is still performed. If the function returns zero, you know that the thread still *exists*.

But what does it mean when the thread exists? Does it mean that it is still *executing*? Or does it mean that it has not been reclaimed as part of a pthread_join(3), or as a consequence of pthread_detach(3) cleanup?

It turns out that when the thread *exists*, it means that it is still executing. In other words, it *has not returned* from the thread function that was started. If the thread has returned, it is considered to be incapable of receiving a signal.

Based on this, you know that you will get a zero returned when the thread is still executing. When error code ESRCH is returned instead, you know that the thread has completed.

Mutexes

While not strictly a CPU topic, mutexes are inseparable from a discussion about threads. A *mutex* is a locking device that allows the software designer to stop one or more threads while another is working with a shared resource. In other words, one thread receives exclusive access. This is necessary to facilitate inter-thread communication. I'm simply going to describe the mutex API here, rather than the theory behind the application of mutexes.

pthread_mutex_create(3)

A mutex is initialized with the system call to pthread_mutex_init(3):

```
int pthread_mutex_init(
    pthread_mutex_t *mutex,
    const pthread_mutexattr_t *attr
);
```

> mutex: A pointer to a pthread_mutex_t object, to be initialized.
>
> attr: A pointer to a pthread_mutexattr_t object, describing mutex options. Supply zero (or NULL), if you can accept the defaults.
>
> returns: Returns zero if the call is successful; otherwise, returns an error code (not in errno).

Error	Description
EAGAIN	The system lacks the necessary resources (other than memory) to initialize another mutex.
ENOMEM	Insufficient memory exists to initialize the mutex.
EPERM	The caller does not have the privilege to perform the operation.
EBUSY	The implementation has detected an attempt to reinitialize the object referenced by mutex, a previously initialized, but not yet destroyed, mutex.
EINVAL	The value specified by attr is invalid.

An example of mutex initialization is provided here:

```
pthread_mutex_t mutex;
int rc;

rc = pthread_mutex_init(&mutex,0);
assert (!rc);
```

pthread_mutex_destroy(3)

When the application no longer needs a mutex, it should use pthread_mutex_destroy(3) to release its resources:

```
pthread_mutex_t mutex ;
int rc;
...
rc = pthread_mutex_destroy(&mutex);
assert(!rc);
```

mutex: The address of the mutex to release resources for.

returns: Returns zero when successful, or an error code when it fails (not in errno).

Error	Description
EBUSY	Mutex is locked or in use in conjunction with a pthread_cond_wait(3) or pthread_cond_timedwait(3).
EINVAL	The value specified by mutex is invalid.

pthread_mutex_lock(3)

When a thread needs exclusive access to a resource, it must lock the resource's mutex. As long as the cooperating threads follow the same procedure of locking first, they cannot both access the shared object at the same time.

```
int pthread_mutex_lock(pthread_mutex_t *mutex);
```

> mutex: A pointer to the mutex to lock.

> returns: Returns zero if the mutex was successfully locked; otherwise, an error code is returned (not in errno).

Error	Description
EINVAL	The mutex was created with the protocol attribute having the value PTHREAD_PRIO_PROTECT, and the calling thread's priority is higher than the mutex's current priority ceiling. Or the value specified by the mutex does not refer to an initialized mutex object.
EAGAIN	Maximum number of recursive locks for mutex has been exceeded.
EDEADLK	The current thread already owns the mutex.

The following shows the function being called:

```
pthread_mutex_t mutex;
int rc;

...

rc = pthread_mutex_lock(&mutex);
```

pthread_mutex_unlock(3)

When exclusive access to a resource is no longer required, the mutex is unlocked:

```
int pthread_mutex_unlock(pthread_mutex_t *mutex);
```

> mutex: A pointer to the mutex to be unlocked.
>
> returns: Returns zero if the mutex was unlocked successfully; otherwise, an error code is returned (not in errno).

Error	Description
EINVAL	The value specified by mutex does not refer to an initialized mutex object.
EPERM	The current thread does not own the mutex.

A simple example of unlocking a mutex is provided here:

```
pthread_mutex_t mutex;
int rc;

...

rc = pthread_mutex_unlock(&mutex);
```

Condition Variables

Sometimes mutexes alone are not enough for efficient scheduling of CPU between different threads. Mutexes and condition variables are often used together to facilitate inter-thread communication. New comers might struggle with this concept, at first.

Why do we need condition variables when we have mutexes?

Consider what is necessary in building a software queue that can hold a maximum of eight items. Before we can queue something, we need to first see if the queue is full. But we cannot test that until we have the queue locked—otherwise, another thread could be changing things under our own noses.

So we lock the queue but find that it is full. What do we do now? Do we simply unlock and try again? This works but it wastes CPU time. Wouldn't it be better if we had some way of being alerted when the queue was no longer full?

The condition variable works in concert with a mutex and a "signal" (of sorts). In pseudo code terms, a program trying to queue an item on a queue would perform the following steps:

1. Lock the mutex. We cannot examine anything in the queue until we lock it.

2. Check the queue's capacity. Can we place a new item in it? If so:

   a. Place the new item in the queue.

   b. Unlock and exit.

3. If the queue is full, the following steps are performed:

   a. Using a condition variable, "wait" on it, with the associated mutex.

   b. When control returns from the wait, return to step 2.

How does the condition variable help us? Consider the following steps:

1. The mutex is locked (1).

2. The wait is performed (3a). This causes the kernel to do the following:

    a. Put the calling thread to sleep (put on a kernel wait queue).

    b. Unlock the mutex that was locked in step 1.

Unlocking of the mutex in step 2b is necessary so that another thread can do something with the queue (hopefully, take an entry from the queue so that it is no longer full). If the mutex remained locked, no thread would be able to move.

At some future point in time, another thread will do the following:

1. Lock the mutex.

2. Find entries in the queue (it was currently full), and pull one item out of it.

3. Unlock the mutex.

4. Signal the condition variable that the "waiter" is using, so that it can wake up.

The waiting thread then awakens:

1. The kernel makes the "waiting" thread ready.

2. The mutex is successfully relocked.

Once that thread awakens with the mutex locked, it can recheck the queue to see whether there is room to queue an item. Notice that *the thread is awakened only when it has already reacquired the mutex lock.* This is why condition variables are paired with a mutex in their use.

pthread_cond_init(3)

Like any other object, a condition variable needs to be initialized:

```
int pthread_cond_init(
    pthread_cond_t              *cond,
    const pthread_condattr_t    *attr
);
```

> cond: A pointer to the pthread_cond_t structure to be initialized.
>
> attr: A pointer to a cond variable attribute if one is provided, or supply zero (or NULL).
>
> returns: Zero is returned if the call is successful; otherwise, an error code is returned (not in errno).

Error	Description
EAGAIN	The system lacked the necessary resources.
ENOMEM	Insufficient memory exists to initialize the condition variable.
EBUSY	The implementation has detected an attempt to reinitialize the object referenced by cond, a previously initialized, but not yet destroyed, condition variable.
EINVAL	The value specified by attr is invalid.

pthread_cond_destroy(3)

When a condition (cond) variable is no longer required, its resources should be released with the following call:

```
int pthread_cond_destroy(pthread_cond_t *cond);
```

92

cond: Condition variable to be released.

returns: Zero if the call was successful; otherwise, returns an error code (not in errno).

Error	Description
EBUSY	Detected an attempt to destroy the object referenced by cond while it is referenced by pthread_cond_wait() or pthread_cond_timedwait() in another thread.
EINVAL	The value specified by cond is invalid.

pthread_cond_wait(3)

This function is one-half of the queue solution. The pthread_cond_wait(3) function is called with the mutex already locked. The kernel will then put the calling thread to sleep (on the wait queue) to release the CPU, while at the same time unlocking the mutex. The calling thread remains blocked until the condition variable cond is signaled in some way (more about that later).

When the thread is awakened by the kernel, the system call returns with the mutex locked. At this point, the thread can check the application condition (like queue length) and then proceed if things are favorable, or call pthread_cond_wait(3) again to wait further.

```
int pthread_cond_wait(pthread_cond_t *cond, pthread_mutex_t *mutex);
```

cond: Pointer to the condition variable to be used for the wake-up call.

mutex: Pointer to the mutex to be associated with the condition variable.

returns: Returns zero upon success; otherwise, an error code is returned (not in errno).

Error	Description
EINVAL	The value specified by cond, mutex is invalid. Or different mutexes were supplied for concurrent pthread_cond_timedwait() or pthread_cond_wait() operations on the same condition variable.
EPERM	The mutex was not owned by the current thread at the time of the call.

The following code snippet shows how a queuing function would use this. (Initialization of mutex and cond is assumed.)

```
pthread_mutex_t mutex;
pthread_cond_t cond;

...
pthread_mutex_lock(&mutex);

while ( queue.length >=max_length )
    pthread_cond_wait(&cond,&mutex);

// queue the item
...
pthread_mutex_unlock(&mutex);
```

The while loop retries the test to see whether the queue is "not full." The while loop is necessary when multiple threads are inserting into the queue. Depending on timing, another thread could beat the current thread to queuing an item, making the queue full again.

pthread_cond_signal(3)

When an item is taken off the queue, a mechanism needs to wake up the thread attempting to put one entry into the full queue. One wake-up option is the pthread_cond_signal(3) system call:

```
int pthread_cond_signal(pthread_cond_t *cond);
```

> cond: A pointer to the condition variable used to signal one thread.

> returns: Returns zero if the function call was successful; otherwise, an error number is returned (not in errno).

Error	Description
EINVAL	The value cond does not refer to an initialized condition variable.

It is *not* an error if no other thread is waiting. This function does, however, wake up one waiting thread, if one or more are waiting on the specified condition variable.

This call is preferred for *performance* reasons if signaling one thread will "work." When there are special conditions whereby some threads may succeed and others would not, you need a *broadcast* call instead. When it can be used, waking *one* thread saves CPU cycles.

pthread_cond_broadcast(3)

This is the broadcast variant of pthread_cond_signal(3). If multiple waiters have different tests, a broadcast should be used to allow *all* waiters to wake up and consider the conditions found.

```
int pthread_cond_broadcast(pthread_cond_t *cond);
```

> cond: A pointer to the condition variable to be *signaled*, waking *all* waiting threads.

> returns: Zero is returned when the call is successful; otherwise, an error number is returned (not in errno).

Error	Description
EINVAL	The value cond does not refer to an initialized condition variable.

It is *not* an error to broadcast when there are no waiters.

Summary

This chapter has introduced the CPU as a resource to be exploited. The /proc/cpuinfo driver was described, which provides a quick summary of your CPU capabilities (and number of processors).

An introduction to ARM architecture was provided, allowing you to view architecture differs from implementation—that the BCM2837 is Broadcom's implementation of the ARMv8-A architecture, for example. For the C programmer, the chapter finished with a whirlwind tour of the pthread API, as supported by Linux.

CHAPTER 7

USB

The USB port has become ubiquitous in the digital world, allowing the use of a large choice of peripherals. The Raspberry Pi models support one to four USB ports, depending upon the model.

This chapter briefly examines some power considerations associated with USB support and powered hubs. The remainder of this chapter examines the device driver interface available to the Raspbian Linux developer by programming access to an EZ-USB FX2LP developer board.

Power

Very early models of the Raspberry Pi limited each USB port to 100 mA because of the polyfuses on board. Revision 2.0 models and later did away with these, relieving you from the different failures that could occur. The USB 2 power limit is 500 mA from a single port. Keep this in mind when designing your IoT (internet of things).

Note   Wireless USB adapters consume between 350 mA and 500 mA.

© Warren Gay 2018
W. Gay, *Advanced Raspberry Pi*, https://doi.org/10.1007/978-1-4842-3948-3_7

Powered Hubs

Some applications will require a powered USB hub for high-current peripherals. This is particularly true for wireless network adapters, since they require up to 500 mA. But a USB hub requires coordination with the Linux kernel and thus requires software support. A number of hubs have been reported not to work. The following web page is a good resource for listing hubs that are known to work with Raspbian Linux:

`http://elinux.org/RPi_Powered_USB_Hubs`

With the powered USB hub plugged in, you can list the USB devices that have registered with the kernel by using the `lsusb` command:

```
$ lsusb
Bus 001 Device 008: ID 1a40:0101 Terminus Technology Inc. Hub
Bus 001 Device 007: ID 1a40:0101 Terminus Technology Inc. Hub
Bus 001 Device 004: ID 045e:00d1 Microsoft Corp. Optical Mouse
                       with Tilt Wheel
Bus 001 Device 005: ID 04f2:0841 Chicony Electronics Co., Ltd
                       HP Multimedia Keyboard
Bus 001 Device 006: ID 0424:7800 Standard Microsystems Corp.
Bus 001 Device 003: ID 0424:2514 Standard Microsystems Corp.
                       USB 2.0 Hub
Bus 001 Device 002: ID 0424:2514 Standard Microsystems Corp.
                       USB 2.0 Hub
Bus 001 Device 001: ID 1d6b:0002 Linux Foundation 2.0 root hub
```

The first two in the example session show my Terminus Technology Inc. powered hub, registered after it was plugged into the Pi. The mouse (Microsoft) and keyboard (HP) are two peripherals plugged into the Pi. The remaining are drivers supporting the Pi hub for the USB ports. The hub used in this session is shown in Figure 7-1.

Figure 7-1. *A powered USB hub*

EZ-USB FX2LP

In this chapter, we're not just going to talk about USB. Instead we're going to interface your Pi to an economical board known as the EZ-USB FX2LP, which is available on eBay for the low cost of about $4. The chip on board is CY7C68013A and is manufactured by Cypress. If you do an eBay search for "EZ-USB FX2LP board," you should be able to find several sources.

There is an FX3LP chip available but it is not hobby priced. Furthermore, it requires special instructions to get driver support installed. If you stay with the FX2LP, the Raspbian Linux kernel drivers should automatically support it.

Figure 7-2 illustrates the unit that the author is using, with a USB Mini-b (5-pin) cable plugged in. You will need to order the cable if you don't already own one. By using a USB developer board, you can control both ends of the USB connection. Yet the EZ-USB is simple enough to use, allowing us to avoid rocket science.

Figure 7-2. *The FX2LP EZ-USB developer board*

When you first get the device, you should be able to test it simply by plugging it into a Pi USB port. Then use the lsusb command to see if the Linux kernel sees it (the line shown below is wrapped to make it fit the page width).

```
$ lsusb
Bus 001 Device 011: ID 04b4:8613 Cypress Semiconductor Corp.
CY7C68013 EZ-USB FX2 \
        USB 2.0 Development Kit
...
```

Device Introduction

Anchor Chips Inc. was acquired in 1999 by Cypress Semiconductor Corp.[8] Anchor had designed an 8051 chip that allowed software to be uploaded into its SRAM over USB, to support various peripheral functions. This approach allowed one hardware device to be configured by software for ultimate flexibility. Cypress has since improved and extended its capabilities in new designs like the FX2LP (USB 2.0) and later. One of the best features of this device is how much USB support is built into the hardware.

A complete PDF manual can be downloaded from:

```
http://www.cypress.com/file/126446/download
```

In this document, you will find a wealth of information about the device and USB in general. An entire book could be written about this device but let's simply list some of the salient features:

- 8051 microcontroller architecture with Cypress extensions

- 16 KB of SRAM, for microcontroller code and data

- Hardware FIFO for fast software-free transfers (up to 96 MB/s)

- GPIF (general programming interface) for fast state-machine transfers

- 2 x UART serial communications

- I2C master peripheral for I/O with FLASH

- Hardware USB 2.0 serial engine

One of the reasons I chose this product is that you can program all of the software on the Pi and try out your changes without having to flash anything. And no special microcontroller programmer is required.

USB API Support

On the Linux side, we also obviously need software support. USB devices are normally supported by device drivers and appear as generic peripherals like keyboards, mice, or storage. What is interesting about the EZ-USB device is that we have support enough in the Linux kernel to upload FX2LP firmware to the device. Once uploaded to the FX2LP's SRAM, the device will *ReNumerate*™.

USB Enumeration

When a USB device is first plugged into a USB network (or first seen at boot time), it must go through the job of *enumeration* to discover what devices exist on the bus and know their requirements.

The master of the bus is the host (PC/laptop/Pi). All devices plugged into the bus are slave devices and must wait for the host to request a reply. With very few exceptions, slaves only speak when the master tells them to.

The process of discovery requires the host to query the device by using address zero (all devices must respond to this). The request is a Get-Descriptor-Device request that allows the device to describe some of its attributes. Next the host will assign a specific device address, with a Set-Address request. Additional Get-Descriptor requests are made by the host to gain more information. From these information transfers the host learns about the number of endpoints, power requirements, bus bandwidth required, and what driver to load, etc.

ReNumeration™

This is a term that Cypress uses to describe how an active EZ-USB device disconnects from the USB bus, and enumerates again, possibly as a different USB device. This is possible when executing the downloaded firmware in the EZ-USB SRAM. Alternatively, EZ-USB can be configured to download its firmware into SRAM from the onboard flash storage, using its I2C bus.

Raspbian Linux Installs

To demonstrate USB on the Pi, we must first be able to get software compiled, uploaded, and running on the FX2LP board. To do this, we need some software tools installed. All of these installs must be performed from the root account. Use sudo for that:

```
$ sudo -i
#
```

Install sdcc

The sdcc package includes the 8051 cross compiler and libraries. Thankfully, it is only a command away:

```
# apt-get install sdcc
Reading package lists... Done
Building dependency tree
Reading state information... Done
The following additional packages will be installed:
  gputils gputils-common gputils-doc sdcc-doc sdcc-libraries
Suggested packages:
  sdcc-ucsim
The following NEW packages will be installed:
  gputils gputils-common gputils-doc sdcc sdcc-doc sdcc-
  libraries
0 upgraded, 6 newly installed, 0 to remove and 2 not upgraded.
Need to get 0 B/4,343 kB of archives.
```

After this operation, 53.6 MB of additional disk space will be
used.
Do you want to continue? [Y/n] y
Selecting previously unselected package sdcc-libraries.
(Reading database ... 128619 files and directories currently
installed.)
Preparing to unpack .../0-sdcc-libraries_3.5.0+dfsg-2_all.deb
...
Unpacking sdcc-libraries (3.5.0+dfsg-2) ...
Selecting previously unselected package sdcc.
Preparing to unpack .../1-sdcc_3.5.0+dfsg-2_armhf.deb ...
Unpacking sdcc (3.5.0+dfsg-2) ...
Selecting previously unselected package sdcc-doc.
Preparing to unpack .../2-sdcc-doc_3.5.0+dfsg-2_all.deb ...
Unpacking sdcc-doc (3.5.0+dfsg-2) ...
Selecting previously unselected package gputils-common.
Preparing to unpack .../3-gputils-common_1.4.0-0.1_all.deb ...
Unpacking gputils-common (1.4.0-0.1) ...
Selecting previously unselected package gputils.
Preparing to unpack .../4-gputils_1.4.0-0.1_armhf.deb ...
Unpacking gputils (1.4.0-0.1) ...
Selecting previously unselected package gputils-doc.
Preparing to unpack .../5-gputils-doc_1.4.0-0.1_all.deb ...
Unpacking gputils-doc (1.4.0-0.1) ...
Setting up sdcc-libraries (3.5.0+dfsg-2) ...
Setting up gputils-common (1.4.0-0.1) ...
Setting up gputils-doc (1.4.0-0.1) ...
Setting up sdcc-doc (3.5.0+dfsg-2) ...
Setting up sdcc (3.5.0+dfsg-2) ...
Processing triggers for man-db (2.7.6.1-2) ...
Setting up gputils (1.4.0-0.1) ...
#

This next package is *optional* but is one you may want to use someday. It allows you to simulate the 8051 code on the Pi:

```
# apt-get install sdcc-ucsim
Reading package lists... Done
Building dependency tree
Reading state information... Done
The following NEW packages will be installed:
  sdcc-ucsim
0 upgraded, 1 newly installed, 0 to remove and 2 not upgraded.
Need to get 705 kB of archives.
After this operation, 1,952 kB of additional disk space will be
used.
Get:1 http://raspbian.mirror.colo-serv.net/raspbian stretch/
main armhf sdcc-ucsim armhf 3.5.0+dfsg-2 [705 kB]
Fetched 705 kB in 2s (268 kB/s)
Selecting previously unselected package sdcc-ucsim.
(Reading database ... 131104 files and directories currently
installed.)
Preparing to unpack .../sdcc-ucsim_3.5.0+dfsg-2_armhf.deb ...
Unpacking sdcc-ucsim (3.5.0+dfsg-2) ...
Processing triggers for man-db (2.7.6.1-2) ...
Setting up sdcc-ucsim (3.5.0+dfsg-2) ...
# sync
```

The sync command (at the end) is a good idea on the Pi after making significant changes. It causes the kernel to flush the disk cache out to the flash file system. That way, if your Pi crashes for any reason, you can at least be sure that those changes are now saved in flash. This is a lifesaver if you have cats sniffing around your Pi.

Install cycfx2prog

Next install the cycfx2prog package. We will use the cycfx2prog command to upload our firmware to the FX2LP.

```
# apt-get install cycfx2prog
Reading package lists... Done
Building dependency tree
Reading state information... Done
The following NEW packages will be installed:
  cycfx2prog
0 upgraded, 1 newly installed, 0 to remove and 2 not upgraded.
Need to get 12.6 kB of archives.
After this operation, 52.2 kB of additional disk space will be
used.
Get:1 http://muug.ca/mirror/raspbian/raspbian stretch/main
armhf cycfx2prog armhf 0.47-1 [12.6 kB]
Fetched 12.6 kB in 1s (8,007 B/s)
Selecting previously unselected package cycfx2prog.
(Reading database ... 131163 files and directories currently
installed.)
Preparing to unpack .../cycfx2prog_0.47-1_armhf.deb ...
Unpacking cycfx2prog (0.47-1) ...
Setting up cycfx2prog (0.47-1) ...
# sync
```

Install libusb-1.0-0-dev

The first thing you should do at this point is to update your system, if you haven't done so recently. There was a problem installing the dev package originally, so perform the following as root to correct the issue:

```
# apt-get update
# apt-get upgrade
```

106

Once that is done, install libusb:

```
# apt-get install libusb-1.0-0-dev
```

Installing that package will also install libusb-1.0-0 (without the "dev") if it isn't already installed. Check for the presence of the header file, which is going to be critical:

```
# ls -l /usr/include/libusb-1.0/libusb.h
-rw-r--r-- 1 root root 71395 Oct 26  2016 /usr/include/
libusb-1.0/libusb.h
```

Blacklist usbtest

This step is probably necessary, unless it has been done before. It disables the Linux kernel module usbtest, which will attach to unclaimed devices. Unless this is disabled, our code will not be able to attach to the FX2LP device. From root, perform the following to make the change permanent:

```
# sudo -i
# echo 'blacklist usbtest' >> /etc/modprobe.d/blacklist.conf
```

If you'd prefer not to make this change, you can remove the loaded module manually when required (as root):

```
# rmmod usbtest
```

Obtain Software from github.com

Let's now download the source code for this book, from github.com. From your top-level (home) directory perform:

```
$ git clone https://github.com/ve3wwg/Advanced_Raspberry_Pi.git
Cloning into './Advanced_Raspberry_Pi'...
```

If you don't like the subdirectory name used, you can simply rename it:

```
$ mv ./Advanced_Raspberry_Pi ./RPi
```

Alternatively, you can clone it directly to a subdirectory name of your choosing (notice the added argument):

```
$ git clone https://github.com/ve3wwg/Advanced_Raspberry_Pi.git
./RPi
Cloning into './RPi'...
```

Test EZ-USB FX2LP Device

Before we get into the actual USB project, let's make sure that our tools and our EZ-USB device are working correctly. Change to the following subdirectory:

```
$ cd ~/RPi/libusb/blink
```

Listing the files there, you should see:

```
$ ls
blink.c  Makefile
$
```

The Makefile there also references the following file:

```
../ezusb/Makefile.incl
```

If you're an advanced user and need to make changes, be sure to examine that file. This is used to define how to upload to the FX2LP device, etc. There are also some customized FX2LP include files there.

Compile blink

Using the sdcc cross compiler, we can compile the blink.c module as
follows (long lines are broken with a backslash):

```
$ make
sdcc --std-sdcc99 -mmcs51 --stack-size 64 --model-small --xram-
loc 0x0000 \
   --xram-size 0x5000 --iram-size 0x0100 --code-loc 0x0000 -I../
ezusb blink.c
```

The generated file of interest is named blink.ihx (Intel Hex):

```
$ cat blink.ihx
:03000000020006F5
:03005F0002000399
:0300030002009068
:20006200AE82AF837C007D00C3EC9EED9F501E7AC87B00000000EA24FFF8E
B34FFF9880279
:200082008903E84970ED0CBC00DE0D80DB2275B203D280C2819003E8120062
C280D2819041
:0700A20003E812006280EA8E
:06003500E478FFF6D8FD9F
:200013007900E94400601B7A009000AD780075A000E493F2A308B8000205
A0D9F4DAF275E7
:02003300A0FF2C
:20003B007800E84400600A790075A000E4F309D8FC7800E84400600
C7900900000E4F0A3C5
:04005B00D8FCD9FAFA
:0D0006007581071200A9E582600302000366
:0400A900758200223A
:00000001FF
```

This is the Intel hexadecimal format file for the compiled blink firmware that will be uploaded to the FX2LP device to be executed.

EZ-USB Program Execution

This part requires a bit of special care because the Makefile does not know how the FX2LP enumerated as far as bus and device number. First list the devices on the USB bus:

```
$ lsusb
Bus 001 Device 010: ID 045e:00d1 Microsoft Corp. Optical Mouse
                    with Tilt Wheel
Bus 001 Device 009: ID 04f2:0841 Chicony Electronics Co., Ltd
                    HP Multimedia Keyboard
Bus 001 Device 011: ID 04b4:8613 Cypress Semiconductor Corp.
                    CY7C68013 EZ-USB \
    FX2 USB 2.0 Development Kit
Bus 001 Device 006: ID 0424:7800 Standard Microsystems Corp.
Bus 001 Device 003: ID 0424:2514 Standard Microsystems Corp.
                    USB 2.0 Hub
Bus 001 Device 002: ID 0424:2514 Standard Microsystems Corp.
                    USB 2.0 Hub
Bus 001 Device 001: ID 1d6b:0002 Linux Foundation 2.0 root hub
```

From this session, locate the EZ-USB device. Here the bus number is 001 and the device number 011. Using this information, type the following (modify to match your own bus and device numbers):

```
$ make BUS=001 DEV=011 prog
sudo cycfx2prog -d=001.011 reset prg:blink.ihx run
Using ID 04b4:8613 on 001.011.
Putting 8051 into reset.
Putting 8051 into reset.
```

Programming 8051 using "blink.ihx".
Putting 8051 out of reset.
$

If all went well as it did in this session, you should now see the two
built-in LEDs alternately flashing on your FX2LP board. The source code is
presented in Listing 7-1.

Listing 7-1. The EZ-USB FX2LP blink.c source code

```
0006: #include <fx2regs.h>
0007: #include <fx2sdly.h>
0008:
0009: static void
0010: delay(unsigned times) {
0011:    unsigned int x, y;
0012:
0013:    for ( x=0; x<times; x++ ) {
0014:        for ( y=0; y<200; y++ ) {
0015:            SYNCDELAY;
0016:        }
0017:    }
0018: }
0019:
0020: void
0021: main(void) {
0022:
0023:    OEA = 0x03;      // PA0 & PA1 is output
0024:
0025:    for (;;) {
0026:        PA0 = 1;
0027:        PA1 = 0;
```

```
0028:         delay(1000);
0029:         PA0 = 0;
0030:         PA1 = 1;
0031:         delay(1000);
0032:   }
0033: }
```

If you are using a different manufactured board, you might need to track down the LED pins and make small changes to the code. As far as I know, all available boards use these same LEDs. The board I am using has the LEDs connected to GPIO port A pin 0 (PA0) and PA1. If yours are different, substitute for PA0 and PA1 in the code.

Additionally, you will need to change the following line:

```
0023:   OEA = 0x03;     // PA0 & PA1 is output
```

OEA is the register name for port A output enable. The bits set to 1 in this register, and configure the corresponding port A pins as an output pin. For example, if your board uses PA2 and PA3 instead, you would need to change that line to:

```
0023:   OEA = 0x0C;     // PA2 & PA3 is output (bits 2 & 3)
```

If the LEDs are located on a different port altogether, then change the "A" in OEA to match the port being used.

USB Demonstration

Now we can finally perform a demonstration of the Raspberry Pi using libusb to communicate with a USB device (FX2LP). To keep this simple, our assignment is rather trivial, except for the use of USB in between the two ends. The goal is to be able to turn on/off the LEDs on the FX2LP device from the Raspberry Pi side. At the same time the Pi will read confirmation information about the current state of the LEDs from the USB device. In effect, this demonstration exercises the sending of command information to the FX2LP, while also receiving updates from the FX2LP about the LED states.

FX2LP Source Code

Our main focus is the Raspberry Pi side, but let's examine the important aspects of the FX2LP source code so that you can see what is going on in the remote device. First change to the following subdirectory:

```
$ cd ~/RPi/libusb/controlusb
```

The FX2LP source file of interest is named ezusb.c with the main program illustrated in Listing 7-2.

Listing 7-2. FX2LP main program in ezusb.c

```
0091: void
0092: main(void) {
0093:
0094:   OEA = 0x03;        // Enable PA0 and PA1 outputs
0095:   initialize();   // Initialize USB
0096:
0097:   PA0 = 1;           // Turn off LEDs..
0098:   PA1 = 1;
0099:
0100:   for (;;) {
0101:       if ( !(EP2CS & bmEPEMPTY) )
0102:           accept_cmd();   // Have data in EP2
0103:
0104:       if ( !(EP6CS & bmEPFULL) )
0105:           send_state();   // EP6 is not full
0106:   }
0107: }
```

Lines 94 to 98 configure the GPIO pins of the FX2LP as outputs. Then it runs the loop in lines 100 to 106 forever. The if statement in line 101 tests if there is any data received in USB endpoint 2, and when not empty, it calls the function accept_cmd().

Line 104 checks to see if endpoint 6 is not full. If not full, the function send_state() is called to send status information. Now let's examine those two functions in more detail.

Function accept_cmd

The function is displayed in Listing 7-3.

Listing 7-3. The FX2LP function accept_cmd() in ezusb.c

```
0047: static void
0048: accept_cmd(void) {
0049:     __xdata const unsigned char *src = EP2FIFOBUF;
0050:     unsigned len = ((unsigned)EP2BCH)<<8 | EP2BCL;
0051:
0052:     if ( len < 1 )
0053:         return;            // Nothing to process
0054:     PA0 = *src & 1;        // Set PA0 LED
0055:     PA1 = *src & 2;        // Set PA1 LED
0056:     OUTPKTEND = 0x82;      // Release buffer
0057: }
```

The magic of the FX2LP is that most of the USB stuff is handled in silicon. Line 50 accesses a register in the silicon that indicates how much data was delivered to endpoint 2. If there is no data, the function simply returns in line 53.

Otherwise the data is accessed through a special pointer, which was obtained in line 49. Line 54 sets the LED output pin PA0 according to bit 0 of the first byte received (the Raspberry Pi program will only be sending one byte). PA1 is likewise set by bit 1 of that same command byte.

Last of all, line 56 tells the silicon that the data in endpoint 2 can be released. Without doing this, no more data would be received.

Function send_state

The send_state() function reads the current status of GPIO ports PA0 and PA1 and forms an ASCII message to send back to the Raspberry Pi (Listing 7-4). The verbose message format was chosen as an illustration for sending/receiving several bytes of information.

Listing 7-4. The FX2LP function send_state() in ezusb.c

```
0063: static void
0064: send_state(void) {
0065:     __xdata unsigned char *dest = EP6FIFOBUF;
0066:     const char *msg1 = PA0 ? "PA0=1" : "PA0=0";
0067:     const char *msg2 = PA1 ? "PA1=1" : "PA1=0";
0068:     unsigned char len=0;
0069:
0070:     while ( *msg1 ) {
0071:         *dest++ = *msg1++;
0072:         ++len;
0073:     }
0074:     *dest++ = ',';
0075:     ++len;
0076:     while ( *msg2 ) {
0077:         *dest++ = *msg2++;
0078:         ++len;
0079:     }
0080:
0081:     SYNCDELAY;
0082:     EP6BCH=0;
```

```
0083:    SYNCDELAY;
0084:    EP6BCL=len; // Arms the endpoint for transmission
0085: }
```

Line 65 accesses the endpoint 6 FIFO buffer, for placing the message into. Lines 66 and 67 simply choose a message depending upon whether the GPIO port is a 1-bit or a 0-bit. Lines 70 to 73 then copy this message into the endpoint buffer from line 65. Lines 74 and 75 add a comma, and then the loop in lines 76 to 79 copy the second message to the endpoint buffer.

The SYNCDELAY macros are a timing issue unique to the FX2LP, when running at its top clock speed. Line 82 sets the high byte of the FIFO length to zero (our messages are less than 256 bytes). Line 84 sets the low byte of the FIFO length to the length we accumulated in variable len. Once the low byte of the FIFO length has been set, the silicon runs with the buffer and sends it up to the Pi on the USB bus.

Apart from the initialization and setup of the endpoints for the FX2LP, that is all there is to the EZ-USB implementation. The initialization source code is also in ezusb.c, for those that want to study it more closely.

EZ-USB Initialization

To initialize the FX2LP device, a few registers have values stuffed into them in order to configure it. Ignore the SYNCDELAY macro calls—these are simply placed there to give the FX2LP time enough to accept the configuration changes while the device operates at the top clock rate. Listing 7-5 illustrates the configuration steps involved.

Listing 7-5. The EZ-USB initialization code from ezusb.c

```
0010: static void
0011: initialize(void) {
0012:
```

```
0013:    CPUCS = 0x10;          // 48 MHz, CLKOUT disabled.
0014:    SYNCDELAY;
0015:    IFCONFIG = 0xc0;       // Internal IFCLK @ 48MHz
0016:    SYNCDELAY;
0017:    REVCTL = 0x03;         // Disable auto-arm + Enhanced
                                   packet handling
0018:    SYNCDELAY;
0019:    EP6CFG = 0xE2;         // bulk IN, 512 bytes, double-
                                   buffered
0020:    SYNCDELAY;
0021:    EP2CFG = 0xA2;         // bulk OUT, 512 bytes, double-
                                   buffered
0022:    SYNCDELAY;
0023:    FIFORESET = 0x80;      // NAK all requests from host.
0024:    SYNCDELAY;
0025:    FIFORESET = 0x82;      // Reset EP 2
0026:    SYNCDELAY;
0027:    FIFORESET = 0x84;      // Reset EP 4..
0028:    SYNCDELAY;
0029:    FIFORESET = 0x86;
0030:    SYNCDELAY;
0031:    FIFORESET = 0x88;
0032:    SYNCDELAY;
0033:    FIFORESET = 0x00;      // Back to normal..
0034:    SYNCDELAY;
0035:    EP2FIFOCFG = 0x00;     // Disable AUTOOUT
0036:    SYNCDELAY;
0037:    OUTPKTEND = 0x82;      // Clear the 1st buffer
0038:    SYNCDELAY;
0039:    OUTPKTEND = 0x82;      // ..both of them
0040:    SYNCDELAY;
0041: }
```

Line 13 configures the CPU clock for 48 MHz, while line 15 configures an interface clock also for 48 MHz. Line 19 configures endpoint 6 to be used for bulk input (from the hosts perspective), while line 21 configures endpoint 2 for bulk output. Lines 23 to 31 perform a FIFO reset. Lines 37 and 39 clear the double-buffered FIFO and then the FX2LP silicon is ready to handle USB requests.

Raspberry Pi Source Code

Now let's turn our attention to the Raspberry Pi code, using libusb. Listing 7-6 illustrates the main program source code found in controlusb. cpp. We're still in the directory:

```
$ cd ~/RPi/libusb/controlusb
```

Listing 7-6. The main program in controlusb.cpp for the Raspberry Pi

```
0164: int
0165: main(int argc,char **argv) {
0166:     Tty tty;
0167:     int rc, ch;
0168:     char buf[513];
0169:     unsigned id_vendor = 0x04b4,
0170:         id_product = 0x8613;
0171:     libusb_device_handle *hdev;
0172:     unsigned state = 0b0011;
0173:
0174:     hdev = find_usb_device(id_vendor,id_product);
0175:     if ( !hdev ) {
0176:         fprintf(stderr,
0177:             "Device not found. "
0178:             "Vendor=0x%04X Product=0x%04X\n",
```

```
0179:                 id_vendor,id_product);
0180:         return 1;
0181:     }
0182:
0183:     rc = libusb_claim_interface(hdev,0);
0184:     if ( rc != 0 ) {
0185:         fprintf(stderr,
0186:             "%s: Claiming interface 0.\n",
0187:             libusb_strerror(libusb_error(rc)));
0188:         libusb_close(hdev);
0189:         return 2;
0190:     }
0191:
0192:     printf("Interface claimed:\n");
0193:
0194:     if ( (rc = libusb_set_interface_alt_setting(hdev,0,1))
         != 0 ) {
0195:         fprintf(stderr,"%s: libusb_set_interface_alt_
             setting(h,0,1)\n",
0196:             libusb_strerror(libusb_error(rc)));
0197:         return 3;
0198:     }
0199:
0200:     tty.raw_mode();
0201:
0202:     // Main loop:
0203:
0204:     for (;;) {
0205:         if ( (ch = tty.getc(500)) == -1 ) {
0206:             // Timed out: Try to read from EP6
0207:             rc = bulk_read(hdev,0x86,buf,512,10/*ms*/);
```

```
0208:            if ( rc < 0 ) {
0209:                fprintf(stderr,
0210:                    "%s: bulk_read()\n\r",
0211:                    libusb_strerror(libusb_error(-rc)));
0212:                break;
0213:            }
0214:
0215:            assert(rc < int(sizeof buf));
0216:            buf[rc] = 0;
0217:            printf("Read %d bytes: %s\n\r",rc,buf);
0218:            if ( !isatty(0) )
0219:                break;
0220:        } else {
0221:            if ( ch == 'q' || ch == 'Q' || ch == 0x04
                 /*CTRL-D*/ )
0222:                break;
0223:            if ( ch == '0' || ch == '1' ) {
0224:                unsigned mask = 1 << (ch & 1);
0225:
0226:                state ^= mask;
0227:                buf[0] = state;
0228:                rc = bulk_write(hdev,0x02,buf,1,10/*ms*/);
0229:                if ( rc < 0 ) {
0230:                    fprintf(stderr,
0231:                        "%s: write bulk to EP 2\n",
0232:                        libusb_strerror(libusb_error(-
                         rc)));
0233:                    break;
0234:                }
0235:                printf("Wrote %d bytes: 0x%02X  (state
                     0x%02X)\n",
```

```
0236:                        rc,unsigned(buf[0]),state);
0237:              } else {
0238:                  printf("Press q to quit, else 0 or 1 to "
                           "toggle LED.\n");
0239:              }
0240:          }
0241:      }
0242:
0243:      rc = libusb_release_interface(hdev,0);
0244:      assert(!rc);
0245:      libusb_close(hdev);
0246:
0247:      close_usb();
0248:      return 0;
0249: }
```

C++ was used for the Raspberry Pi code to simplify some things. The non C++ programmer need not fear. Many Arduino students are using C++ without realizing it. The Arduino folks are likely wincing at me for saying this because they don't want to scare anyone. For this project, we'll focus on what mostly looks and works like C.

Line 166 defines a class instance named tty. Don't worry about its details because we'll just use it to do some terminal I/O stuff that is unimportant to our focus.

Lines 169 and 170 define the vendor and product ID that we are going to be looking for on a USB bus somewhere. Line 174 calls upon the libusb function find_usb_device based upon these two ID numbers. If the device is not found, it returns a null pointer, which is tested in line 175.

When the device is found, control passes to line 183, where we claim interface zero. If this fails it is likely because it is claimed by another driver (like usbtest).

121

The alternate interface 1 is chosen in line 194. This is the last step in the sequence leading up to the successful USB device access for the loop that follows, starting in line 204. Once the loop exits (we'll see how shortly), the interface is released in line 243 and then closed in 245. Line 247 closes the libusb library.

USB I/O Loop

Line 200 uses the tty object to enable "raw mode" for the terminal. This permits this program to receive one character at a time. Normally a RETURN key must be pressed before the program sees any input, which is inconvenient for this demo.

Within the loop, line 205 tries to read a terminal character, waiting for up to 500 ms. If none is received within that time, the call returns -1 to indicate a timeout. When that happens, the code starting in line 207 tries to read from USB endpoint 6 (the high bit in 0x86 indicates that this is an OUT port, from the host's point of view). This is the endpoint that our FX2LP will be sending us status updates on (as character string messages).

Lines 150 and 152 are executed when a character from the Raspberry Pi keyboard is received. If the character is a 'q', the program exits the loop in line 151. This allows for a clean program exit.

Lines 224 to 236 are executed if a '0' or '1' is typed. Line 224 turns the character into a 0-bit or a 1-bit in the variable mask. In other words, mask is assigned 0x01 or 0x02, depending upon the input character being a '0' or '1' respectively. Line 226 tracks the state of the LED bit in the variable named state. The value of mask then toggles the respective bit on or off, depending upon its prior state.

Line 227 places the state byte into the first buffer byte. This 1-byte buffer is then written to endpoint 2 (argument 0x02), timing out if necessary after 10 ms in line 228. If the timeout occurred, the return value of rc will be negative. Otherwise the bytes written are displayed on the terminal from line 235.

Line 238 is executed if the program didn't understand the character typed at the terminal.

Listing 7-7 illustrates the source code for the function find_usb_device.

Listing 7-7. The function find_usb_device in file controlusb.cpp

```
0080: static libusb_device_handle *
0081: find_usb_device(unsigned id_vendor,unsigned id_product) {
0082:
0083:    if ( !usb_devs ) {
0084:        libusb_init(nullptr);          // Initialize
0085:        // Fetch list of devices
0086:        n_devices = libusb_get_device_list(nullptr,&usb_
               devs);
0087:        if ( n_devices < 0 )
0088:            return nullptr;     // Failed
0089:    }
0090:    return libusb_open_device_with_vid_pid(
0091:        nullptr,id_vendor,id_product);
0092: }
```

The first time libusb is called, the function libusb_init must be called. This is done in line 84 if variable usb_devs is a null pointer (note that the variable usb_devs is a static variable and is initialized as null (nullptr in C++)). After that, line 86 fetches a list of USB devices and stores a pointer into usb_devs for future use.

Once that formality is out of the way, we call upon libusb_open_device_with_vid_pid to locate and open our device.

Function bulk_read

Within the main loop shown in Listing 7-6, the function bulk_read was called from line 207. Listing 7-8 illustrates the code for that function.

Listing 7-8. The bulk_read function in controlusb.cpp

```
0111: static int
0112: bulk_read(
0113:    libusb_device_handle *hdev,
0114:    unsigned char endpoint,
0115:    void *buffer,
0116:    int buflen,
0117:    unsigned timeout_ms
0118: ) {
0119:    unsigned char *bufp = (unsigned char*)buffer;
0120:    int rc, xlen = 0;
0121:
0122:    assert(endpoint & 0x80);
0123:    rc = libusb_bulk_transfer(hdev,endpoint,
               bufp,buflen,&xlen,timeout_ms);
0124:    if ( rc == 0 || rc == LIBUSB_ERROR_TIMEOUT )
0125:        return xlen;
0126:    return -int(rc);
0127: }
```

Essentially, this function is a simple interlude to the library function libusb_bulk_transfer in line 123. The number of bytes actually read is returned into the int variable xlen in this call. For larger packets, this could be broken into segments of data. Here we use the simple assumption that we will receive all of our data in one transfer.

Note that if the transfer times out, we can still have some data transferred (line 124 tests for this). The number of bytes read is returned at line 125. Otherwise we return the negative integer of the error code.

Function bulk_write

The bulk_write function is more involved because it must ensure that the full message is transmitted, even when it is sent in small chunks. Listing 7-9 illustrates.

Listing 7-9. The bulk_write function in controlusb.cpp

```
0133: static int
0134: bulk_write(
0135:    libusb_device_handle *hdev,
0136:    unsigned char endpoint,
0137:    void *buffer,
0138:    int buflen,
0139:    unsigned timeout_ms
0140: ) {
0141:    unsigned char *bufp = (unsigned char*)buffer;
0142:    int rc, xlen = 0, total = 0;
0143:
0144:    assert(!(endpoint & 0x80));
0145:
0146:    for (;;) {
0147:        rc = libusb_bulk_transfer(hdev,endpoint,
                   bufp,buflen,&xlen,timeout_ms);
0148:        if ( rc == 0 || rc == LIBUSB_ERROR_TIMEOUT ) {
0149:            total += xlen;
0150:            bufp += xlen;
0151:            buflen -= xlen;
0152:            if ( buflen <= 0 )
0153:                return total;
```

```
0154:        } else {
0155:            return -int(rc); // Failed
0156:        }
0157:    }
0158: }
```

The message transfer uses libusb_bulk_transfer again but knows this is being sent to the host based upon the endpoint number (the assertion in line 144 checks). The number of bytes actually sent by the call is returned in the xlen variable (argument five). The the transfer was successful, or timed out, the total number of bytes are returned as a positive number (line 153). Otherwise the negative error code is returned.

Note that the routine tracks total bytes transferred in line 149. The buffer start pointer is incremented in line 150 and the count to be sent reduced in line 151. The routine only returns when all bytes are sent or the request has timed out. Ideally, better handling should be provided for the timeout case.

The Demonstration

Now let's perform the illustration. With the FX2LP device plugged into the USB port, find out its bus and device number for the firmware upload to it:

```
$ lsusb
Bus 001 Device 007: ID 04b4:8613 Cypress Semiconductor Corp.
                    CY7C68013 \ EZ-USB FX2 USB 2.0 Development
                    Kit
Bus 001 Device 006: ID 0424:7800 Standard Microsystems Corp.
Bus 001 Device 003: ID 0424:2514 Standard Microsystems Corp.
                    USB 2.0 Hub
```

```
Bus 001 Device 002: ID 0424:2514 Standard Microsystems Corp.
                    USB 2.0 Hub
Bus 001 Device 001: ID 1d6b:0002 Linux Foundation 2.0 root hub
$
```

Knowing now that it is on bus 001 and device 007, upload the firmware to it. You should see session output like the following:

```
$ sudo make BUS=001 DEV=007 prog
sudo cycfx2prog -d=001.007 prg:ezusb.ihx run delay:10
dbulk:6,-512,5
Using ID 04b4:8613 on 001.007.
Putting 8051 into reset.
Programming 8051 using "ezusb.ihx".
Putting 8051 out of reset.
Delay: 10 msec
Reading <=512 bytes from EP adr 0x86  ...etc.
```

One the cycfx2prog takes the FX2LP out of reset, our firmware code starts executing, which is what the "Reading <=512 bytes" messages are all about. Now make the Raspberry Pi program, if you've not already done so:

```
$ make -f Makefile.posix
g++ -c -std=c++11 -Wall -Wno-deprecated  -I. -g -O0 controlusb.
cpp \ -o controlusb.o
g++  controlusb.o -o controlusb -lusb
```

Now launch it:

```
$ sudo ./controlusb
Interface claimed:
Read 11 bytes: PA0=1,PA1=1
Read 11 bytes: PA0=1,PA1=1
Read 11 bytes: PA0=1,PA1=1
```

```
Wrote 1 bytes: 0x01  (state 0x01)
Read 11 bytes: PA0=1,PA1=1
Read 11 bytes: PA0=1,PA1=1
Read 11 bytes: PA0=1,PA1=0
Read 11 bytes: PA0=1,PA1=0
Read 11 bytes: PA0=1,PA1=0
Read 11 bytes: PA0=1,PA1=0
Wrote 1 bytes: 0x00  (state 0x00)
Read 11 bytes: PA0=1,PA1=0
Read 11 bytes: PA0=1,PA1=0
Wrote 1 bytes: 0x02  (state 0x02)
Read 11 bytes: PA0=0,PA1=0
Read 11 bytes: PA0=0,PA1=0
Wrote 1 bytes: 0x00  (state 0x00)
Read 11 bytes: PA0=0,PA1=1
```

The program requires root so launch it with sudo. Otherwise it will find the device but not be able to claim the interface. The first line:

```
Wrote 1 bytes: 0x01  (state 0x01)
```

is written when I typed a 1. Shortly after, the LED on PA1 lights up (the LEDs are active low, so a 0-bit turns on the LED). Two lines later, the FX2LP is able to send us a message reporting that PA1=0 (LED on). This is not tardiness on the FX2LP's part but is the reality that it was unable to send a message about it until the prior USB messages were read by the Pi.

Some other doodling with '0' and '1' was performed until the 'q' key ended the demonstration.

Summary

A lot of ground was covered in this chapter. A whirlwind introduction to the FX2LP EZ-USB device was presented. The curious mind should look at the PDF documents for the EZ-USB device and seek out books and online resources for it. This chapter only scratched the surface of what that silicon can do.

The main focus of this chapter was to see how to handle USB I/O directly from a user mode program on the Raspberry Pi. The libusb library makes this rather easy, once you know the basics. These were covered in the controlusb.cpp source code. Now that you're armed and dangerous, you can take your USB knowledge to a new level by designing new applications using USB.

CHAPTER 8

Ethernet

Networking has become an important part of everyday life, whether by wire or wireless. Having a network adapter on your Raspberry Pi allows you to connect to it and work from the comfort of your desktop or laptop computer. It also allows your application on the Pi to communicate with the outside world. Even when the Raspberry Pi is deployed as part of an embedded project, the network interface continues to shine. Remote logging and control are just a couple of examples.

Wired Ethernet

The standard Raspbian SD card image provides a wired network connection, using DHCP (dynamic host configuration protocol) to automatically assign an IP address to it. If you are using the HDMI output and keyboard devices to work on the Pi, the dynamically assigned IP address is not a problem. But if you would like to eliminate the attached display and keyboard and operate "headless," connecting to the Pi over the network is attractive. The only problem is the potentially changing IP address assigned by DHCP.

DHCP will not always use a different IP address because it *leases* the address for a time. But a dynamically assigned address makes it difficult to connect to your Raspberry Pi from another computer when it changes. As discussed in Chapter 2, you can use the nmap command to scan for it, but this is inconvenient (this example is from Devuan Linux):

```
root@devuan:~# nmap -sP 192.168.1.1-250
```

© Warren Gay 2018
W. Gay, *Advanced Raspberry Pi*, https://doi.org/10.1007/978-1-4842-3948-3_8

```
Starting Nmap 6.47 ( http://nmap.org ) at 2018-06-01 19:59 EDT
Nmap scan report for 192.168.1.1
Host is up (0.00026s latency).
MAC Address: C0:FF:D4:95:80:04 (Unknown)
Nmap scan report for 192.168.1.12
Host is up (0.044s latency).
MAC Address: 00:1B:A9:BD:79:12 (Brother Industries)
Nmap scan report for 192.168.1.77
Host is up (0.15s latency).
MAC Address: B8:27:EB:ED:48:B1 (Raspberry Pi Foundation)
Nmap scan report for 192.168.1.121
Host is up (0.00027s latency).
MAC Address: 40:6C:8F:11:8B:AE (Apple)
Nmap scan report for 192.168.1.89
Host is up.
Nmap done: 250 IP addresses (4 hosts up) scanned in 7.54 seconds
root@devuan:~#
```

If you use your Pi at school or away from home, using DHCP may still be the best option for you. If you are plugging it into different networks as you travel, DHCP sets up your IP address properly and *takes care of the name server configuration*. However, if you are using your unit at home, or your school can assign you a valid IP address to use, a static IP address simplifies access.

Note   Be sure to get approval and an IP address assigned to prevent network conflicts.

Static Wired Address

The simplest way to set up your static wired ethernet address is to use the graphical desktop and open the dialog for "Wireless & Wired Network Settings." This is available at the top right of your screen by right-clicking on the WIFI icon, to the left of the speaker icon. Figure 8-1 illustrates.

Figure 8-1. *The pop-up menu containing the Wireless and Wired Network Settings dialog*

Select and click the selection "Wireless & Wired Network Settings." A dialog like Figure 8-2 should appear.

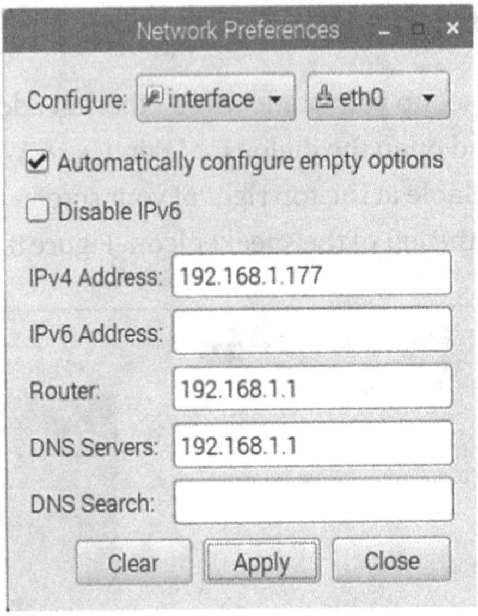

Figure 8-2. *The Network Preferences dialog box*

To configure the wired interface, choose "interface" and then "eth0". Leave the "Automatically configure empty options" checked if you like, as I did in the figure. Fill in your address, router, and DNS Servers info and click "Apply" and then "Close." What is updated by this action? The following lines will be appended to the file /etc/dhcpcd.conf:

```
interface eth0
inform 192.168.1.177
static routers=192.168.1.1
static domain_name_servers=192.168.1.1
```

With these settings established, the wired ethernet port should automatically be assigned the static IP address 192.168.1.177 in this example.

Wireless Configuration

The wireless network interface is configured in a similar way to the wired adapter. Bring up the dialog box that you saw in Figure 8-2, except that you will choose "SSID" instead of "interface." Figure 8-3 shows the wireless configuration dialog.

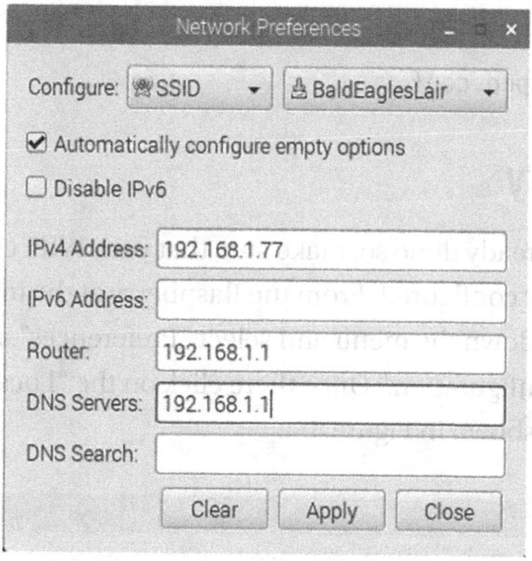

Figure 8-3. *The Wireless configuration dialog*

At the right of "SSID," choose the wireless network you wish to join. Click Apply and then Close. After you have done this, the file /etc/dhcpcd. conf is updated with:

```
SSID BaldEaglesLair
inform 192.168.1.77
static routers=192.168.1.1
static domain_name_servers=192.168.1.1
```

Bugs

The graphical dialog works great except that if you repeat the configuration of the wireless network, you will get added entries at the bottom of the file. If these multiple settings for the same SSID are in conflict, your wireless network may never work. If that is the case, you need to edit the file to remove the conflicting duplicates:

```
# sudo -i
# nano /etc/dhcpcd.conf
```

WIFI Country

If you have not already done so, make sure that your WIFI country has been properly configured. From the Raspberry at the top left of the desktop, pull down the menu and select "Preferences" and then "Raspberry Pi Configuration." Once there click on the "Localisation" tab with an example shown in Figure 8-4.

Figure 8-4. The "Localisation" tab with the WIFI Country setting

Once there, it is a simple matter to click on "Set WIFI Country" to select your country. This is an important configuration item because it determines the legal operating frequencies for your wireless LAN (local area network) adapter in your country.

Test Static IP Addresses

Once you have configured things, the simplest thing to do is to reboot your Raspberry Pi to make the new settings take effect. Usually, the graphical dialogs will make your changes take effect almost immediately.

A good manual check is to use the ifconfig command:

```
$ ifconfig eth0
eth0: flags=4163<UP,BROADCAST,RUNNING,MULTICAST>  mtu 1500
        inet 192.168.1.177  netmask 255.255.255.0  broadcast
        192.168.1.255
        inet6 fe80::8cc8:d1d2:61ba:d377  prefixlen 64  scopeid
        0x20<link>
        ether b8:27:eb:b8:1d:e4  txqueuelen 1000  (Ethernet)
        RX packets 10505  bytes 900810 (879.6 KiB)
        RX errors 0  dropped 0  overruns 0  frame 0
        TX packets 26412  bytes 14866204 (14.1 MiB)
        TX errors 0  dropped 0 overruns 0  carrier 0  collisions 0
```

From this you can see your IP address for the wired network adapter is configured:

```
inet 192.168.1.177  netmask 255.255.255.0  broadcast 192.168.1.255
```

Likewise you can check the wireless adapter:

```
$ ifconfig wlan0
wlan0: flags=4163<UP,BROADCAST,RUNNING,MULTICAST>  mtu 1500
        inet 192.168.1.77  netmask 255.255.255.0  broadcast
        192.168.1.255
```

```
inet6 fe80::dd0c:a1af:9a22:a0c0  prefixlen 64  scopeid
0x20<link>
ether b8:27:eb:ed:48:b1  txqueuelen 1000  (Ethernet)
RX packets 24977  bytes 1777643 (1.6 MiB)
RX errors 0  dropped 0  overruns 0  frame 0
TX packets 6924  bytes 7627770 (7.2 MiB)
TX errors 0  dropped 0 overruns 0  carrier 0  collisions 0
```

Let's now check that the names are *resolving*. Normally, I would recommend nslookup or dig commands for this, but neither comes preinstalled on Raspbian. So let's just use the ping command:

```
$ ping -c 1 google.com
PING google.com (172.217.0.238) 56(84) bytes of data.
64 bytes from yyz10s03-in-f14.1e100.net (172.217.0.238): icmp_
seq=1 ttl=55 time=17.9 ms

--- google.com ping statistics ---
1 packets transmitted, 1 received, 0% packet loss, time 0ms
rtt min/avg/max/mdev = 17.931/17.931/17.931/0.000 ms
```

In this example, we see that google.com was looked up and translated to the IP address 172.217.0.238 (your attempt may differ). From this, we conclude that the name service is working. The -c1 option on the ping command line causes only one ping to be performed. Otherwise, ping will keep trying and you may need to ^C to interrupt its execution.

If the name google.com does not resolve, you'll need to troubleshoot /etc/resolv.conf. It should look something like this (note the nameserver line):

```
$ cat /etc/resolv.conf
# Generated by resolvconf
search subversive.cats.ca
nameserver 192.168.1.1
```

For more information about this file, consult:

```
$ man 5 resolv.conf
```

USB Adapters

If you have a wired USB ethernet adapter, you can set up networking for that also. An example of a cheap unit is shown in Figure 8-5. It should appear in your dialog as "interface" "eth1" when you have already have a built-in wired adapter like the Raspberry Pi 3 B+. When used for the Raspberry Pi Zero (not Zero W), it will appear as "eth0". This is a great way to temporarily communicate with your Zero.

Wireless USB adapters can also be used, if your Raspbian Linux supports it. Often device specific firmware needs to be loaded for support. Also keep in mind that the wireless adapter can require from 350 to 500 mA of current from the USB port.

Radicom advertises that their non-wireless model LUHM200 model requires a maximum of 165 mA (unconfirmed if it is supported by Raspbian Linux). A Pi compatibility list is found at this website:

```
https://elinux.org/RPi_USB_Ethernet_adapters
```

That site lists a few other current consumption figures, including an Apple adapter that requires 250 mA. In general, a *wired* adapter should consume considerably less than a wireless adapter, and when supported, should require no special driver. My unit shown in Figure 8-5 used about 45 mA.

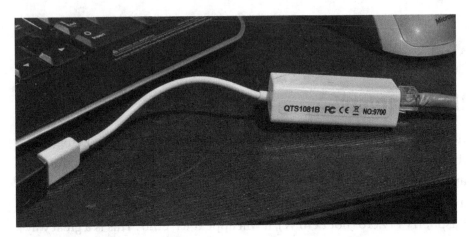

Figure 8-5. *A wired USB ethernet adapter plugged into an USB extension cable*

/etc/hosts File

If you have a static IP address for your Raspberry Pi, why not update your Linux, or OS X /etc/hosts file (Windows, typically C:\Windows\system32\ drivers\etc\hosts), with a hostname? For example, your hosts file could have the following line added:

```
$ cat /etc/hosts
. . .
192.168.1.177 rasp raspi rpi pi # My Raspberry Pi
```

Now you can use a hostname of rasp, raspi, rpi, or pi to access your Raspberry Pi on the network.

Pi Direct

Given the low cost of Raspberry Pi SBCs (single board computers), you might run another Pi as a satellite off of your main Raspberry Pi 3 B+. If you're a game developer, you might want to take advantage of the satellite

Pi for a VR (virtual reality) display. This offers you 2 x HDMI outputs, if the network connection between the two is fast enough. For lighter graphics loads, you might even use a Raspberry Pi Zero.

To explore this possibility, let's outline the steps to link two Raspberry Pi's directly through a wired ethernet connection. I will use a Raspberry Pi 3 B+ accessed through the WIFI (interface wlan0), but link the satellite Pi (Raspberry Pi 3 B, *not plus*) through the wired ethernet ports on both (interface eth0 on both). The remote (satellite) Pi is to have full access to the internet, via the Pi 3 B+.

It used to be necessary to use an ethernet *cross-over* cable but now this is unnecessary. The ethernet firmware now auto configures the ports with straight cables. Figure 8-6 illustrates the example network that I will use to make this discussion easier. Take a moment now to soak it in.

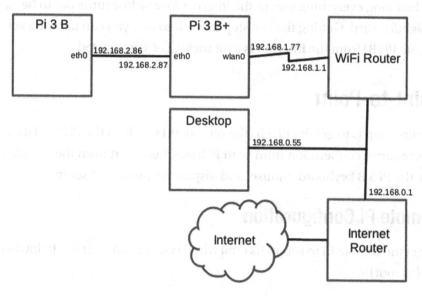

Figure 8-6. *Example network for Pi 3 B+ and point-to-point connected Pi 3 B*

We're going to focus on the Pi 3 B+ and the Pi 3 B in this example. But note that the internet access for the B+ node arrives over WIFI (interface wlan0), via the WIFI router (192.168.1.1). This is fed through an ISP router at 192.168.0.1. Desktop access to the B+ node is over WIFI as well, using the IP address 192.168.1.77.

The problems to be solved are the following:

- Setting up a point-to-point connection between the B+ and the B, using a cable from eth0 to eth0 on both Pi's.

- Enabling IP routing so that all connect requests go through the B+ (from B).

- Enable forwarding from the B to the internet (this includes setting up name server access).

Enabling everything except the internet forwarding turns out to be straightforward. Getting the last step to work so that you can upgrade your remote Pi (B) from the internet is a bit tricky. Let's get started.

Point-to-Point

The first step is to get the Pi 3 B (the remote Pi) to talk to the Pi 3 B+ (B+). This requires cooperation from both Pi hosts. Let's start from the remote Pi (use the Pi 3 B keyboard, mouse, and display for this initial setup).

Remote Pi Configuration

To get the remote Pi to set up its eth0 wired connection, edit the following file (as root):

```
# nano /etc/dhcpcd.conf
```

Add/edit lines so that you end up with:

```
interface eth0
inform 192.168.2.86
static ip_address=192.168.2.86/24
static domain_name_servers=192.168.1.1
static routers=192.168.2.87
```

If you've been here before, make sure you comment out or otherwise disable old references to the interface eth0.

- The `inform` option tells the DHCP at boot time that ethernet interface eth0 is to be brought up with the IP address 192.168.2.86.

- The `static ip_address` line specifies the same, except that the /24 indicates the boundary between the network and host address.

- The `static domain_name_servers` line configures where name server requests should go. Here we forward name server requests to the WIFI router at 192.168.1.1.

- The `static routers` line is vital here. It directs that all traffic to unknown hosts to be "thrown over the wall" to the Pi 3 B+ host.

192.168.2.87 is the B+ end of that directly connected wired link (review Figure 8-6). It is important that the IP address be the *B+ end of that link*. If you mistakenly provide 192.168.2.86 instead, it would end up trying to forward to itself (B).

Save those changes and reboot. After it comes up, you should be able to verify its IP address and routing tables as follows (from the keyboard and display):

```
# ifconfig eth0
eth0:  flags=4163<UP,BROADCAST,RUNNING,MULTICAST>   mtu 1500
        inet 192.168.2.86  netmask 255.255.255.0  broadcast
        192.168.2.255
        inet6 fe80::595f:6363:5a8:d68  prefixlen 64  scopeid
        0x20<link>
        ether b8:27:eb:4d:56:6f  txqueuelen 1000  (Ethernet)
        RX packets 163  bytes 13423 (13.1 KiB)
        RX errors 0  dropped 0  overruns 0  frame 0
        TX packets 143  bytes 22865 (22.3 KiB)
        TX errors 0  dropped 0 overruns 0  carrier 0  collisions 0
```

If the link isn't up (running), don't worry about that yet. We still have work to do on the B+ end of the connection. Check the routing:

```
# route -n
Kernel IP routing table
Destination  Gateway      Genmask         Flags Metric Ref Use Iface
0.0.0.0      192.168.2.87 0.0.0.0         UG    202    0   0   eth0
192.168.2.0  0.0.0.0      255.255.255.0 U     202    0   0   eth0
```

- The destination of 0.0.0.0 represents a default destination. We see from the first line that it is configured to be sent to 192.168.2.87 (the B+ end of the point-to-point) link.

- The second line indicates that any network requests for 192.168.2.0 will also be routed by the default.

This should complete the remote Pi (B) configuration.

WIFI Pi (B+)

Now we must configure the Pi 3 B+ so that it also brings up the point-to-point interface eth0. Edit its file /etc/dhcpcd.conf so that the following lines remain for eth0:

```
auto eth0
interface eth0
inform 192.168.2.87
static ip_address=192.168.2.87/24
nogateway
```

- The line auto eth0 brings up the interface when it is available.

- The line interface eth0 causes all following lines to apply to this interface.

- The inform line tells the DHCP server that interface eth0 will have the IP address 192.168.2.87.

- The static ip_address line specifies the IP address and indirectly specifies the netask with the /24.

- The nogateway option indicates that there is no gateway to configure (there are no other hosts to be found on the 192.168.2.0 network).

After rebooting your Pi 3 B+ (and Pi 3 B), you should now have a direct link between the two. Check the Pi 3 B+:

```
# ifconfig eth0
eth0: flags=4163<UP,BROADCAST,RUNNING,MULTICAST>  mtu 1500
        inet 192.168.2.87  netmask 255.255.255.0  broadcast
        192.168.2.255
```

```
inet6 fe80::8cc8:d1d2:61ba:d377  prefixlen 64  scopeid
0x20<link>
ether b8:27:eb:b8:1d:e4  txqueuelen 1000  (Ethernet)
RX packets 26  bytes 3670 (3.5 KiB)
RX errors 0  dropped 0  overruns 0  frame 0
TX packets 31  bytes 4206 (4.1 KiB)
TX errors 0  dropped 0 overruns 0  carrier 0  collisions 0
```

Hopefully your link has both the address 192.168.2.87 but is also up ("RUNNING"). Check the routine also:

```
# route -n
Kernel IP routing table
Destination  Gateway       Genmask          Flags Metric Ref Use Iface
0.0.0.0      192.168.1.1   0.0.0.0          UG    303    0   0   wlan0
192.168.1.0  0.0.0.0       255.255.255.0 U        303    0   0   wlan0
192.168.2.0  0.0.0.0       255.255.255.0 U        202    0   0   eth0
```

From this display, note the following:

- The default gateway is 192.168.1.1 (from an earlier WIFI setup). So anything the host doesn't know how to route will be thrown over the wall to the WIFI router to handle.

- Anything that pertains to the WIFI router network (192.168.1.0), also is routed to the WIFI router.

- Anything being directed to network 192.168.2.0, is sent to the interface eth0, which is our point-to-point link to the remote Pi.

From this B+ side, let's test logging into the remote Pi (B), using the remote end's IP number:

```
$ ssh pi@192.168.2.86
pi@192.168.2.86's password:
Linux raspberrypi3 4.14.34-v7+ #1110 SMP ...
```

So far so good.

WIFI Pi iptables

I wish I could tell you that we were done. Unfortunately, there are two more steps remaining. On the B+ we must:

- Enable IP forwarding

- Configure iptables so it knows how and which packets to forward.

IP forwarding as a feature that is disabled by default because it could lead to a security breach. Having this single setting set to off provides peace of mind when you need it.

Enable IP Forwarding

To turn on IP forwarding, perform:

```
# sysctl -w net.ipv4.ip_forward=1
net.ipv4.ip_forward = 1
```

The -w option causes a system file to be updated to save your setting. Without this option, the setting would not be restored upon the next reboot. IP forwarding is not yet in operation yet—this simply gives permission to forward packets.

Configure IP Forwarding

Now we turn our attention to the iptables facility within Linux. If you're like me, you might be groaning "do I really have to learn all this stuff about firewalls?" Or perhaps "Sigh, I just want it to work!" Bear with me—only a little more is required.

If you've not messed with iptables at all, then you can probably skip the clear step. If you already have firewall rules installed that you want to keep, you'll also want to avoid clearing. Otherwise, let's check iptables and then clear the rules. First list the filters:

```
# iptables -L
Chain INPUT (policy ACCEPT)
target     prot opt source                destination

Chain FORWARD (policy ACCEPT)
target     prot opt source                destination

Chain OUTPUT (policy ACCEPT)
target     prot opt source                destination
```

If all is clear, this is all you should see in the display. When you don't use the -t option, you are referring implicitly to a table named filters. However, we must also check the table named nat:

```
# iptables -L -t nat
Chain PREROUTING (policy ACCEPT)
target     prot opt source                destination

Chain INPUT (policy ACCEPT)
target     prot opt source                destination

Chain OUTPUT (policy ACCEPT)
target     prot opt source                destination

Chain POSTROUTING (policy ACCEPT)
target     prot opt source                destination
```

The display is empty of any added rules. If you see rules you want to get rid off, use the -F and -X options to clear them all out:

```
# iptables -F
# iptables -F -t nat
# iptables -X
# iptables -X -t nat
```

After running these commands, you should be able to get the empty lists as shown before. The -F option deletes all the rule chains. The -X deletes any special user-defined chains. Again, when -t option is absent, it is as if you specified -t filters. The option -t nat applies to the network address translation (NAT) table.

Now we are in a position to tell iptables to forward our packets and apply NAT when necessary.

```
# iptables -t nat -A POSTROUTING -o wlan0 -j MASQUERADE
```

This command appends to the nat table to direct any forwarded packet destined to interface wlan0, to be network address translated (NATted). The packets are "masqueraded" to look like they came from 192.18.1.77 (B+), rather than the remote Pi (B).

With this in place, let's retest on the remote Pi (B).

Second Remote Pi Test

Log into the remote Pi (B) with keyboard, and test the link routing:

```
$ ping 192.168.1.1
PING 192.168.1.1 (192.168.1.1) 56(84) bytes of data.
64 bytes from 192.168.1.1: icmp_seq=1 ttl=63 time=3.22 ms
64 bytes from 192.168.1.1: icmp_seq=2 ttl=63 time=4.12 ms
^C
```

```
--- 192.168.1.1 ping statistics ---
2 packets transmitted, 2 received, 0% packet loss, time 1001ms
rtt min/avg/max/mdev = 3.229/3.675/4.121/0.446 ms
```

If things are correct, this ping of your WIFI gateway should be successful, as this example shows. So far, so good.

Another good test is to ping google with:

```
$ ping 8.8.8.8
```

If this fails, it is probably an indication of problems in the rest of your network (or google).

Assuming that was successful, try testing the name resolver:

```
# ping google.com
PING google.com (172.217.0.110) 56(84) bytes of data.
...
```

The fact that it shows you 192.217.0.110 (in this example) an IP number for the name google.com means that the name server is working.

As a final test, you should be able to do an apt-get update:

```
# apt-get update
Hit:1 http://archive.raspberrypi.org/debian stretch InRelease
Hit:2 http://raspbian.raspberrypi.org/raspbian stretch
InRelease
Reading package lists... Done
```

At this point, you should be able to follow this with the usual:

```
# apt-get upgrade
```

Persistent iptables

To avoid having to set up iptables every time, we need to make the rules restorable at boot time. But before we save the rules, let's make sure we're not clobbering existing files. The /etc/iptables directory should not exist yet:

```
# ls -d /etc/iptables
ls: cannot access '/etc/iptables': No such file or directory
```

If not, then create it now:

```
# mkdir /etc/iptables
```

If the directory did exist, check that a file named rules doesn't already exist or has no important content:

```
# cat /etc/iptables/rules
```

Assuming the rules file doesn't yet exist or has no material content, we can save our iptables rules to this file:

```
# iptables-save >/etc/iptables/rules
```

To have iptables rules automatically restored at boot time, create/edit the following file:

```
# nano /etc/dhcpcd.enter-hook
```

Add the following line to it:

```
iptables-restore </etc/iptables/rules
```

Save the edit. Now when you boot, the DHCP server should perform a restore of your iptables rules, from that file.

Rule Checking

Even when things are going well, it is nice to have verification that this iptables stuff is working. The iptables command can show you what rules are being exercised by listing the rules with counts by the addition of the -v option:

```
# iptables -L -v
Chain INPUT (policy ACCEPT 1277 packets, 122K bytes)
 pkts bytes target     prot opt
in     out     source                  destination
```

```
Chain FORWARD (policy ACCEPT 258 packets, 83716 bytes)
 pkts bytes target     prot opt
in    out    source                destination
Chain OUTPUT (policy ACCEPT 1181 packets, 120K bytes)
 pkts bytes target     prot opt
in    out    source                destination
```

From this display we can confirm that 258 packets were forwarded, in addition to the information about INPUT and OUTPUT rules. The same reporting is available for the nat table by adding the -t nat option.

Access

The procedure that was just outlined permits you to log into your remote Pi in an indirect way. Using this chapter's example, you would first ssh to 192.168.1.77, and from there ssh into 192.168.2.86. Without additional configuration, you would not be able to ssh into 192.168.2.86 directly from the desktop computer. It can be done, but that topic is beyond our scope.

The present arrangement does, however, allow the two Pi's to communicate directly with each other. Gaming applications can make use of the shared CPU resources and exploit the use of two HDMI displays. As an added bonus, the remote Pi also has the luxury of internet access, which includes the ability to update with apt-get.

Security

This presentation is a *get-started* example. There are more options and rules that could be applied for greater protection. But if you're already operating behind a firewall, the added complexity of managing that may not be necessary.

If your Pi is not behind a firewall and you plan to expose your device directly on the internet, then you must take the time to learn more about `iptables` and firewalling principles.

Summary

This chapter has shown how the wireless and wired ethernet adapters can be configured using the graphical desktop. This is quite suitable for normal and routine cases.

For special configurations, however, things get more involved. The remainder of the chapter covered the editing of files and `iptables` setup, to build a point-to-point connection. This allows the remote Pi to access the internet through the first Pi. Knowing how to save the `iptables` configuration and coax the DHCP server to restore those rules at boot time completes the picture. From this starting point, you can expand your knowledge of configuring your network to specialized needs.

CHAPTER 9

SD Card Storage

The file system is central to the Unix system design from which Linux
borrows. The mass storage requirements have traditionally been
fulfilled through hard disk subsystems. However, as hosts become as
small as credit cards, flash memory technology has replaced the bulky
mechanical drive.

SD Card Media

The first Pi's used a standard-sized SD card. All newer models, however,
now use the MicroSD card shown in Figure 9-1, along with the standard SD
adapter.

Figure 9-1. *SD MicroSD adapter (left) and 8 GB MicroSD card
at right*

© Warren Gay 2018
W. Gay, *Advanced Raspberry Pi*, https://doi.org/10.1007/978-1-4842-3948-3_9

The 8 pins of the underside of the MicroSD are shown in Figure 9-2.

Figure 9-2. *The underside of the MicroSD card, with its 8 pins exposed*

SD Card Basics

The SD card includes an internal controller, also known as a Flash Storage Processor (FSP). In this configuration, the host merely provides a command and waits for the response. The FSP takes care of all erase, programming, and read operations necessary to complete the command. In this way, Flash card designs are permitted to increase in complexity as new performance and storage densities are implemented.

The SD card manages data with a sector size of 512 bytes. This was intentionally made the same as the IDE magnetic disk drive for compatibility with existing operating systems. Commands issued by the host include a sector address to allow read/writes of one or more sectors.

Note   Operating systems may use a multiple of the 512-byte sector.

Commands and data are protected by a CRC (cyclic redundancy check) code generated by the FSP. The FSP also automatically performs a read after write to verify that the data was written correctly.[9] If the write was defective, the FSP automatically corrects it, replacing the physical sector with another if necessary.

The SD card soft error rate is much lower than a magnetic disk drive. In the rare case when errors are discovered, the last line of defense is a correcting ECC (error correction code), which allows for data recovery. These errors are corrected in the media to prevent future unrecoverable errors. All of this activity is transparent to the host.

Raspbian Block Size

The block size used by the operating system may be a multiple of the media's sector size. To determine the physical block size used under Raspbian, we first discover how the root file system is mounted (the following listing has been trimmed):

```
$ mount
/dev/mmcblk0p2 on / type ext4 (rw,noatime,data=ordered)
...
/dev/mmcblk0p1 on /boot type vfat (rw,relatime,fmask=0022,dma
sk=0022, \
        codepage=437,iocharset=ascii,shortname=mixed,
        errors=remount-ro)
```

From this we deduce that the device used for the root file system is /dev/mmcblk0p2. The naming convention used tells us the following:

Component	Name	Number	Type
Prefix	/dev/mmcblk		MMC block
Device number	0	0	
Partition number	p2	2	

From the earlier mount command output, notice that the /boot file system was mounted on /dev/mmcblk0p1. This indicates that the /boot file system is from partition 1 of the same SD card device.

Using the device information, we consult the /sys pseudo file system to find out the physical and logical sector sizes. Here we supply mmcblk0 as the third-level pathname qualifier to query the device:

```
$ cat /sys/block/mmcblk0/queue/physical_block_size
  512
$ cat /sys/block/mmcblk0/queue/logical_block_size
  512
$
```

The result shown informs us that the Raspbian Linux used in this example uses a block (sector) size of 512 bytes, both physically and logically. This precisely matches the SD card's sector size.

Disk Cache

While we're examining mounted SD card file systems, let's also check the type of device node used:

```
$ ls -l /dev/mmcblk0p?
brw-rw---- 1 root disk 179, 1 Jun 19 07:42 /dev/mmcblk0p1
brw-rw---- 1 root disk 179, 2 Jun 19 07:42 /dev/mmcblk0p2
```

The example output displays a b at the beginning of the brw-rw---- field. This tells us that the disk device is a *block* device as opposed to a *character* device. (The associated character device would show a c instead.) Block devices are important for file systems because they provide a disk cache capability to vastly improve the file system performance. The output shows that both the root (partition 2) and the /boot (partition 1) file systems are mounted using block devices.

Capacities and Performance

SD cards allow a configurable data bus width within limits of the media. All SD cards start with one data bit line until the capabilities of the memory card are known. After the capabilities of the media are known, the data bus can be expanded under software control, as supported. Table 9-1 summarizes SD card capabilities.[10]

Table 9-1. *SD Card Capabilities*

Standard	Description	Greater Than	Up To	Data Bus
SDSC	Standard capacity	0	2 GB	1-bit
SDHC	High capacity	2 GB	32 GB	4-bit
SDXC	Extended capacity	32 GB	2 TB	4-bit

Transfer Modes

There are three basic data transfer modes used by SD cards:

- SPI Bus mode
- 1-bit SD mode
- 4-bit SD mode

SPI Bus Mode

The SPI Bus mode is used mainly by consumer electronics using small microcontrollers supporting the SPI bus. Examining Table 9-2 reveals that data is transmitted 1 bit at a time in this mode (pin 2 or 7).

Table 9-2. *MicroSD SPI Bus Mode*

Pin	Name	I/O	Logic	Description	SPI
1	NC				
2	/CS	I	PP	Card select (active low)	CS
3	DI	I	PP	Data in	MOSI
4	VDD	S	S	Power	
5	CLK	I	PP	Clock	SCLK
6	VSS	S	S	Ground	
7	DO	O	PP	Data out	MISO
8				Reserved	

The various SD card connections are used in different ways, as documented by the Table 9-2 mnemonics in the columns I/O and Logic. Table 9-3 is a legend for these and also applies to Table 9-4.

Table 9-3. *Legend for I/O and Logic*

Notation	Meaning	Notes
I	Input	Relative to card
O	Output	
I/O	Input or output	
PP	Push/pull logic	
OD	Open drain	
S	Power supply	
NC	Not connected	Or logic high

SD Mode

SD mode allows for varying data bus width for added I/O rates supported by SDHC and SDXC cards. Higher data clock rates also improve transfer rates. Table 9-4 lists the pin assignments.

Table 9-4. *Micro SD Mode Pins*

Pin	Name	I/O	Logic	Description
1	DAT2	I/O	PP	Data 2
2	CD/DAT3	I/O	PP	Card Detect/Data 3
3	CMD	I/O	PP/OD	Command/response
4	VDD	S	S	Power
5	CLK	I	PP	Clock
6	VSS	S	S	Ground
7	DAT0	I/O	PP	Data 0
8	DAT1	I/O	PP	Data 1

Wear Leveling

Unfortunately, Flash memory is subject to *wear* for each *write* operation performed (as each write requires erasing and programming a block of data). The design of Flash memory requires that a large block of memory be erased and rewritten, even if a single sector has changed value. For this reason, wear leveling is used as a technique to extend the life of the media. Wear leveling extends life by moving data to different physical blocks while retaining the same logical address.

Whether or not a given memory card supports wear leveling is an open question without supporting documentation. Some manufacturers may not implement wear leveling at all or use a lower level of overprovisioning. Wear leveling is not specified in the SD card standard, so no manufacturer is compelled to follow SanDisk's lead.

Direct File System Mounts

There are times when it is convenient to make changes to a SD card file system with the Pi offline, using Linux. If you have an USB card adapter, this could also be done by a different Pi. Using the SD card slot or a SD card reader attached to your Linux box, you can mount the file systems directly.

But how do you know what to mount? There are at least two helpful commands you can apply:

- lsblk

- blkid

The lsblk command is great for showing you the block devices and the partition arrangements:

```
# lsblk
NAME       MAJ:MIN   RM     SIZE   RO   TYPE MOUNTPOINT
sda          8:0      0   149.1G    0   disk
├─sda1       8:1      0   147.3G    0   part /
├─sda2       8:2      0      1K     0   part
└─sda5       8:5      0     1.8G    0   part [SWAP]
sdb          8:16     1    14.5G    0   disk
├─sdb1       8:17     1    41.8M    0   part
└─sdb2       8:18     1    14.5G    0   part
sr0         11:0      1    1024M    0   rom
#
```

From that display, you can see the Linux root file system is mounted from /dev/sda1. Our SD card appears on /dev/sdb, with partitions sdb1 and sdb2. The blkid command gives us some more information, including the partition labels:

```
# blkid
/dev/sda1: UUID="51d355c1-2fe1-4f0e-aaae-01d526bb27b5"
TYPE="ext4" PARTUUID="61c63d91-01"
/dev/sda5: UUID="83a322e3-11fe-4a25-bd6c-b877ab0321f9"
TYPE="swap" PARTUUID="61c63d91-05"
/dev/sdb1: LABEL="boot" UUID="A75B-DC79" TYPE="vfat"
PARTUUID="2e37b5e0-01"
/dev/sdb2: LABEL="rootfs" UUID="485ec5bf-9c78-45a6-9314-
32be1d0dea38" TYPE="ext4" \
            PARTUUID="2e37b5e0-02"
```

This display shows that our Pi /boot partition is on /dev/sdb1, while its root partition is available on /dev/sdb2. These can be mounted directly. First make sure you have directory entries to mount them on (if they don't exist already):

```
# mkdir /mnt/1
# mkdir /mnt/2
```

Now they can be mounted:

```
# mount /dev/sdb1 /mnt/1
# mount /dev/sdb2 /mnt/2
```

Once mounted like this, you can list or change files at will in directories /mnt/1 or /mnt/2.

Read-Only Problem

What do you do when Linux complains that your SD card is read-only?

```
# mount /dev/sdb1 -o rw /mnt/1
mount: /dev/sdb1 is write-protected, mounting read-only
```

This problem can stem from at least three possible sources:

- The switch on the MicroSD adapter has slipped to the "Protect" (or locked) position.

- Linux has a software lock on the device.

- Or the MicroSD adapter is faulty (bad connection).

MicroSD Adapter Switch

The slide switch for the MicroSD adapter can be a real nuisance as it accidentally gets slid into the "locked" position. The solution is to pull it back out and fix the switch setting.

Software Protection

Another possibility is that Linux has a software lock on the device. The -r1 option turns this feature on:

```
# hdparm -r1 /dev/sdb1

/dev/sdb1:
 setting readonly to 1 (on)
 readonly      = 1 (on)
# mount /dev/sdb1 /mnt/1
mount: /dev/sdb1 is write-protected, mounting read-only
#
```

The hdparm command using the -r1 command can set a software lock for the device. Attempting to mount the file system with this lock enabled results in a read-only mount. The solution to this is to disable this protection using option -r0:

```
# hdparm -r0 /dev/sdb1
```

164

```
/dev/sdb1:
 setting readonly to 0 (off)
 readonly      = 0 (off)
# mount /dev/sdb1 /mnt/1
```

MicroSD Adapter Quality

When this read-only issue happened to me for the first time, I thought
the issue was with the hardware in the Linux computer I was using.
Researching this I discovered that some people had reported that their
MicroSD adapter was the problem. After trying three different MicroSD
adapters, I was eventually successful. The first two adapters failed with a
bad connection making the device read-only.

If you got an adapter with your MicroSD card, that is probably the
adapter you want to use. However, that may not guarantee success.

Image Files

If you lack a way to mount the SD card directly, then you can still
manipulate the image file. This might be the downloaded Raspbian
image or perhaps a friend was able to get it to you somehow. Perhaps they
created the image from the SD card from their computer:

```
# dd if=/dev/sdb of=/tmp/sdcard.img bs=1024k
```

That dd command copies the input disk (/dev/sdb) to an output file (/
tmp/sdcard.img), using a block size of 1 MB (1024k). The large block size
is used for greater efficiency.

The problem with the image file is that it contains two partitions. If it
were a single partition, then it could be mounted directly. The partitions
require us to do a bit more work. Installing kpartx will make this task
easier:

```
# apt-get install kpartx
```

Now when we have an image file to mount we can use it as follows:

```
# kpartx -v -a /tmp/sdcard.img
add map loop0p1 (254:0): 0 85611 linear /dev/loop0 8192
add map loop0p2 (254:1): 0 30351360 linear /dev/loop0 98304
```

Notice the names loop0p1 and loop0p2? Use them to mount the file system partitions in the image file:

```
# mount /dev/mapper/loop0p1 /mnt/1
# mount /dev/mapper/loop0p2 /mnt/2
```

Now you will find your /boot files in /mnt/1 and the Pi root partition mounted at /mnt/2. When you are done with making your changes, unmount the partitions:

```
# umount /mnt/1
# umount /mnt/2
```

After unmounting the file systems, you can copy the image file back to your SD card.

Summary

This chapter briefly introduced the SD card and its operation. Then two different ways of working with the SD card file system outside of the Raspberry Pi were examined—mounting the SD card on Linux directly and mounting an image file. Both have their uses, particularly in rescue operations.

CHAPTER 10

UART

The Raspberry Pi has a UART interface to allow it to perform serial data communication. The data lines used are 3.3 V logic-level signals and should *not* be connected to TTL logic (+5 V) (they also are *not RS-232 compatible*). To communicate with equipment using RS-232, you will need a converter module.

RS-232 Converter

While an industrious person could build their own RS-232 converter, there is little need to do so when cheap converters on a pcb are available.

Figure 10-1 shows a MAX232CSE chip pcb that I have used. This particular unit supports only the RX and TX lines with no hardware flow control. When searching for a unit, get one that works with 3.3 V logic levels. Some units will only work with TTL (+5 V) logic, which would be harmful to your Pi. The MAX232CSE chip supports 3.3 V operation when its VCC supply pin is connected to +3.3 V.

© Warren Gay 2018
W. Gay, *Advanced Raspberry Pi*, https://doi.org/10.1007/978-1-4842-3948-3_10

Figure 10-1. *MAX232CSE interface*

I also recommended that you choose a unit supporting *the hardware flow control signals*. Look for the CTS and DTR signals. A full RS-232 converter would also include DTR, DSR, and CD signals.

Note   Throughout this text, we'll refer to *3 V*, knowing that it is more precisely 3.3 V.

TTL Adapters

You can also use TTL adapters instead of converting the signal to the +/- voltages required by RS-232. The Pi requirement is that the signaling side (TTL) should be capable of operating at +3.3 V instead of the usual +5 V. Using a +5 V adapter could damage your Pi. Units that can interface +3.3 V will likely have a jumper to select the voltage.

DTE or DCE

When choosing your RS-232 converter, keep in mind that there are two types of serial connections:

DCE: Data communications equipment (female connector)

DTE: Data terminal equipment (male connector)

A normal USB serial adapter (for a laptop, for example) will present a DTE (male) connector. The wiring of this cable is such that it expects to plug into to a DCE (female) connection. When this holds true for your Raspberry Pi's adapter, the laptop's serial adapter can plug straight into the DCE (female) connector, *eliminating* the need for a crossover cable or null modem.

Consequently, for your Pi, choose a RS-232 converter that provides a female (DCE) connector. Likewise, make sure that you acquire for the laptop/desktop a cable or USB device that presents a male (DTE) connection. Connecting DTE to DTE or DCE to DCE requires a crossover cable, and depending on the cable, a "gender mender" as well. It is best to get things "straight" right from the start.

Assuming that you used a DCE converter for the Pi, connect the RS-232 converter's 3 V logic TX to the Pi's TXD0 and the RX to the Pi's RXD0 data lines.

All this business about DCE and DTR has always been rather confusing. If you also find this confusing, there is another practical way to look at it. Start with the connectors and the cable(s) that you plan to use. Make sure they mate at both ends and that the serial cable is known to be a *straight cable* (vs. a *crossover*). Once those physical problems are taken care of, you can get the wiring correct. Connect the TX to RX, and RX to TX. In other words, *you* wire the crossover in your own wiring between the RS-232 adapter and the Raspberry Pi. The important thing to remember is that somewhere the transmitting side needs to send a signal into the RX (receiving) side, in both directions.

169

Note   A straight serial cable will connect pin 2 to pin 2, and pin 3 to pin 3 on a DB9 or DB25 cable. A crossover cable will cross these two, among other signal wires.

RS-232

RS-232 is the traditional name for a series of standards related to serial communication. It was first introduced by the Radio Sector of the EIA in 1962. The first data terminals were teletypewriters (DTE) communicating with modems (DCE). Early serial communications were plagued by incompatibilities until later standards evolved.

A serial link includes two data lines, with data being transmitted from a terminal and received by the same terminal. In addition to these data lines are several handshaking signals (such as RTS and CTS). By default, these are not provided for by the Raspberry Pi.

Figure 10-2 shows a serial signal transmission, with time progressing from left to right. RS-232 equipment expects a signal that varies between –15 V and +15 V.

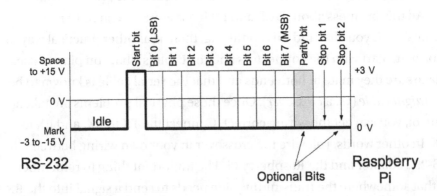

Figure 10-2. Serial signal

The standard states that the signal is considered to be in a *mark state*, when the voltage is between –3 and –15 V. The signal is considered in a *space state* if the voltage is between +3 and +15 V. The RS-232 data line is in the mark state when the line is idle.

Start Bit

When an asynchronous character of data is to be sent, the line first shifts to a space level for the duration of 1 bit. This is known as the *start bit* (0). Data bits immediately follow.

Asynchronous lines do not use a clock signal like synchronous links. The asynchronous receiver must have a clock matching the same baud rate as the transmitter. The receiver samples the line 16 times in the bit cell time to determine its value. Sampling helps to avoid a noise pulse from triggering a false data read.

Data Bits

Data bits immediately follow the start bit, with the least significant bit first. A space is a 0 data bit, while mark represents a 1 bit. Early teletype equipment used 5 data bits sending characters in the 5-bit Baudot code.[11] For this reason, serial ports can be configured for 5, 6, 7, or 8 data bits. Before the ASCII character set was extended to 8 bits, it was common to use 7-bit serial data.

Parity Bit

An optional parity bit can be generated when transmitting or can be detected on the receiving side. The parity can be odd, even, or stick (mark or space). The most commonly used setting today is No Parity, which saves 1-bit time for faster communication. Older equipment often used parity

171

to guard against errors from noisy serial lines. Odd parity is preferred over even because it forces at least one signal transition in the byte's transmission. This helps with the data reliability.

Mark or space parity is unusual and has limited usefulness. Mark parity could be used along with 2 stop bits to effectively provide 3 stop bits for very slow teletypewriter equipment. Mark or space parity reduces the effective throughput of data without providing any benefit, except possibly for diagnostic purposes. Table 10-1 summarizes the various parity configurations.

Table 10-1. *RS-232 Parity Settings*

Parity	X	Notes
None	N	No parity bit
Even	E	1 if even number of data 1-bits
Odd	O	1 if odd number of data 1-bits
Mark	M	Always at mark level (1)
Space	S	Always at space level (0)

Stop Bits

Asynchronous communication requires synchronizing the receiver with the transmitter. For this reason, 1 or more stop bits exist so that the receiver can synchronize with the leading edge of the next start bit. In effect, each stop bit followed by a start bit provides built-in synchronization.

Many UARTs support 1, 1.5, or 2 stop bits. The Broadcom SoC supports 1 or 2 stop bits only. The use of 2 stop bits was common for teletypewriter equipment and probably rarely used today. Using 1 stop bit increases the overall data throughput. Table 10-2 summarizes the stop-bit configurations.

Table 10-2. *Stop-Bit Configuration*

Stop Bits	Description
1	1 stop bit
1.5	1.5 stop bits (†)
2	2 stop bits

†*Unsupported by the Raspberry Pi*

Baud Rate

The *baud rate* is calculated from bits per second, which includes the start, data, parity, and stop bits. A link using 115200 baud, with no parity and 1 stop bit, provides the following data byte rate:

$$D_{rate} = \frac{B}{s+d+p+S}$$
$$= \frac{115200}{1+8+0+1}$$
$$= 11,520 bytes\,/\,s$$

where

B is the baud rate.

s is the start bit (always 1 bit).

d is the number of data bits (5, 6, 7, or 8).

p is the parity bit (0 or 1).

S is the stop bit (1, 1.5, or 2).

The 115200 baud link allows 11,250 bytes per second. If a parity bit is added, the throughput is reduced:

$$D_{rate} = \frac{115200}{1+8+1+1}$$
$$= 10,472.7 bytes\,/\,s$$

The addition of a parity bit reduces the transmission rate to 10,472.7 bytes per second.

Table 10-3 lists the standard baud rates that a serial link can be configured for on the Raspberry Pi.

Table 10-3. *Standard Baud Rates*

Rate	Notes
75	Teletypewriters
110	Teletypewriters
300	Low-speed (acoustic) modem
1200	
2400	
4800	
9600	
19200	
38400	
57600	
115200	Raspberry Pi console

Break

With asynchronous communication, it is also possible to send and receive a *break signal*. This is done by stretching the start bit beyond the data bits and the stop bit(s), and eventually returning the line to the mark state. When the receiver sees a space instead of a mark for the stop bit, it sees a *framing error*.

Some UARTs distinguish between a framing error and a break by noting how long the line remains in the space state. A simple framing error can happen as part of noisy serial line communications (particularly when modems were used) and normally attributed to a received character error. Without break detection, it is possible to assume that a break has been received when several framing errors occur in a sequence. Short sequences of framing errors, however, can also just indicate a mismatch in baud rates between the two endpoints.

Flow Control

Any link that transmits from one side to a receiver on the other end has the problem of flow control. Imagine a factory assembly line where parts to be assembled arrive at the worker's station faster than he/she can assemble them. At some point, the conveyor belt must be temporarily stopped, or some parts will not get assembled. Alternatively, if the conveyor belt is reduced in speed, the assembly worker will be able to keep up, but at a slower than optimal pace.

Unless the serial link receiver can process every character of data as fast as it arrives, it will need flow control. The simplest approach is to simply reduce the baud rate, so that the receiver will always keep up. But this isn't always satisfactory. A logging application might be able to write the information quickly, except when writes occur to an SD card, for example.

A better approach is to signal to the transmitter to stop sending when the receiver is bogged down. Once the receiver catches up, it can then tell the transmitter to resume transmission. Note that this problem exists for both sides of a serial link:

- Data transmitted to the terminal (DTE)

- Data transmitted to the data communications equipment (DCE)

Two forms of flow control are used:

- Hardware flow control

- Software flow control

Hardware Flow Control

Hardware flow control uses additional signal lines to regulate the flow of data. The RS-232 standards have quite an elaborate set of signals defined, but the main signals needed for flow control are shown in Table 10-4. Unlike the data line, these signals are inactive in the space state and active in the mark state.

Table 10-4. *Hardware Flow Controls*

DTE	Direction	DCE	Description	Active
RTS	→	RTS	Request to send(†)	Low
CTS	←	CTS	Clear to send(†)	
DSR	←	DSR	Data set ready	Low
DTR	→	DTR	Data terminal ready	

† Primary flow control signals

The most important signals are the ones marked with a dagger in Table 10-4. When CTS is active (mark), for example, the DCE (Pi) is indicating that it is OK to send data. If the DCE gets overwhelmed by the volume of data, the CTS signal will change to the inactive (space) state. Upon seeing this, the DTE (desktop) is required to stop sending data. Otherwise, loss of data may occur.

Similarly, the desktop operating as the DTE is receiving data from the DCE (Pi). If the laptop gets overwhelmed with the volume of incoming data, the RTS signal is changed to the inactive state (space). The remote end (DCE) is then expected to cease transmitting. When the desktop has caught up, it will reassert RTS, giving the DCE permission to resume.

The DTR and DSR signals are intended to convey the readiness of the equipment at each end. If the terminal was deemed not ready (DTR), DSR is not made active by the DCE. Similarly, the terminal will not assert DTR unless it is ready. In modern serial links, DTR and DSR are often assumed to be true, leaving only CTS and RTS to handle flow control.

Where flow control is required, hardware flow control is considered more reliable than software flow control.

Software Flow Control

To simplify the cabling and the supporting hardware for serial communications, the hardware flow controls can be omitted/ignored. In its place, a data protocol is used instead.

Initially, each end of the link assumes readiness for reception of data. Data is sent until an XOFF character is received, indicating that transmission should stop. The receiver sends the XON character when it is ready to resume reception again. These software flow control characters are shown in Table 10-5.

Table 10-5. *Software Flow Control Characters*

Code	Meaning	ASCII	Hex	Keyboard
XOFF	Pause transmission	DC3	13	Control-S
XON	Resume transmission	DC1	11	Control-Q

In a terminal session, the keyboard commands can be used to control the serial connection. For example, if information is displaying too fast, the user can type Ctrl-S to cause the transmission to stop. Pressing Ctrl-Q allows it to resume.

The disadvantages of software flow control include the following:

1. Line noise can prevent the receiver from seeing the XOFF character and can lead to loss of data (due to data overrun).

2. Line noise can prevent the remote end from seeing the XON character and can fail to resume transmission (causing a link "lockup").

3. Line noise can cause a false XON/XOFF character to be received (data loss or link lockup).

4. The delay in the remote end seeing a transmitted XOFF character can cause loss of data if the receiving buffer is full.

5. The XON and XOFF characters cannot be used for data in the transmission link.

Problems 1 to 3 can cause link lockups or data loss. Problem 4 is avoidable if the buffer notifies the other end early enough to prevent overflow. Problem 5 is an issue for binary data transmission.

Raspberry Pi UARTs

The Raspberry Pi supports two UARTs:

UART	Hardware	Node	GPIO	ALT
UART0	PL011	/dev/ttyAMA0	14 & 15	0
UART1	**Mini UART**	**/dev/ttyS0**	14 & 15	5

Whether the PL011 or the mini UART is used depends upon the model of the Raspberry Pi. Originally, this question was simple to answer. The Model B and Model A Pi's simply used the PL011 (/dev/ttyAMA0) device for the console. The mini UART (/dev/ttyS0) is a different hardware block and was also available, albeit with limited features.

With the addition of Wireless and Bluetooth on the Pi 3 and the Pi Zero W, the PL011 UART was commandeered for the BT (Bluetooth) and WIFI support while the mini UART was substituted for the serial console. All other models use the preferred PL011 device for the console instead.

However, the rules for what is assigned is more complicated now that the device tree overlays are being used. More detail is available from raspberrypi.org. The following online document, which doesn't include a date-stamp, has more of the gory details:

```
https://www.raspberrypi.org/documentation/configuration/uart.md
```

Which Is in Use?

You can verify which serial device is being used as follows:

```
$ cat /boot/cmdline.txt
dwc_otg.lpm_enable=0 console=serial0,115200 console=tty1 ...
```

The console= option can appear multiple times in the kernel command line. In this Raspberry Pi 3 Model B example, we see that there are two consoles defined, but only one is the serial port (serial0). Listing the serial device shows:

```
$ ls -l /dev/serial0
lrwxrwxrwx 1 root root 5 Jun 19 22:04 /dev/serial0 -> ttyS0
```

The name /dev/serial0 is a symlink to the actual device /dev/ttyS0.

```
$ ls -l /dev/ttyS0
crw--w---- 1 root tty 4, 64 Jun 19 22:04 /dev/ttyS0
```

So this Pi is configured to use the mini UART (/dev/ttyS0).

Listing the boot command line on my Raspberry Pi 3 B+ yielded:

```
$ cat /boot/cmdline.txt
dwc_otg.lpm_enable=0 console=serial0,115200 console=tty1 ...
```

It claims to be using /dev/serial0, but there is *no* serial0 *device* for this configuration:

```
$ ls /dev/serial0
ls: cannot access '/dev/serial0': No such file or directory
```

The raspberrypi.org page also states:

If cmdline.txt uses the alias serial0 to refer to the user-accessible port, the firmware will replace it with the appropriate port whether or not this overlay is used.

Disabling the Serial Console

If you want to make use of the serial device for a *non-console* purpose, then obviously we must disable the console. The easiest way to do this is to become root and use `raspi-config`:

```
# raspi-config
```

Cursor down to select "Interface Options" and press Return (Figure 10-3).

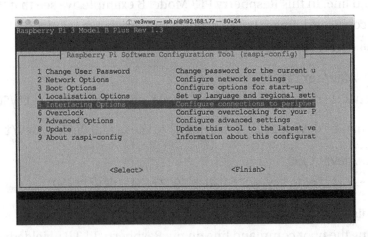

Figure 10-3. *The opening dialog for raspi-config, with "Interface Options" selected*

Then cursor down (Figure 10-4) to select "Serial" and press Return.

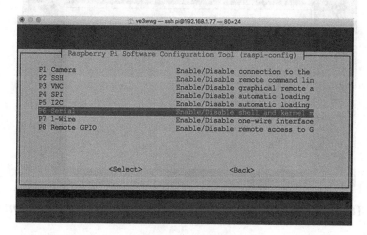

Figure 10-4. *Select "Serial" in raspi-config and press Return*

Then choose "<No>" to disable the console and press Return
(Figure 10-5).

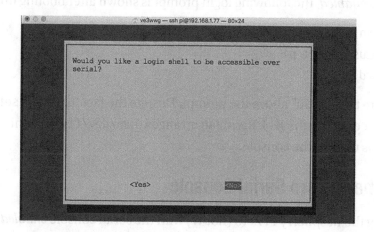

Figure 10-5. *Choose "<No>" to disable the console in raspi-config*

The dialog completes (Figure 10-6) by prompting if you want to reboot.
This is necessary for a console change in the kernel. This prompt may be
skipped if you already had the chosen setting.

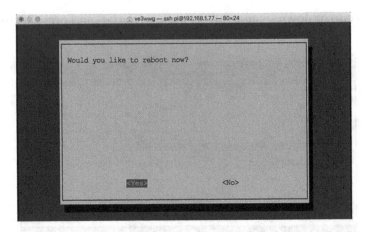

Figure 10-6. *The raspi-config dialog ends by asking if you want to reboot*

Raspberry Pi 3 Serial Console

When booting the Raspberry Pi 3 with the serial port connected and console *enabled*, the following login prompt is shown after booting up:

```
Raspbian GNU/Linux 9 rpi3bplus ttyS0
rpi3bplus login: pi
Password:
```

Note the "ttyS0" above the prompt. Despite the fact that /dev/serial0 does not exist (on the B+), Raspbian arranges that /dev/ttyS0 (mini UART) is used as the console.

Raspberry Zero Serial Console

Booting the Raspberry Pi Zero (not W) with the serial console *enabled* confirms that it uses the PL011 (/dev/ttyAMA0) device for the console:

```
Raspbian GNU/Linux 8 raspberrypi ttyAMA0

raspberrypi login: pi
Password:
```

182

The Raspberry Pi Zero shown in Figure 10-7 has a female header strip soldered into the board. The serial port adapter is a true RS232C converter using the MAX232CSE IC. The connections are:

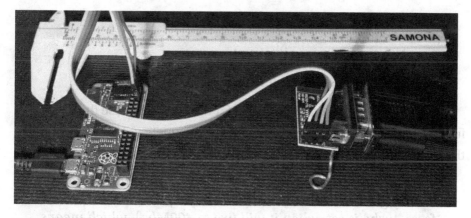

Figure 10-7. *Raspberry Pi Zero with serial console wired to RS232C adapter. The adapter has a true RS232C to USB plugged into it.*

- P1-01 (+3.3 V) to VCC
- P1-06 to Gnd
- P1-08 (GPIO14) to TX
- P1-10 (GPIO15) to RX

With this arrangement, there is no flow control. Given the high baud rate involved, if improved data integrity is needed, drop the baud rate to something lower like 9600 baud.

PL011 and Mini UART Differences

The mini UART has smaller FIFOs and does not support hardware flow control. Without flow control, it will be prone to losing data at high data rates. The mini's baud rate is also linked to the VPU clock, leading to other problems.

183

The mini UART also is deficient in the following ways:

- No break detection

- No framing error detection

- No parity bit support

- No receive timeout interrupt

- No DCD, DSR, DTR, or RI signals

The VPU clock presents a problem for the UART because the VPU frequency governor normally varies the core frequency. This would cause the UART baud rate to vary also. The raspberrypi.org states:

The Linux console can be re-enabled by adding enable_uart=1 to config.txt. This also fixes the core_freq to 250Mhz (unless force_turbo is set, when it will fixe to 400Mhz), which means that the UART baud rate stays consistent.

Avoid the mini UART if you can.

PL011 UART Features

The Broadcom *BCM2835 ARM Peripherals* manual states that the following features are *unsupported*:

- *No* Infrared Data Association (IrDA) support

- *No* Serial InfraRed (SIR) protocol encoder/decoder (endec)

- *No* direct memory access (DMA)

- *No* support for signals DCD, DSR, DTR, and RI

The following features *are* supported, however:

- Separate 16×8 transmit and 16×12 receive FIFO buffers

- Programmable baud rate generator

- False start-bit detection

- Line-break generation and detection

- Support of control functions CTS and RTS

- Programmable hardware flow control

- Fully programmable serial interface characteristics:

  - Data can be 5, 6, 7, or 8 bits.

  - Even, odd, mark, space, or no-parity bit generation and detection.

  - 1 or 2 stop-bit generation.

  - Baud rate generation, DC up to UARTCLK/16.

Broadcom also states that there are some differences between its implementation of the UART and the 16C650 UART. But these are mostly device driver details:

- Receive FIFO trigger levels are 1/8, 1/4, 1/2, 3/4, and 7/8.

- Transmit FIFO trigger levels are 1/8, 1/4, 1/2, 3/4, and 7/8.

- The internal register map address space and the bit function of each register differ.

- 1.5 stop bits is *not* supported.

- *No* independent receive clock.

The only real concern to the application developer is that the 1.5 stop-bits configuration option is *not* available, which is rarely used these days.

If you need the RS-232 DCD, DSR, DTR, and RI signals, these can be implemented using GPIO input and output pins (along with the appropriate RS-232 line-level shifters). These are relatively slow-changing signals, which can easily be handled in user space. The one limitation of this approach, however, is that the hang-up TTY controls provided by the device driver will be absent. To change that, the device driver source code could be modified to support these signals using GPIO. The Raspbian Linux module of interest for this is as follows:

```
drivers/tty/serial/amba-pl011.c
```

UART GPIO Pins

By default, the transmit and receive pins are GPIO 14 (TX) and 15 (RX), which are pins P1-08 and P1-10 respectively on the GPIO header. When the PL011 device is available, the hardware flow control signals can also be made to appear on the GPIO header when alternate function 5 is chosen. Table 10-6 lists these connections.

Table 10-6. *UART Pins*

Function	GPIO	P1/P5	ALT	Direction	Description
TXD	14	P1-08	0	Out	DTE transmitted data
RXD	15	P1-10	0	In	DTE received data
RTS	17	P1-11	5	Out	Request to send
CTS	30	P1-36	5	In	Clear to send

RTS/CTS Access

Hardware flow controls CTS and RTS are available on GPIO 30 (P1-26) and 17 (P1-11), respectively, when configured. By default these are GPIO inputs, but this can be reconfigured. To gain access to the UART's CTS and RTS signals, configure GPIO 30 and 17 to *alternate function 5*.

Summary

As the Raspberry Pi has matured into new models, the features associated with the serial device have become more complicated. Yet the Raspberry Pi Foundation has provided you with the `raspi-config` tool to simplify the configuration of the serial console or exclusive use serial line.

Armed with the information presented, you will be able to log into your headless Raspberry Pi Zero using the serial adapter. This information puts you in the best possible position to make use of this valuable resource.

CHAPTER 11

GPIO Hardware

General-purpose I/O is a topic near to the hearts of Raspberry Pi owners because this is the interface to the outside world. The Pi is flexibly designed to allow I/O pins to be reconfigured under software control. For example, GPIO 14 can be an input, an output, or operate as a serial port TX data line.

One of the challenges related to the Pi's GPIO interface is that it uses a weak CMOS 3.3 V interface. The GPIO pins are also susceptible to ESD (electrostatic discharge) damage and are weak drivers (2 to 16 mA). Finally, the limited GPIO power must be budgeted from the total spare current capacity (50 mA on the original Pi Model B). Using adapter boards overcomes these problems but can add considerably to the cost. Consequently this provides a fertile area for coming up with cheap and effective roll-your-own solutions.

Pins and Designations

Tables 11-1 and 11-2 illustrate the GPIO connections for modern Raspberry Pi models. Table 11-1 lists the odd-numbered pins while Table 11-2 provides the even-numbered pins on the 20x2 header strip.

© Warren Gay 2018
W. Gay, *Advanced Raspberry Pi*, https://doi.org/10.1007/978-1-4842-3948-3_11

189

Table 11-1. *Odd-Numbered GPIO Pins for the Modern Raspberry Pi*

Pin	GPIO	Name	Description
P1-01			+3.3 V Power supply, from regulator
P1-03	GPIO-2		I2C SDA1(with 1.8 kΩ pull-up resistor)
P1-05	GPIO-3		I2C SCL1 (with 1.8 kΩ pull-up resistor)
P1-07	GPIO-4	GPIO_GCLK	General-purpose clock output or 1-Wire
P1-09			Ground
P1-11	GPIO-17	GPIO_GEN0	
P1-13	GPIO-27	GPIO_GEN2	
P1-15	GPIO-22	GPIO_GEN3	
P1-17			+3.3 V Power supply, from regulator
P1-19	GPIO-10	SPI_MOSI	
P1-21	GPIO-9	SPI_MISO	
P1-23	GPIO-11	SPI_CLK	
P1-25			Ground
P1-27		ID_SD	I2C ID EEPROM Data
P1-29	GPIO-5		
P1-31	GPIO-6		
P1-33	GPIO-13		
P1-35	GPIO-19		
P1-37	GPIO-26		
P1-39			Ground

Table 11-2. *Even-Numbered GPIO Pins for the Modern Raspberry Pi*

Pin	GPIO	Name	Description
P1-02			+5 V Power supply
P1-04			+5 V Power supply
P1-06			Ground
P1-08	GPIO-14	TXD0	UART transmit
P1-10	GPIO-15	RXD0	UART receive
P1-12	GPIO-18	GPIO_GEN1	
P1-14			Ground
P1-16	GPIO-23	GPIO_GEN4	
P1-18	GPIO-24	GPIO-GEN5	
P1-20			Ground
P1-22	GPIO-25	GPIO-GEN6	
P1-24	GPIO-8	SPI_CE0_N	
P1-26	GPIO-7	SPI_CE1_N	
P1-28		ID_SC	I2C ID EEPROM Clock
P1-30			Ground
P1-32	GPIO-12		
P1-34			Ground
P1-36	GPIO-16		
P1-38	GPIO-20		
P1-40	GPIO-21		

GPIO Cross Reference

Frequently you may know the GPIO that you want, but finding the pin number requires a little searching. Table 11-3 is a convenient cross reference, sorted by GPIO number and listing the corresponding pin number.

Table 11-3. *GPIO Cross Reference*

GPIO	Pin	GPIO	Pin	GPIO	Pin	GPIO	Pin
GPIO-2	P1-03	GPIO-9	P1-21	GPIO-16	P1-36	GPIO-23	P1-16
GPIO-3	P1-05	GPIO-10	P1-19	GPIO-17	P1-11	GPIO-24	P1-18
GPIO-4	P1-07	GPIO-11	P1-23	GPIO-18	P1-12	GPIO-25	P1-22
GPIO-5	P1-29	GPIO-12	P1-32	GPIO-19	P1-35	GPIO-26	P1-37
GPIO-6	P1-31	GPIO-13	P1-33	GPIO-20	P1-38	GPIO-27	P1-13
GPIO-7	P1-26	GPIO-14	P1-08	GPIO-21	P1-40		
GPIO-8	P1-24	GPIO-15	P1-10	GPIO-22	P1-15		

Configuration After Reset

Upon reset, most GPIO pins are configured as general-purpose inputs with some exceptions. However, as Raspbian Linux changes and new Pi models get introduced, there is probably no boot GPIO state that is safe to assume. If you use a GPIO, then it should be configured before use.

Pull-Up Resistors

As noted earlier, GPIO 2 and 3 (I2C pins) have an external resistor tied to the +3.3 V rail to meet I2C requirements. The remaining GPIO pins are pulled high or low by an internal 50 $k\Omega$ resistor in the SoC. The internal pull-up resistor is weak and effective at only giving an unconnected

GPIO input a defined state. A CMOS (complementary metal oxide semiconductor) input should not be allowed to float midway between its logic high and low. When pull-up resistance is needed for an external circuit, it is probably best to provide the external pull-up resistor, rather than relying on the weak internal one.

Configuring Pull-Up Resistors

The pull-up configuration of a GPIO pin can be configured in a C program using the SoC registers GPPUP and GPPUDCLK0/1. The Pi GPPUP register is laid out as in Table 11-4.

Table 11-4. The Raspberry Pi GPPUP Register

Bits	Field	Description	Type	Reset
31-2	-	Unused, GPIO pin pull-up/down	R	0
1-0	PUD	00 Off—disable pull-up/down	R/W	0
		01 Pull-down enable		
		10 Pull-up enable		
		11 Reserved		

The layout of the GPPUDCLK0 register layout is illustrated in Table 11-5.

Table 11-5. The GPPUDCLK0 Register Layout

Bits	Field	Description	Type	Reset
31-0	PUDCLKn	n = 0..31	R/W	0
		0 No effect		
		1 Assert clock		

Finally, the GPPUDCLK1 register layout is illustrated in Table 11-6.

Table 11-6. *The GPPUDCLK1 Register Layout*

Bits	Field	Description		Type	Reset
31-22	-	Reserved		R	0
21-0	PUDCLKn	n = 32..53		R/W	0
		0	No effect		
		1	Assert clock		

The Broadcom documentation describes the general procedure for programming the pull-up resistor as follows:

1. Write the pull-up configuration desired in the rightmost 2 bits of the 32-bit GPPUP register. The configuration choices are as follows:

   00: Disable pull-up control.

   01: Enable pull-down control.

   10: Enable pull-up control.

2. Wait 150 cycles to allow the preceding write to be registered.

3. Write a 1-bit to every GPIO position, in the group of 32 GPIO pins being configured.
   GPIOs 0–31 are configured by register GPPUDCLK0.

4. Wait another 150 cycles to allow step 3 to register.

5. Write 00 to GPPUP to remove the control signal.

6. Wait another 150 cycles to allow step 5 to register.

7. Finally, write to GPPUDCLK0/1 to remove the clock.

The Broadcom procedure may seem confusing because of the word *clock*. Writing to GPPUP and GPPUDCLK0/1 registers by using the preceding procedure is designed to provide a *pulse* to the internal pull-up resistor flip-flops (their data clock input). First a state is established in step 1, and then the configured 1 bits are clocked high in step 3 (for selected GPIO pins). Step 5 establishes a zero state, which is then sent to the flip-flop clock inputs in step 7.

The documentation also states that the current settings for the pull-up drivers *cannot* be read (there is no register access available to read these flip-flops). This makes sense when you consider that the state is held by these internal flip-flops that were changed by the procedure. Fortunately, when configuring the state of a particular GPIO pin, you change only the pins that you select by the GPPUDCLK0/1 register. The others remain unchanged. Chapter 16 will demonstrate how to change the pull-up resistors in a C program.

Drive Strength

How much drive can a GPIO pin provide in terms of current? The design of the SoC (system on chip) is such that each GPIO pin can safely sink or source up to 16 mA without harm. The drive strength is software configurable from 2 to 16 mA.

Table 11-7 lists the SoC registers for configuring the drive strength of the GPIO. There are three registers, affecting GPIO pins in three groups of 28 (two groups affect user-accessible GPIOs). The slew rate, hysteresis, and drive strength settings all apply at the group level. The drive strength is configured through a 3-bit value from 2 mA to 16 mA, in increments of 2 mA. When writing to these registers, the field PASSWRD must contain the hexadecimal value 0x5A, as a guard against accidental changes.

Table 11-7. *GPIO Pads Control*

Bits	Field	Description		I/O	Reset
31:24	PASSWRD	0x5A	Must be 0x5A when writing	W	0x00
23:05	Reserved	0x00	Write as zero, read as don't care	R/W	
04:04	SLEW	Slew rate			
		0	Slew rate limited	R/W	1
		1	Slew rate not limited		
03:03	HYST	Enable input hysterisis			
		0	Disabled	R/W	1
		1	Enabled		
02:00	DRIVE	Drive strength		R/W	3
		0	2 mA		
		1	4 mA		
		2	6 mA		
		3	8 mA (default except 28 to 45)		
		4	10 mA		
		5	12 mA		
		6	14 mA		
		7	16 mA (GPIO 28 to 45)		

To visualize how the Raspberry Pi controls drive strength, see
Figure 11-1. The control lines Drive0 through Drive2 are enabled by bits
in the DRIVE register. With these three control lines disabled (zero), only
the bottom 2 mA amplifier is active (this amplifier is always enabled for
outputs). This represents the weakest drive-strength setting.

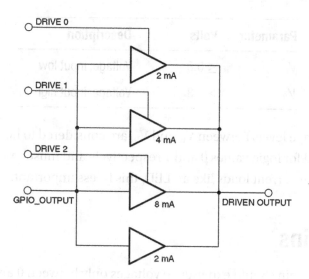

Figure 11-1. *Drive-strength control*

With Drive 0 set to a 1, the top amplifier is enabled, adding another 2 mA of drive, for a total of 4 mA. Enabling Drive 1 adds a further 4 mA of drive, totaling 8 mA. Enabling Drive 2 brings the total drive capability to 16 mA.

It should be mentioned that these drive capabilities are *not current limiters*. What they do is apply more or less amplifier drive. If the GPIO output is wired up to a light load like a CMOS chip or MOSFET transistor where little current is drawn, then the minimum drive of 2 mA suffices. When the GPIO output is loaded with a higher current load, the single 2 mA buffer may not be enough to keep the logic level within spec. By applying more drive, the output voltage levels are coerced into the correct operating range.

Logic Levels

The Raspberry Pi GPIO pins use 3.3 V logic levels. The precise logic-level specifications from the original BCM2835 SoC are as follows (newer models may vary slightly).

Parameter	Volts	Description
V_{IL}	≤ 0.8	Voltage, input low
V_{IH}	≥ 1.3	Voltage, input high

The voltage levels between V_{IL} and V_{IH} are considered to be ambiguous or undefined for logic values 0 and 1 respectively and must be avoided. When driving current loads like an LED, this is less important.

Input Pins

A GPIO input pin should experience voltages only between 0 and the 3.3 V maximum. Exercise caution when interfacing to other circuits that use higher voltages like TTL logic, where 5 V is used. The SoC is not tolerant of overvoltages and can be damaged.

While there exist protection diodes on chips to prevent negative input swings and overvoltage, these are weak and intended only to bleed away static charges. Broadcom does not document the current capacity of these protective diodes.

Output Pins

As an output GPIO pin, the user bears full responsibility for current limiting. There is *no* current limiting provided. When the output pin is in the high state, as a voltage source, it tries to supply 3.3 V (within the limits of the transistor and the supplying voltage regulator).

If this output is shorted to ground, then as much current as can be supplied will flow. This could lead to permanent damage.

The outputs also work to the voltage specifications listed earlier. But the attached load can skew the operating voltage range. An output pin can *source* or *sink* current. The amount of current required and the amount of *output drive* configured alters the operating voltage profile. As long as you keep within the current limits for the configured drive capability, the voltage specifications should be met by your Pi.

Sourcing Current

Figure 11-2 illustrates how a GPIO port sources current into its load (illustrated as a resistor). Current flows from the +3.3 V supply, through transistor M_1, out the GPIO pin, into *the load and then* to ground. Because of this, it takes a high (logic 1) to send current into the load. This is an example of an *active high* configuration.

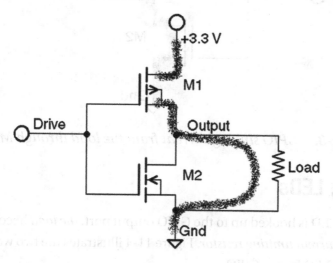

Figure 11-2. *The GPIO sourcing current through the load from transistor M1*

Sinking Current

Figure 11-3 illustrates how the GPIO output can sink current through the load to ground using transistor M2. Because *the load* is connected to the +3.3 V supply, current flows from the supply *into* the load and then into GPIO output pin to ground through M_2. To send current through the load, a logic 0 is written to the output port making this the *active low* configuration.

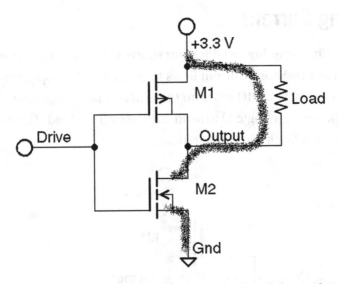

Figure 11-3.   *GPIO sinking current from the load through M2*

Driving LEDs

When an LED is hooked up to the GPIO output port, *the load* becomes the LED and *current limiting resistor*. Figure 11-4 illustrates the two ways of driving an LED from a GPIO.

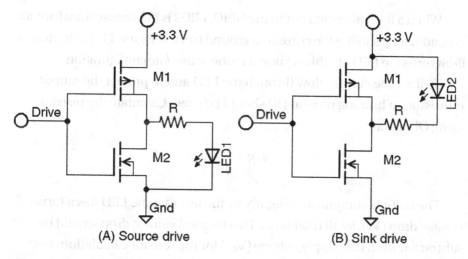

Figure 11-4. *Raspberry Pi GPIO driving two LEDs through a limiting resistor. Active high configuration at (A) left. Active low configuration at (B) right.*

The MOSFETs used in the GPIO output driver, are complementary. Notice how the arrow in the symbol for M1 differs from M2. These transistors act as switches. The drive signal is inverted from the GPIO output bit written. The drive signal to the gate of M1 and M2 is low when a 1-bit is written to the output. A low turns M1 on while simultaneously turning off M2. In this manner, only the upper or lower transistor is on for a given drive signal.

When the GPIO is written with a 1-bit, LED1 is lit because the GPIO transistor M1 is sourcing current through LED1 (review Figure 11-2). Because a 1-bit turns on the LED, this is known as the active *high* configuration.

When a 0-bit is written out to the GPIO, LED2 is lit because transistor M2 is conducting, sinking the current to ground (review Figure 11-3). Because a 0-bit turns the LED on, this is known as the active *low* configuration.

To limit the current flow through the LED and to protect the output transistors, a limiting resistor (R) should be used. Calculate the resistor using Ohm's law:

$$R = \frac{V}{I}$$

The math is complicated slightly by the fact that the LED has a forward voltage drop (V_F), as all diodes do. This forward voltage drop should be subtracted from the supply voltage (V_{CC}) for the resistor calculation. For red LEDs, the voltage drop is usually between 1.63 and 2.03 V.

Knowing the desired current draw for the LED, the resistance needed can be calculated from the following:

$$R = \frac{V_{CC} - V_{LED}}{I_{LED}}$$

where:

V_{CC} is the supply voltage (+3.3 V).

V_{LED} is the forward voltage drop for the LED.

I_{LED} is the required current draw for the LED.

For V_{LED} it is best to assume the worst case and assume the lowest voltage drop of 1.63 V. About 8 mA is reasonable for brightness from a 5 mm LED, allowing us to calculate the resistance of the limiting resistor:

$$R = \frac{3.3 - 1.63}{0.008}$$
$$= 208.75\,\Omega$$

Since resistors come in standard values, we round up to the nearest standard 10% component value of 220 Ω.

Note   Rounding resistance down would lead to higher current. It is better to err on the side of less current.

The LED and the 220 Ω limiting resistor can be wired according to Figure 11-4, either in the active high (A) or low (B) configuration.

Other LED Colors

Some pure-green, blue, white and UV (ultra violet) LEDs have a V_F of about 3.3 V. These LEDs would have you compute a resistance at or near zero ohms. In this case, no limiting resistor is required.

Yellow LEDs, on the other hand, can have a V_F of about 1.8 V. It normally happens that you don't have the datasheet when working with LEDs. Especially when you've pulled them out from a junk box. It is best to measure V_F, using the breadboard circuit of Figure 11-5. In this measurement, use 5 V or more as the supply. That way, if your V_F measures near or above 3.3 V, you can get a good reading. Attach your DMM (digital multi-meter) probes at the points indicated and measure the voltage. Assume a resistor of about 220 to 330 ohms (higher when using 3 mm or smaller LEDs).

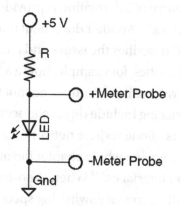

Figure 11-5. *Measuring forward voltage (V_F) of an unknown LED*

203

Despite all the precaution of measuring the forward voltage, you may still compute the 10% resistor value of 220 or 330 ohms. But this gives you reassurance that no harm will occur to the GPIO. For higher voltage LEDs, the limiting resistor can be safely eliminated. If there is any doubt, measure the current consumed by the LED when it is on. It should not exceed 16 mA to stay within the Pi's driving limit.

Driving Logic Interfaces

For LEDs, the requirements of the interface are rather simple. The interface is a success if the LED is lit when the output port is in one state, and the LED is dark in the other. The precise voltage appearing at the GPIO output pin in these two states is of little concern if the maximum current limits are respected.

When interfacing to logic, the output *voltage* is critical. For the receiving logic, the output level must be at least V_{IH} to reliably register a 1 bit (for the BCM2835, this is 1.3 V). Likewise, the output should present less than V_{IL} to reliably register a 0 in the receiver (for the BCM2835, this is 0.8V). Any voltage level between these limits is *ambiguous* and can cause the receiver to randomly see a 0 or a 1.

There are a large number of approaches to interfacing between different logic families. A good source of information is provided by the document "Microchip 3V Tips'n Tricks."[12] Another document titled "Interfacing 3V and 5V Applications, AN240" describes the issues and challenges of interfacing between systems.[13] It describes, for example, how a 5 V system can end up raising the 3.3 V supply voltage if precautions are not taken.

Approaches to interfacing include direct connections (when safe), voltage-dividing resistors, diode resistor networks, and the more-complex op-amp comparators. There is a whole chapter devoted to the subject in "Custom Raspberry Pi Interfaces."[14] When choosing an approach, remember to consider the necessary switching speed of the interface.

Driving Bi-color LEDs

This is a good place to mention driving bi-color LEDs. Some of these are configured so that one LED is forward biased while the other is reversed biased but using two leads. Or you can just use a pair of LEDs connected together as shown in Figure 11-6. This has the advantage of needing only two GPIO outputs. To change colors, you simply change the polarity of the pair of GPIO outputs.

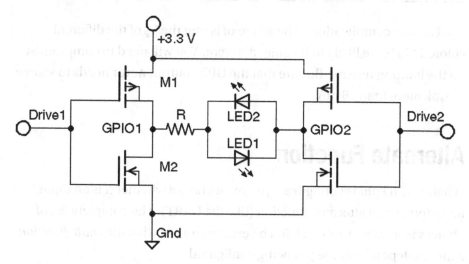

Figure 11-6. *Driving a bi-color LED or LED pair*

Table 11-8 summarizes a truth table for the possible states of the GPIO pair. When the two GPIO outputs have different states, one LED or the other is lit because current can flow. When both GPIOs have the same state, no current can flow turning off both LEDs. When LED1 and LED2 provide different colors, you choose the color output by selecting which LED is forward biased.

Table 11-8. *Truth Table for Driving Bi-color LEDs in Figure 11-6*

GPIO-1	GPIO-2	Result
Low	Low	Both LEDs are off (off)
Low	High	LED2 is forward biased (on), LED1 is off
High	Low	LED1 is forward biased (on), LED2 is off
High	High	Both LEDs are off (off)

The one complication to be aware of is that the V_F of the different colored LEDs are likely to be quite different. You will need to compromise on the limiting resistor. Be sure that the GPIO output never needs to source or sink more than 16 mA.

Alternate Function

When a GPIO pin is configured, you must choose whether it is an input, an output, or an alternate function (like the UART). The complete list of choices is shown in Table 11-9. The exact nature of what *alternate function x* means depends on the pin being configured.

Table 11-9.   *Alternate Function Selection*

Code	Function Selected	ALT
000	GPIO pin is an input.	
001	GPIO pin is an output.	
100	GPIO pin is alternate function 0.	0
101	GPIO pin is alternate function 1.	1
110	GPIO pin is alternate function 2.	2
111	GPIO pin is alternate function 3.	3
011	GPIO pin is alternate function 4.	4
010	GPIO pin is alternate function 5.	5

The values shown in the table's Code column are used in the configuration register itself. The alternate function numbers are listed in the ALT column. Keeping these two straight can be confusing when programming. Once the function has been selected, the configuration is then fine-tuned according to its peripheral type.

Output Pins

When a pin is configured for output, the remaining elements of configuration consist of the following:

- Logic sense
- Output state

The output state of the GPIO pins can either be set as a 32-bit word affecting 32 GPIOs at a time or set or cleared individually. Having individual set/clear operations allows the host to change individual bits without disturbing the state of others, or having to know their state.

Input Pins

Input pins are more complex because of the additional hardware functionality offered. This requires that the input GPIO pin be configured for the following:

- Detect rising input signals (synchronous/ asynchronous)

- Detect falling input signals (synchronous/ asynchronous)

- Detect high-level signals

- Detect low-level signals

- Logic sense

- Interrupt handling (handled by driver)

- Choose no pull-up; use a pull-up or pull-down resistor

Once these choices have been made, it is possible to receive data related to input signal changes, or simply query the pin's current state.

Floating Potentials

The *unconnected* GPIO input can "float" if there is no pull-up or pull-down resistor provided or configured. When the input is *connected* to a driving circuit, that circuit will provide a non-floating voltage level. The GPIO input uses a MOSFET transistor. The nature of that is that it is sensitive only to voltage (not current, like a bipolar transistor). So when the input is left unconnected, the GPIO input can sense voltages, including static electricity nearby (like a cat).

Output GPIO pins are clamped to the output level, which leaves the internal input transistor in a safe state. When a GPIO is configured as an input, it is normally best to configure it with a pull-up or pull-down resistance. This will pull the signal high or to ground. When otherwise left to float, the static electricity will be random and require the ESD (electrostatic discharge diodes) protection diodes to bleed away the charge.

Summary

This chapter has introduced a number of hardware traits of the Raspberry Pi GPIO. This gives you a solid foundation of its capabilities as well as its limitations. The design of the Pi allows considerable GPIO flexibility, from drive level, pull-up resistors and alternate functions.

The chapters following will introduce different ways of working with the GPIO ports, including direct access from a C program.

CHAPTER 12

Sysfs GPIO

This chapter examines GPIO driver access using the Raspbian Linux sysfs pseudo file system. Using the Raspbian driver allows even a shell script to configure, read, or write to GPIO pins.

The C/C++ programmer might be quick to dismiss this approach as too slow. But the driver does provide reasonable edge detection that is not possible with the direct register access approach. The driver has the advantage of receiving interrupts about GPIO state changes. This information can be passed onto the program using system calls such as poll(2).

/sys/class/gpio

Explore the top level directory by changing to it as root:

```
$ sudo -i
# cd /sys/class/gpio
```

At this point you should be able to see two main pseudo files of interest:

- export

- unexport

These are write-only pseudo files, which cannot be read—not even by the root user:

```
# cat export
cat: export: Input/output error
```

© Warren Gay 2018
W. Gay, *Advanced Raspberry Pi*, https://doi.org/10.1007/978-1-4842-3948-3_12

```
# cat unexport
cat: unexport: Input/output error
```

Normally, the kernel manages the use of GPIO pins, especially for peripherals like the UART that need them. The purpose of the export pseudo file is to allow the user to reserve it for use, much like opening a file. The unexport pseudo file is used to return the resource back to the Raspbian kernel's care.

Exporting a GPIO

To obtain exclusive use of GPIO17, the export pseudo file is written to as follows:

```
# echo 17 >/sys/class/gpio/export
# echo $?
0
```

Notice that the return code was 0, when $? was queried. This indicates no error occurred. If we had supplied an invalid GPIO number, or one that was not relinquished, we get an error returned instead:

```
# echo 170 >/sys/class/gpio/export
-bash: echo: write error: Invalid argument
# echo $?
1
```

After the successful reservation of gpio17, a new pseudo subdirectory should appear named gpio17.

```
# ls /sys/class/gpio/gpio17
active_
low device direction edge power subsystem uevent value
```

Configuring GPIO

Once you have access to a GPIO from an export, the main pseudo files are of interest:

- direction: To set I/O direction

- value: To read or write a GPIO value

- active_low: To alter the sense of logic

- edge: To detect interrupt driven changes

gpioX/direction:

The values that can be read or written to the direction pseudo file are described in Table 12-1.

Table 12-1. The Values for the gpiox/direction file

Value	Meaning
in	The GPIO port is an input.
out	The GPIO port is an output.
high	Configure as output and output a high to the port.
low	Configure as output and output a low to the port.

To configure our gpio17 as an output pin, perform the following:

```
# echo out > /sys/class/gpio/gpio17/direction
# cat /sys/class/gpio/gpio17/direction
out
```

The cat command that follows is not necessary but verifies that we have configured gpio17 as an output.

It is also possible to use the direction pseudo file to configure the GPIO as an output *and* set its value in one step:

```
# echo high > /sys/class/gpio/gpio17/direction
# echo low > /sys/class/gpio/gpio17/direction
```

gpioX/value

The value pseudo file permits you to set values for the configured GPIO. With the GPIO set to output mode, we can now write a high to the pin:

```
# echo 1 > /sys/class/gpio/gpio17/value
```

Legal values are simply are simply 1 or 0. When reading inputs, the value 1 or 0 is returned.

If you have an LED hooked up to GPIO17, it should now be lit. Use Figure 11-4 (A) for the wiring of the LED and resistor. Whatever we write out to the GPIO can also be read back in:

```
# cat /sys/class/gpio/gpio17/value
1
```

Writing a zero to the pseudo file, sets the output value to low, turning off the LED.

```
# echo 0 > /sys/class/gpio/gpio17/value
```

Figure 12-1 illustrates the author's "iRasp" setup—Raspberry Pi 3 B+ screwed to the back of an old Viewsonic monitor, using the Pi Cobbler cable and adapter to bring the GPIO signals to the breadboard. Attached to GPIO17 is a red LED, in series with a 330 ohm current limiting resistor. Given that the Pi 3 B+ has WIFI, this makes a convenient iMac-like workstation that can be moved about. In the figure, it is operating headless, but the four USB ports make it a simple matter to add a keyboard and mouse. Observant folks may notice that the monitor stand was adapted from another for this monitor.

Figure 12-1. *Raspberry Pi 3 B+ using Pi Cobbler to breadboard, with red LED wired to GPIO17 in active high configuration*

gpioX/active_low

Sometimes the polarity of a signal is inconvenient. Active low configuration recognizes the fact that the signal is *active* when the signal is *low*, rather than the normal *high*. If this proves inconvenient, you can change the sense of the signal using the active_low pseudo file:

```
# cat /sys/class/gpio/gpio17/active_low
0
# echo 1 > /sys/class/gpio/gpio17/active_low
# cat /sys/class/gpio/gpio17/active_low
1
```

The first command (cat) simply reads the current setting. Zero means that normal active high logic is in effect. The second command (echo) changes the active high configuration to active low. The third command confirms the setting was made. Now send a 1 to the gpio17/value pseudo file:

```
# echo 1 > /sys/class/gpio/gpio17/value
```

With the active low configuration established, this should cause the LED to go off. If we follow this with a write of zero to the pseudo file, the LED will now go on:

```
# echo 0 > /sys/class/gpio/gpio17/value
```

The sense of the logic has been inverted. If you change the wiring of the LED so that it corresponds to Figure 11-4 (B), writing a zero will turn on the LED. In this scenario, the sense of the logic matches the sense of the wiring.

gpioX/edge and gpioX/uevent

Some applications require the detection of changes of a GPIO. Since a user mode program does not receive interrupts, its only option is to continually poll a GPIO for a change in state. This wastes CPU resources and is like kids in the back seat of the car asking, "Are we there yet? Are we there yet?" The driver provides an indirect way for a program to receive a notification of the change.

Acceptable values to be written to this pseudo file are listed in Table 12-2.

Table 12-2. *Acceptable Values for Pseudo File Edge*

Value	Meaning
none	No edge detection.
rising	Detect a rising signal change.
falling	Detect a falling signal change.
both	Detect a rising or falling signal change.

These values can only be set on an input GPIO and exact case must be used.

```
# echo in > /sys/class/gpio/gpio17/direction
# echo both > /sys/class/gpio/gpio17/edge
# cat /sys/class/gpio/gpio17/edge
both
```

Once configured, it is possible to use the uevent pseudo file to check for changes. This must be done using a C/C++ program that can use poll(2) or selectl(2) to get notifications. When using poll(2), request events POLLPRI and POLLERR. When using select(2), the file descriptor should be placed into the exception set. The uevent file is no help to the shell programmer unfortunately.

GPIO Test Script

A simple test script is provided in the directory ~/RPi/scripts/gp and listed in Listing 12-1. To run it on GPIO17, invoke it as follows (from root):

```
$ sudo -i
# ~pi/RPi/scripts/gp 17
GPIO 17: on
GPIO 17: off  Mon Jul  2 02:48:49 +04 2018
GPIO 17: on
GPIO 17: off  Mon Jul  2 02:48:51 +04 2018
GPIO 17: on
GPIO 17: off  Mon Jul  2 02:48:53 +04 2018
GPIO 17: on
GPIO 17: off  Mon Jul  2 02:48:55 +04 2018
```

If you had an LED wired up to GPIO17, you should see it blinking slowly.

Listing 12-1. The ~/RPi/scripts/gp test script

```
0001: #!/bin/bash
0002:
0003: GPIO="$1"
0004: SYS=/sys/class/gpio
0005: DEV=/sys/class/gpio/gpio$GPIO
0006:
0007: if [ ! -d $DEV ] ; then
0008:     # Make pin visible
0009:     echo $GPIO >$SYS/export
0010: fi
0011:
0012: # Set pin to output
0013: echo out >$DEV/direction
```

```
0014:
0015: function put() {
0016:     # Set value of pin (1 or 0)
0017:     echo $1 >$DEV/value
0018: }
0019:
0020: # Main loop:
0021: while true ; do
0022:     put 1
0023:     echo "GPIO $GPIO: on"
0024:     sleep 1
0025:     put 0
0026:     echo "GPIO $GPIO: off  $(date)"
0027:     sleep 1
0028: done
0029:
0030: # End
```

GPIO Input Test

Another simple script is shown in Listing 12-2, which will report the state of an input GPIO as it changes. It requires three arguments:

1. Input GPIO number (defaults to 25)

2. Output GPIO number (defaults to 24)

3. Active sense: 0=active high, 1=active low (default 0)

The following invocation assumes the input GPIO is 25, the LED output is on 17, and the configuration is active high. Press Control-C to exit.

```
# ~pi/RPi/scripts/input 25 17 0
0000 Status: 0
0001 Status: 1
```

```
0002 Status: 0
0003 Status: 1
0004 Status: 0
^C
```

Listing 12-2. The ~/RPi/scripts/input script

```
0001: #!/bin/bash
0002:
0003: INP="${1:-25}"  # Read from GPIO 25 (GEN6)
0004: OUT="${2:-24}"  # Write to GPIO 24 (GEN5)
0005: ALO="${3:-0}"   # 1=active low, else 0
0006:
0007: set -eu
0008: trap "close_all" 0
0009:
0010: function close_all() {
0011:   close $INP
0012:   close $OUT
0013: }
0014: function open() { # pin direction
0015:   dev=$SYS/gpio$1
0016:   if [ ! -d $dev ] ; then
0017:     echo $1 >$SYS/export
0018:   fi
0019:   echo $2 >$dev/direction
0020:   echo none >$dev/edge
0021:   echo $ALO >$dev/active_low
0022: }
0023: function close() { # pin
0024:   echo $1 >$SYS/unexport
```

```
0025: }
0026: function put() { # pin value
0027:   echo $2 >$SYS/gpio$1/value
0028: }
0029: function get() { # pin
0030:   read BIT <$SYS/gpio$1/value
0031:   echo $BIT
0032: }
0033:
0034: count=0
0035: SYS=/sys/class/gpio
0036:
0037: open $INP in
0038: open $OUT out
0039: put $OUT 1
0040: LBIT=2
0041:
0042: while true ; do
0043:   RBIT=$(get $INP)
0044:   if [ $RBIT -ne $LBIT ] ; then
0045:     put $OUT $RBIT
0046:     printf "%04d Status: %d\n" $count $RBIT
0047:     LBIT=$RBIT
0048:     let count=count+1
0049:   else
0050:     sleep 1
0051:   fi
0052: done
0053:
0054: # End
```

Summary

This chapter has shown how to apply the sysfs driver interface to GPIO ports. While it may seem that this interface is primarily for use with shell scripts, the uevent pseudo file requires a C/C++ program to take advantage of it. These pseudo files otherwise provide a command-line interface, allowing different GPIO actions.

The next chapter will examine program access to the uevent file and explore direct access to the GPIO registers themselves.

CHAPTER 13

C Program GPIO

Whether your application needs fast access or specialized access from GPIO, a C/C++ program is the most convenient way to go. Python programs likewise can have direct access with the help of a module.

This chapter looks at how to access the GPIO ports directly from within a program, starting with the unfinished business of using the uevent file, to detect input GPIO changes with the help of interrupts behind the scenes.

Edge Events

The previous chapter introduced the uevents pseudo file that the GPIO driver provides. There it was explained that you needed to use one of the system calls poll(2) or select(2) to take advantage of this notification. Here I'll illustrate the use of poll(2), since it is the preferred system call of the two.

The idea behind poll(2) is that you supply a structured array of open file descriptors and indicate the events that you are interested in. The structure that poll(2) uses is defined as:

```
struct pollfd {
    int   fd;          /* file descriptor */
    short events;      /* requested events */
    short revents;     /* returned events */
};
```

© Warren Gay 2018
W. Gay, *Advanced Raspberry Pi*, https://doi.org/10.1007/978-1-4842-3948-3_13

The open file descriptor is placed into the fd member, while the events of interest are saved to member events. The structure member revents is populated by the system call, which is available upon return.

In directory ~/RPi/evinput you will find the C program source file evinput.c. The portion that performs the poll(2) call is illustrated in Listing 13-1.

Listing 13-1. The gpio_poll() function, invoking the poll(2) system call

```
0126: static int
0127: gpio_poll(int fd) {
0128:    struct pollfd polls[1];
0129:    char buf[32];
0130:    int rc, n;
0131:
0132:    polls[0].fd = fd;              /* /sys/class/gpio17/value */
0133:    polls[0].events = POLLPRI; /* Events */
0134:
0135:    do  {
0136:        rc = poll(polls,1,-1);  /* Block */
0137:        if ( is_signaled )
0138:            return -1;          /* Exit if ^C received */
0139:    } while ( rc < 0 && errno == EINTR );
0140:
0141:    assert(rc > 0);
0142:
0143:    lseek(fd,0,SEEK_SET);
0144:    n = read(fd,buf,sizeof buf); /* Read value */
0145:    assert(n>0);
0146:    buf[n] = 0;
0147:
0148:    rc = sscanf(buf,"%d",&n);
0149:    assert(rc==1);
```

```
0150:    return n;                       /* Return value */
0151:  }
```

In this program, we are interested in only one GPIO, so the array is declared with one element:

```
0128:    struct pollfd polls[1];
```

Prior to calling poll(2), the structure polls[0] is initialized:

```
0132:    polls[0].fd = fd;              /* /sys/class/gpio17/value */
0133:    polls[0].events = POLLPRI; /* Events */
```

If there was a second entry, then polls[1] would be initialized also. After this, the system call can be invoked:

```
0136:        rc = poll(polls,1,-1);  /* Block */
```

The first argument supplies the address of the first structure entry (equivalent to &polls[0]). The second argument indicates how many entries apply to this call (there is only one). The last argument is a timeout parameter in milliseconds, with the negative value meaning to block forever.

If the system call returns a positive value (rc), this indicates how many structure entries returned an event (in member revents). When this happens, the caller must scan the array (polls) for any returned events. In theory, the program should test:

```
if ( polls[0].revents & POLLPRI )
```

to see if there was activity for this file descriptor. In this program we don't test it because only one file descriptor is provided (it's the only file descriptor that can return activity). But if you were testing for two or more GPIOs, this test would be required.

When the returned value from poll(2) is zero, it simply means that the timeout has occurred. In this program, no timeout is used, so this cannot happen.

If the returned value is -1, then the system call has returned because of an error. There is one special error code, EINTR, which will be explained shortly.

For normal read data, the event macro name to use is POLLIN. For the uevent pseudo file, the event macro name is POLLPRI, indicating urgent data to be read. The data to be read is indeed urgent because the state of the GPIO port could change by the time you read the value pseudo file. So if you're hoping to catch rising events, don't be surprised if you sometimes read back a zero. When that has happened, the rising event has come and gone by the time that the GPIO state was read.

EINTR Error

Unix veterans are quick to come to grips with the EINTR error code. We see reference to it in this loop:

```
0135:    do {
0136:        rc = poll(polls,1,-1);   /* Block */
0137:        if ( is_signaled )
0138:            return -1;           /* Exit if ^C received */
0139:    } while ( rc < 0 && errno == EINTR );
```

The problem with poll(2) is that when no timeout is possible, there is no way to respond to a signal (like the terminal Control-C). The signal handler is limited in what it can do, since it is an asynchronous call, which could be interrupting the middle of a malloc(3) call, for example. For this reason, the evinput.c program specifies a safe interrupt handler for Control-C. It simply sets the variable is_signaled to 1.

```
0018: static int is_signaled = 0;   /* Exit program when
signaled */
...
0156: static void
0157: sigint_handler(int signo) {
```

```
0158:   is_signaled = 1;                 /* Signal to exit program */
0159: }
```

In order for the program to notice that the variable has changed to non-zero, the kernel returns with rc=-1 to indicate an error, and sets the errno=EINTR. The code EINTR simply means that the system call was *interrupted* and should be retried. In the code presented, line 137 tests to see if that variable was set to non-zero. If it was, the function immediately returns. Otherwise, the while loop in line 139 keeps the system call retried in line 136.

Reading uevent

Once it has been determined that there is urgent data to be read, there is a bit of a two-step that needs to happen next. This is *not* a poll(2) requirement but is the driver requirement for the pseudo file uevent:

```
0143:   lseek(fd,0,SEEK_SET);
0144:   n = read(fd,buf,sizeof buf); /* Read value */
0145:   assert(n>0);
0146:   buf[n] = 0;
0147:
0148:   rc = sscanf(buf,"%d",&n);
0149:   assert(rc==1);
0150:   return n;                         /* Return value */
```

Line 143 effectively performs a *rewind* on the file descriptor before it reads it in line 144. This informs the driver to make its event data available for the upcoming read. Line 146 simply puts a null byte at the end of the read data, so that sscanf(3) can use it. Since we are expecting a 0 or 1 in text form, this is converted into the integer value n in line 148 and then returned.

Demonstration

To build a demonstration program, perform the following (do a "make clobber" if you need to force a rebuild):

```
$ make
gcc -c -Wall -O0 -g evinput.c -o evinput.o
gcc evinput.o -o evinput
sudo chown root ./evinput
sudo chmod u+s ./evinput
```

This program will not require you to sudo, because it sets the evinput executable to setuid root. On secure systems, you may want to review that.

Do display usage info, use the -h option:

```
$ ./evinput -h
Usage: ./evinput -g gpio [-f] [-r] [-b]
where:
        -f    detect rising edges
        -r    detect falling edges
        -b    detect both edges

Defaults are: -g17 -b
```

Specify the GPIO you want to input from with the -g option (17 is the default). By default, the program assumes the -b option, to report rising and falling edges. Let's try this now:

```
$ ./evinput -g 17 -b
Monitoring for GPIO input changes:

GPIO 17 changed: 0
GPIO 17 changed: 1
GPIO 17 changed: 0
GPIO 17 changed: 1
```

```
GPIO 17 changed: 0
^C
```

The example session shows a few changes from zero to one and back. This will not always be so clean because of contact bounce and the speed that these changes occur. Try now with rising changes:

```
$ ./evinput -g 17 -r
Monitoring for GPIO input changes:

GPIO 17 changed: 0
GPIO 17 changed: 1
GPIO 17 changed: 1
GPIO 17 changed: 1
GPIO 17 changed: 0
GPIO 17 changed: 1
^C
```

The expected value read is a 1 after a rising edge. However, notice that one zero snuck in there, which is a reminder that contact bounce and timing plays a role. The first value displayed by this program is always the initial state of the GPIO.

Multiple GPIO

The evinput.c program has been kept simple for illustration purposes. But the usefulness of the edge detection may have you applying it to multple GPIO ports at once. The beauty of the poll(2) approach is that your application will not waste CPU cycles waiting for an event to occur. Instead the GPIO *interrupt* will inform the kernel of the change when it occurs, and thus inform the uevent driver. This in turn will inform poll(2) when performed on the pseudo file.

To expand the demo code to multiple GPIOs, you will first need to open multiple uevent pseudo files after putting the GPIO into the correct configuration. Then you will need to expand the array polls[] to include the number of GPIOs of interest (line 128). Then initialize each entry as shown in lines 132 and 133.

The second argument to the poll(2) call in line 136 needs to match the number of initialized array elements. If you are monitoring five GPIOs, then argument two needs to be the value 5.

After the do while loop ending at line 139, you will need to scan the array polls[] to determine which GPIO file descriptors reported an event with something like:

```
for ( x=0; x<rc; ++x ) {
    if ( polls[x].revents & EPOLLPRI ) {
        // read polls[x].fd for GPIO value
    }
}
```

In this manner, your application can very efficiently monitor several GPIO inputs for changes. Your code must however be able to cope with contact bounce. Some ICs like the PCF8574 I2C GPIO expander, sport an *INT* pin that can be monitored using this approach.

Direct Register Access

It is sometimes necessary for a user mode program to have direct access to the GPIO registers for performance or other reasons. This requires root access to control user access and because if done incorrectly, can crash your system. A crash is highly undesirable because it can cause loss of files.

The introduction of new Raspberry Pi models has added the challenge of dealing with different hardware platforms. With the original Raspberry Pi Model B and subsequent Model A, there was one fixed hardware offset to the peripheral registers. However, that has changed, and we now need to calculate the correct register address depending upon the hardware model involved.

Peripheral Base Address

In order to access the GPIO peripheral registers, we need to accomplish two things:

1. Determine base address of our register set

2. Need to map physical memory into our virtual address space

Given that Raspberry Pis now differ on where the registers are physically located, we need to determine the peripheral base address. Listing 13-2 shows how the pseudo file is opened and read, to determine the actual base address.

Listing 13-2. Determining the peripheral base address

```
0315: uint32_t
0316: peripheral_base() {
0317:    static uint32_t pbase = 0;
0318:    int fd, rc;
0319:    unsigned char buf[8];
0320:
0321:    fd = open("/proc/device-tree/soc/ranges",O_RDONLY);
0322:    if ( fd >= 0 ) {
0323:        rc = read(fd,buf,sizeof buf);
0324:        assert(rc==sizeof buf);
0325:        close(fd);
0326:        pbase = buf[4] << 24 | buf[5] << 16 | buf[6] << 8 |
                buf[7] << 0;
```

```
0327:    } else {
0328:        // Punt: Assume RPi2
0329:        pbase = BCM2708_PERI_BASE;
0330:    }
0331:
0332:    return pbase;
0333: }
```

The basic steps are:

1. Open the pseudo file (line 321).

2. Read the first 8 bytes into character array buf (line 323).

3. Once read, the file descriptor can be closed (line 325).

4. Piece together the address in line 326.

5. If step 1 fails, assume the value of macro BCM2708_
   PERI_BASE (which is 0x3F00000).

Mapping Memory

The next step in direct access to GPIO registers involves mapping physical memory into the C/C++ program's virtual memory. Listing 13-3 illustrates how physical memory is mapped.

Listing 13-3. Mapping physical memory

```
0274: void *
0275: mailbox_map(off_t offset,size_t bytes) {
0276:    int fd;
0277:
0278:    fd = open("/dev/mem",O_RDWR|O_SYNC);
0279:    if ( fd < 0 )
0280:        return 0;        // Failed (see errno)
```

```
0281:
0282:    void *map = (char *) mmap(
0283:        NULL,                       // Any address
0284:        bytes,                      // # of bytes
0285:        PROT_READ|PROT_WRITE,
0286:        MAP_SHARED,                 // Shared
0287:        fd,                         // /dev/mem
0288:        offset
0289:    );
0290:
0291:    if ( (long)map == -1L ) {
0292:        int er = errno;     // Save errno
0293:        close(fd);
0294:        errno = er;         // Restore errno
0295:        return 0;
0296:    }
0297:
0298:    close(fd);
0299:    return map;
0300: }
```

The basic steps performed are as follows:

1. First memory is accessed by opening /dev/mem, for read and write (line 278). This step requires root access to protect the integrity of the system.

2. Once that file is open, the mmap(2) system call is used to map it into the caller's virtual memory (lines 282 to 289).

   a. The first argument of the call is NULL, to specify that any virtual memory address is acceptable. This address can be specified, but the call will fail if the kernel finds it unacceptable.

    b.   Argument two is the number of bytes to map for this region. In our demo program, this is set to the kernel's page size. It needs to be a multiple of the page size.

    c.   Argument three indicates that we want to read and write the mapped memory. If you only want to query registers, macro PROT_WRITE can be dropped.

    d.   Argument four is MAP_SHARED allowing our calling program to share with any other processes on the system that might be accessing the same region.

    e.   The fifth argument is the file descriptor that we have open.

    f.   The last argument is the starting offset of physical memory that we wish to have access to.

3.   If the mmap(2) call fails for any reason, the return value will be a long negative one. The value errno will reflect the reason why (lines 291 to 296).

4.   Otherwise, the file can be closed (line 298) since the memory access has already been granted. The virtual memory address is returned in 299.

Register Access

Once the required memory has been *mapped*, it is possible to directly access the peripheral registers. To calculate the correct virtual memory address of a given register, macros are used like this one:

```
0040: #define GPIO_BASE_OFFSET   0x200000     // 0x7E20_0000
```

Additional macros reference a specific register relative to the base offset. For example, this macro provides an offset to the register that permits setting of GPIO bits.

```
0052: #define GPIO_GPSET0    0x7E20001C
```

These register accesses are rather messy. In the example gp.c program, the following gpio_read() function uses a set_gpio32() helper function to determine:

1. The register address (saved to gpiolev, line 232).

2. The bit shift needed (saved to variable shift, line 227).

3. From the required register to be accessed (GPIO_ GPLEV0, line 232).

This procedure provides the calculated word address in gpiolev, and a shift value to use to reference a specific bit. Listing 13-4 illustrates the code for this procedure.

Listing 13-4. C function, gpio_read() to read a GPIO input bit

```
0225: int
0226: gpio_read(int gpio) {
0227:     int shift;
0228:
0229:     if ( gpio < 0 || gpio > 31 )
0230:         return EINVAL;
0231:
0232:     uint32_v *gpiolev = set_gpio32(gpio,&shift,GPIO_
          GPLEV0);
0233:
0234:     return !!(*gpiolev & (1<<shift));
0235: }
```

Line 234 then accesses the register containing the GPIO bit of interest and returns it to the caller.

Write access is similar, except that the register is written with values (Listing 13-5).

Listing 13-5. Writing GPIO registers by writing to the register address

```
0241: int
0242: gpio_write(int gpio,int bit) {
0243:    int shift;
0244:
0245:    if ( gpio < 0 || gpio > 31 )
0246:        return EINVAL;
0247:
0248:    if ( bit ) {
0249:        uint32_v *gpiop = set_gpio32(gpio,&shift,GPIO_
             GPSET0);
0250:            *gpiop = 1u << shift;
0251:    } else {
0252:        uint32_v *gpiop = set_gpio32(gpio,&shift,GPIO_
             GPCLR0);
0253:            *gpiop = 1u << shift;
0254:    }
0255:    return 0;
0256: }
```

The one difference between read and write. however, is that the Pi has different registers to set GPIO bits (line 249) and another to clear them (line 252).

Demonstration Program

Build the source code in ~/RPi/gpio (perform "make clobber" if you wish to force a complete rebuild):

```
$ make
gcc -c -Wall -OO -g gp.c -o gp.o
gcc gp.o -o gp
sudo chown root ./gp
sudo chmod u+s ./gp
```

Once again, this program uses setuid root so that you are not forced to do a sudo to use it. The program has usage information, with the application of the -h option:

```
$ ./gp -h | expand -t 8
Usage: ./gp -g gpio { input_opts | output_opts | -a | drive_
opts} [-v]
where:
        -g gpio GPIO number to operate on
        -A n    Set alternate function n
        -a      Query alt function
        -q      Query drive, slew and hysteresis
        -v      Verbose messages
Input options:
        -i n    Selects input mode, reading for n seconds
        -I      Input mode, but performing one read only
        -u      Selects pull-up resistor
        -d      Selects pull-down resistor
        -n      Selects no pull-up/down resistor
Output options:
        -o n    Write 0 or 1 to gpio output
        -b n    Blink for n seconds
```

```
Drive Options:
        -D n    Set drive level to 0-7
        -S      Enable slew rate limiting
        -H      Enable hysteresis
```

All invocations require the specification of the -g option to provide the GPIO number to operate upon. Option -v can be added to provide additional output.

GPIO Input

The following example session configures the GPIO port 17 as an input and selects pull-up high reading for 60 seconds:

```
$ ./gp -g17 -i60
GPIO = 1
GPIO = 0
GPIO = 1
GPIO = 0
GPIO = 1
GPIO = 0
GPIO = 1
GPIO = 0
```

Your session output might show some contact bounce, so don't expect all transitions to be consistently ones alternating with zeros.

For a one time read of input, use -I instead:

```
$ ./gp -g17 -I
GPIO = 1
```

GPIO Output

To configure a GPIO as an output and write a value to it, use the following command:

```
$ ./gp -g17 -o1 -v
gpio_peri_base = 3F000000
Wrote 1 to gpio 17
$ ./gp -g17 -o0 -v
gpio_peri_base = 3F000000
Wrote 0 to gpio 17
```

In this session, the verbose option was added for visual confirmation.

It is useful to have a blinking output when testing. Do this using the -b option. The argument specifies the number of seconds to blink for:

```
$ ./gp -g17 -b4 -v
gpio_peri_base = 3F000000
GPIO 17 -> 1
GPIO 17 -> 0
GPIO 17 -> 1
GPIO 17 -> 0
```

Drive, Hysteresis, and Slew

The drive, slew rate limiting, and hysteresis options can be both set and queried by the -D and -q options. -D sets the values and -q queries:

```
$ ./gp -g17 -D7, -S1 -H0 -q -v
gpio_peri_base = 3F000000
  Set Drive=7, slew=true, hysteresis=false
  Got Drive=7, slew=true, hysteresis=false
```

The Set Drive line is suppressed without the verbose option. The -q option is performed after the set operation and reports on the configuration after the change. It can be used to query only:

```
$ ./gp -g17 -q
  Got Drive=7, slew=true, hysteresis=false
```

Alternate Mode

The alternate mode of the GPIO can also be queried and set:

```
$ ./gp -g17 -a
GPIO 17 is in Output mode.
```

Setting the alternate mode is done with the -A option:

```
$ ./gp -g17 -A5
$ ./gp -g17 -a
GPIO 17 is in ALT5 mode.
```

Transistor Driver

Before we leave the topic of GPIO, let's review a simple transistor driver that can be used in situations where a complete IC solution might be overkill. The GPIO pins of the Raspberry Pi are limited in their ability to drive current. Even configured for full drive, they are limited to 16 mA.

Rather than enlist a buffer IC, you might find that you only need one signal buffered. A cheap utility transistor like the 2N2222A may be all you need. Figure 13-1 illustrates the circuit.

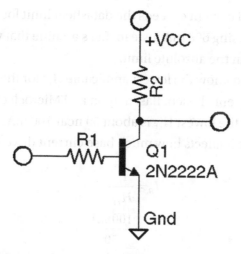

Figure 13-1. *A simple bipolar transistor driver*

The input signal arrives from the GPIO output on the left side of the circuit and flows through resistor R1, through the base emitter junction to ground. R1 limits this current to a safe value. Resistor R2 connects between the collector of Q1 and the power supply, which can be somewhat higher than +3.3 V. This is safe because the collector base junction is reversed biased. Be careful to not exceed the collector base voltage, however.

The maximum power that Q1 can handle is 0.5 W at 25°C. When the transistor is conducting (saturated), the voltage across Q1 (V_{CE}) is between 0.3 and 1 V. The remainder of the voltage is developed across the load. If we assume the worst case of 1 V for V_{CE} we can compute the maximum current for Q1:

$$I_C = \frac{P_{Q1}}{V_{CE}}$$
$$= \frac{1}{0.3}$$
$$= 3.3A$$

This calculated current exceeds the datasheet limit for I_C=600 mA, so we now switch to using 600 mA instead. Let's assume that we only need 100 mA, rather than the absolute limit.

Next we want to know the lowest applicable H_{FE} for the part being used at the collector current chosen. Based upon a STMicroelectronic datasheet, it is estimated that the lowest H_{FE} is about 50 near 100 mA. This value is important because it affects how much base current drive is needed.

$$I_B = \frac{I_C}{H_{FE}}$$
$$= \frac{100mA}{50}$$
$$= 2mA$$

Knowing now, the minimum base current to drive the transistor, we can compute the base resistor R1:

$$R_1 = \frac{GPIO_{HIGH} - V_{BE}}{I_B}$$
$$= \frac{3 - 0.7}{0.002}$$
$$= 1150 ohms$$

The nearest 10% resistor value is 1.2 kohms.

Inductive Loads

It's not unusual to drive a relay coil when larger currents or voltages are involved. The problem with inductive loads, however, is that when the magnetic field collapses, a reverse voltage is induced into the driving circuit. This occurs when the coil current is removed. Special care must be taken to suppress this. Figure 13-2 illustrates a transistor driving a relay coil. The relay opens and closes the load contacts K1.

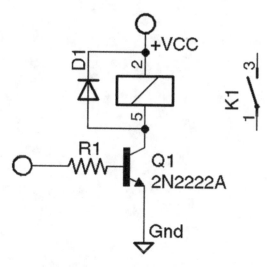

Figure 13-2. *An inductive load driven by Q1*

The relay coil needs a reversed biased diode (D1) across it to bleed any reverse kick that occurs when the current is removed from the coil (pins 5 and 2 in the figure). This will have the effect of slowing the release of the contacts. But this is preferred over the inductive spike causing a system crash.

Summary

The source code provided in gp.c is written entirely in the C language and kept to the bare essentials. It not only demonstrates the direct register access steps involved but provides you with code that you can reuse in your own C/C++ programs.

The chapter finished with a brief look at using a driver transistor when a driver is needed. Often an IC is sought when a cheaper one-transistor solution may be enough.

CHAPTER 14

1-Wire Driver

The 1-Wire protocol was developed by Dallas Semiconductor Corp. initially for the iButton.[15] This communication protocol was attractive enough to be applied to other devices and soon adopted by other manufacturers. This chapter provides an overview of the 1-Wire protocol and how it is supported in the Raspberry Pi.

1-Wire Line and Power

The 1-Wire protocol actually uses two wires, but the ground wire is not counted:

- *Data*: The single wire used for data communication

- *Ground*: The ground or "return" wire

The 1-Wire protocol was designed for communication with low-data content devices like temperature sensors. It provides for low-cost remote sensing by supplying power over the same wire used for data communications. Each sensor can accept power from the data line while the data line is in the high state (which is also the line's idle state). The small amount of power that is siphoned off charges the chip's internal capacitor (usually about 800 pF).[15]

When the data line is active (going low), the sensor chips continue to run off of their internal capacitor (in parasitic mode). Data communications cause the data line to fluctuate between low and high. Whenever the line level returns high again, even for a brief instant, the capacitor recharges.

© Warren Gay 2018
W. Gay, *Advanced Raspberry Pi*, https://doi.org/10.1007/978-1-4842-3948-3_14

The device also provides an optional V_{DD} pin, allowing power to be supplied to it directly. This is sometimes used when parasitic mode doesn't work well enough. This, of course, requires an additional wire, adding to the cost. This chapter will focus on the parasitic mode where V_{DD} is connected to the ground.

Line Driving

The data line is driven by *open drain* transistors in the master and slave devices. The line is held high by a *pull-up* resistor when the transistors are all in the *Off* state. To initiate a signal, one transistor turns on and pulls the line down to ground potential.

Figure 14-1 shows a simplified schematic of the master (GPIO) attached to the bus. Some voltage V (typically, +5 V) is applied to the 1-Wire bus through the pull-up resistor R_{pullup}. When the open drain transistor M_2 is in the *Off* state, the voltage on the bus remains high because of the pull-up resistor. When the master device activates transistor M_2, current will flow from the bus to the ground, acting like a signal short-circuit. Slave devices attached to the bus will see a voltage near zero.

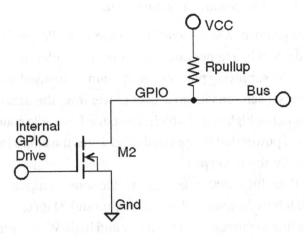

Figure 14-1. *1-Wire driver circuit*

Likewise, when a slave is signaled to respond, the master listens to the bus while the slave activates its driving transistor. Whenever all driving transistors are off, the bus returns to the high idle state.

The master can request that all slave devices reset. After the master has made this request, it relinquishes the bus and allows it to return high. All slave devices that are connected to the bus respond by bringing the line low after a short pause. Multiple slaves will bring the line low at the same time, but this is permitted. This informs the master that at least one slave device is attached to the bus. Additionally, this procedure puts all slave devices into a known reset state.

Master and Slave

The master device is always in control of the 1-Wire bus. Slaves speak only to the master when requested. There is never slave-to-slave device communication.

If the master finds that communication becomes difficult for some reason, it may force a bus reset. This corrects for an errant slave device that might be jabbering on the line.

Protocol

This section presents an introduction to the 1-Wire communication protocol. Knowing something about how the signaling works is not only interesting but may be helpful for troubleshooting. More information is available on the Internet.[16]

Reset

Figure 14-2 provides a simplified timing diagram of the reset procedure for the 1-Wire protocol. When the master driver begins, it resets the 1-Wire bus to put all the slave devices into a known state.

247

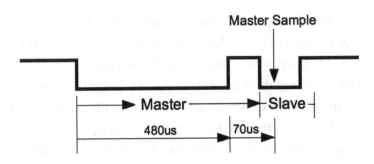

Figure 14-2. *1-Wire reset protocol*

For reset, the bus is brought low and held there for approximately 480 μs. Then the bus is released, and the pull-up resistor brings it high again. After a short time, slave devices connected to the bus start responding by bringing the line low and holding it for a time. Several slaves can participate in this at the same time. The master samples the bus at around 70 μs after it releases the bus. If it finds the line low, it knows that there is at least one slave connected and responding.

Soon after the master sampling point, all slaves release the bus again and go into a listening state. They do not respond again until the master specifically addresses a slave device. For simplicity, we'll omit the discovery protocol used.

Note   Each slave has a guaranteed unique address.

Data I/O

The data protocol is shown in Figure 14-3. Whether writing a 0 or 1 bit, the sending device brings the bus line low. This announces the start of a data bit.

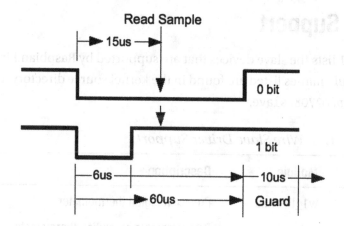

Figure 14-3. *1-Wire read/write of 0 data bit*

When a 0 is being transmitted, the line is held low for approximately 60 µs. Then the bus is released and allowed to return high. When a 1 bit is being transmitted, the line is held low for only about 6 µs before releasing the bus. Another data bit is not begun until 70 µs after the start of the previous bit. This leaves a guard time of 10 µs between bits. The receiver then has ample time to process the bit and gain some signal noise immunity.

The receiver notices a data bit is coming when the line drops low. It then starts a timer and samples the bus at approximately 15 µs. If the bus is still in the low state, a 0 data bit is registered. Otherwise, the data bit is interpreted as a 1. Having registered a data bit, the receiver then waits further until the line returns high (in the case of a 0 bit).

The receiver remains idle until it notices the line going low again, announcing the start of the next bit.

The sender can be either the master or the slave, but the master always controls who can speak next. Slaves do not write to the bus unless the master requested it.

Slave Support

Table 14-1 lists the slave devices that are supported by Raspbian Linux. The module names listed are found in the kernel source directory `arch/arm/machbcm2708/slave`.

Table 14-1. *1-Wire Slave Driver Support*

Device	Module	Description
DS18S20	w1_therm.c	Precision digital thermometer
DS18B20		Programmable resolution thermometer
DS1822		Econo digital thermometer
DS28EA00		9- to 12-bit digital thermometer with PIO
bq27000	w1_bq27000.c	Highly accurate battery monitor
DS2408	w1_ds2408.c	Eight-channel addressable switch
DS2423	w1_ds2423.c	4 KB RAM with counter
DS2431	w1_ds2431.c	1 KB EEPROM
DS2433	w1_ds2433.c	4 KB EEPROM
DS2760	w1_ds2760.c	Precision Li+ battery monitor
DS2780	w1_ds2780.c	Stand-alone fuel gauge

Configuration

With the advent of the Linux device tree, it is now necessary to configure access for the 1-Wire driver. Edit file `/boot/config.txt` and add the following line:

```
dtoverlay=w1-gpio,gpiopin=4,pullup=on
```

The parameter gpiopin=4 specifies that the 1-Wire bus is on GPIO4. This used to be hard-coded in the driver but now permits you to choose differently. It is still the default if the parameter is not specified.

Parameter pullup=on is normally required for successful operation. Even though I had attached a 4.7 kohm resistor to +3.3 V for the bus, I could not get my devices to operate in parasitic mode. I recommend that you provide this parameter. Once you have edited the file, reboot for it to take effect.

There is some interesting documentation available in the /boot directory:

```
$ less /boot/overlays/README
...
Name:   w1-gpio
Info:   Configures the w1-gpio Onewire interface module.
        Use this overlay if you *don't* need a GPIO to drive an
        external
        pullup.
Load:   dtoverlay=w1-gpio,<param>=<val>
Params: gpiopin        GPIO for I/O (default "4")

        pullup         Non-zero, "on", or "y" to enable the
                       parasitic
                       power (2-wire, power-on-data) feature
```

The referenced README file also contains an entry named w1-gpio-pullup, which you should probably avoid unless you know why you are using it. It will require one additional GPIO to be used to pull up the bus (by default GPIO5).

Reading Temperature

The support for the usual temperature sensors is found in the kernel module w1_therm. When you first boot your Raspbian Linux, that module may not be loaded. You can check for it with the lsmod command (root not required for listing):

```
$ lsmod
Module          Size    Used by
snd_bcm2835     12808   1
snd_pcm         74834   1 snd_bcm2835
snd_seq         52536   0
...
```

The module w1_therm depends on another driver module named wire. To verify if the driver modules are loaded, check the pseudo file system:

```
$ ls -l /sys/bus/w1
ls: cannot access /sys/bus/w1 : No such file or directory
```

Having not found the pathname /sys/bus/w1, we have confirmation that the device driver is not loaded.

Loading module w1_therm will bring in most of its module dependents:

```
$ sudo modprobe w1_therm
$ lsmod
Module          Size    Used by
w1_therm        2705    0
wire            23530   1 w1_therm
cn              4649    1 wire
snd_bcm2835     12808   1
snd_pcm         74834   1 snd_bcm2835
...
```

After the wire module is loaded, you'll see the /sys/bus/w1/devices directory. One more module is needed:

```
$ sudo modprobe w1_gpio
$ lsmod
Module            Size    Used by
w1_gpio           1283    0
w1_therm          2705    0
wire              23530   2 w1_therm,w1_gpio
cn                4649    1 wire
snd_bcm2835       12808   1
...
$ cd /sys/bus/w1/devices
$ ls
w1_bus_master1
```

Once module w1_gpio is loaded, there is a bus master driver for the configured GPIO port. The bus master makes its presence known by creating symlink devices/w1_bus_master1. Change to the /sys/bus/w1 directory and list it to see the associated pseudo files within it. The long lines have been abbreviated:

```
# pwd
/sys/bus/w1
# ls -lR .
.:
total 0
drwxr-xr-x 2 root root    0 Jul  6 06:47 devices
drwxr-xr-x 4 root root    0 Jul  6 06:47 drivers
-rw-r--r-- 1 root root 4096 Jul  6 06:47 drivers_autoprobe
--w------- 1 root root 4096 Jul  6 06:47 drivers_probe
--w------- 1 root root 4096 Jul  6 06:47 uevent
```

```
./devices:
total 0
lrwxrwxrwx 1 root root 0 Jul  6 06:47 28-00000478d75e -> ...
lrwxrwxrwx 1 root root 0 Jul  6 06:47 28-0000047931b5 -> ...
lrwxrwxrwx 1 root root 0 Jul  6 06:47 w1_bus_master1 -> ...

./drivers:
total 0
drwxr-xr-x 2 root root 0 Jul  6 06:47 w1_master_driver
drwxr-xr-x 2 root root 0 Jul  6 06:47 w1_slave_driver

./drivers/w1_master_driver:
total 0
--w------- 1 root root 4096 Jul  6 06:47 bind
--w------- 1 root root 4096 Jul  6 06:47 uevent
--w------- 1 root root 4096 Jul  6 06:47 unbind
lrwxrwxrwx 1 root root    0 Jul  6 06:47 w1_bus_master1 -> ...

./drivers/w1_slave_driver:
total 0
lrwxrwxrwx 1 root root    0 Jul  6 06:47 28-00000478d75e -> ...
lrwxrwxrwx 1 root root    0 Jul  6 06:47 28-0000047931b5 -> ...
--w------- 1 root root 4096 Jul  6 06:47 bind
--w------- 1 root root 4096 Jul  6 06:47 uevent
--w------- 1 root root 4096 Jul  6 06:47 unbind
```

The pseudo file names 28-00000478d75e and 28-0000047931b5 are device entries for the author's two DS18B20 devices. Don't worry if you don't see your entries immediately, since it takes time for the discovery protocol to find them.

Slave Devices

Figure 14-4 shows the pin-out of the Dallas DS18B20 slave device. This temperature sensor is typical of many 1-wire slave devices.

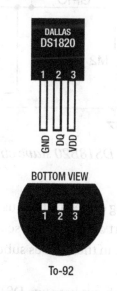

PIN DESCRIPTION

GND   - Ground
DQ   - Data In/Out
V_{DD} - Power Supply Voltage

Figure 14-4. *DS18B20 pin-out*

Slave devices are identified by a pair of digits representing the product family, followed by a hyphen and serial number in hexadecimal. The ID 28-00000478d75e is an example. You might also want to try different devices, like the similar DS18S20. Figure 14-5 illustrates the DS18B20 attached to the Raspberry Pi GPIO.

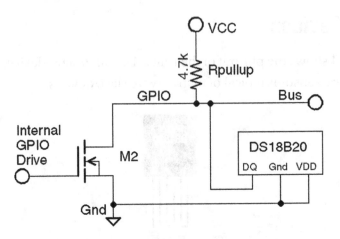

Figure 14-5. *1-Wire with DS18B20 slave circuit, using V_{CC}=3.3 V and 4.7 k pull-up resistor*

When things are working correctly, the bus master detects slave devices automatically as part of its periodic scan. When your device(s) are discovered, they will appear in the devices subdirectory with names like 28-0000028f6667.

The following example shows how two DS18B20 temperature sensors show up on the 1-Wire bus:

```
$ cd /sys/bus/w1/devices
$ ls
28-00000478d75e 28-0000047931b5 w1_bus_master1
$
```

Figure 14-6 illustrates the breadboard setup used by the author.

Figure 14-6. *The breadboard with two DS18B20 temperature sensors wired to the Raspberry Pi*

Reading the Temperature

The slave device's temperature can be read by reading its w1_slave pseudo file. In this example, we read two DS18B20 temperature sensors that are supposed to be accurate to ±0.5 °C. Reading these two sensors together should show fairly good agreement (they were in close proximity of each other):

```
# cd /sys/bus/w1/devices
# cat 28-00000478d75e/w1_slave
a6 01 4b 46 7f ff 0a 10 f6 : crc=f6 YES
a6 01 4b 46 7f ff 0a 10 f6 t=26375
```

The second line ending in t=26375 indicates a reading of 26.375°C.

If the driver is experiencing problems reading from the device, the DS18B20 response may look like this:

```
# cd /sys/bus/w1/devices
# cat 28-00000478d75e/w1_slave
50 05 4b 46 7f ff 0c 10 1c : crc=1c YES
50 05 4b 46 7f ff 0c 10 1c t=85000
```

The value t=85000 is the dead giveaway. If you see this, check your wiring—particularly the pullup resistor. The circuit needs a 4.7 kohm pull-up resistor to +3.3 V.

Summary

In this chapter, the 1-Wire Linux support was put to use to read the Dallas Semiconductor DS18B20 temperature sensor. Table 14-1 lists several other types of 1-wire sensors that you may be able to use. Having driver support makes using sensors like these a breeze.

CHAPTER 15

I²C Bus

The I²C bus, also known as the two-wire interface (TWI), was developed by Philips circa 1982 to allow communication with lower-speed peripherals.[17] It was also economical because it only required two wires (excluding ground and power). Since then, other standards have been devised, building upon this framework, such as the SMBus. However, the original I²C bus remains popular as a simple, cost-effective way to connect peripherals.

I²C Overview

Figure 15-1 shows the I²C bus in the Raspberry Pi context. The Raspberry Pi provides the bus using the BCM2835 device as the bus master. Notice that the Pi also provides the external pull-up resistors R_1 and R_2, shown inside the dotted lines. Table 15-1 lists the two I2C bus lines that are provided on the header strip.

Table 15-1. *I2C Bus Connections*

Connection	GPIO	Description
P1-03	GPIO-2	SDA1 (serial bus data)
P1-05	GPIO-3	SCL1 (serial bus clock)

© Warren Gay 2018
W. Gay, *Advanced Raspberry Pi*, https://doi.org/10.1007/978-1-4842-3948-3_15

The design of the I2C bus allows multiple peripherals to attach to the SDA and the SCL lines. Each slave peripheral has its own unique 7-bit address. For example, the MCP23017 GPIO extender peripheral might be configured with the address of 0x20. Each peripheral is referenced by the master by using this address. Nonaddressed peripherals are expected to remain quiet.

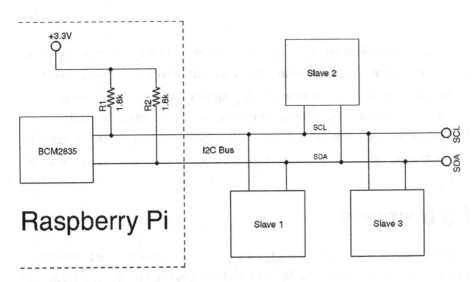

Figure 15-1. *The I²C bus on the Raspberry Pi*

SDA and SCL

Both masters and slaves take turns at "grabbing the bus" at various times. Master and slave use open-drain transistors to drive the bus lines. It is because all participants are using open-drain drivers that pull-up resistors must be used (provided by the Pi). Otherwise, the data and clock lines would float between handoffs.

The open-drain driver design allows all participants to drive the bus lines—just not at the same time. Slaves, for example, turn off their line drivers, allowing the master to drive the signal lines. The slaves just listen, until the master calls them by address. When the slave is required to answer, the slave will then assert its driver, grabbing the line. It is assumed by the slave that the master has already released the bus at this point. When the slave completes its own transmission, it releases the bus, allowing the master to resume.

The idle state for both lines is high. The high state for the Raspberry Pi is +3.3 V. Other systems may use +5 V signaling. When shopping for I²C peripherals, choose ones that will operate at the 3.3 V level. Sometimes 5 V peripherals can be used with careful signal planning or using adapters.

Bus Signaling

The start and stop bits are special in the I²C protocol. The start bit is illustrated in Figure 15-2. Notice the SDA line transition from high to low, while the clock remains in the high (idle) state. The clock will follow by going low after 1/2 bit time following the SDA transition. This special signal combination informs all connected devices to "listen up," since the next piece of information transmitted will be the device address.

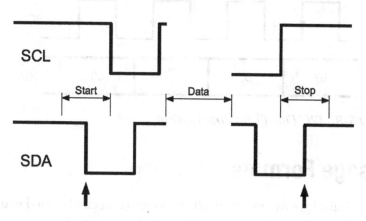

Figure 15-2. *I2C start/stop signaling*

The stop bit is also special in that it allows slave devices to know whether more information is coming. When the SDA line transitions from low to high midway through a bit cell, it is interpreted as a *stop bit*. The stop bit signals the end of the message.

There is also the concept of a *repeated start*, often labeled in diagrams as *SR*. This signal is electrically identical to the start bit, except that it occurs within a message in place of a stop bit. This signals to the peripheral that more data is being sent or required as part of another message.

Data Bits

Data bit timings are approximately as shown in Figure 15-3. The SDA line is expected to stabilize high or low according to the data bit being sent, prior to the SCL line going high. The receiver clocks in the data on the falling edge of SCL, and the process repeats for the next data bit. Note that most significant bits are transmitted first (network order, or big endian).

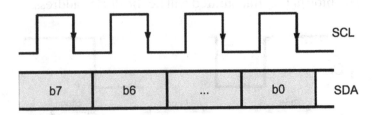

Figure 15-3. *I2C Data bit transmission*

Message Formats

Figure 15-4 displays two example I2C messages that can be used with the MCP23017 chip. The simplest message is the write register request.

MCP23017 <u>Write</u> Register Message:

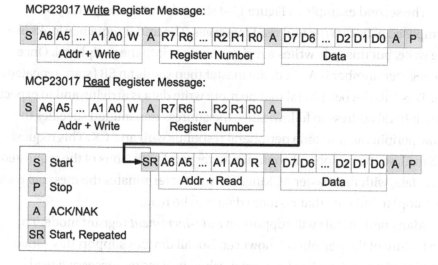

MCP23017 <u>Read</u> Register Message:

Figure 15-4. *Example I2C messages*

The diagram shows each message starting with the S (start) bit and ending with a P (stop) bit. After the start bit, each message begins with a byte containing the 7-bit peripheral address and a read/write bit. Every peripheral must read this byte in order to determine whether the message is addressed to it.

The addressed peripheral is expected to return an ACK/NAK bit after the address is sent. If the peripheral fails to respond for any reason, the line will go high due to the pull-up resistor, indicating a NAK. The master, upon seeing a NAK, will send a stop bit and terminate the transmission.

When the addressed peripheral ACKs the address byte, the master then continues to write when the request is a write. The first example shows the MCP23017 8-bit register number being written next. This indicates which of the peripheral's registers is to be written to. The peripheral will then ACK the register number, allowing the master to follow with the data byte to be written, into the selected register. This too must be ACKed. If the master has no more data to send, the P (stop) bit is sent to end the transmission.

The second example in Figure 15-4 shows how a message may be composed of both write and read messages. The initial sequence looks like the write, but this only writes a register number into the peripheral. Once the register number is ACKed, the master then sends an SR (start, repeated) bit. This tells the peripheral that no more write data is arriving and to expect a peripheral address to follow. Since the address transmitted specifies the *same* peripheral, the same peripheral responds with an ACK. This request is a read, so the peripheral continues to respond with 8 bits of the requested read data, with the master ACKing. The master terminates the message with a P (stop) to indicate that no more data is to be read.

Many peripherals will support an *auto-increment* register mode. This is a feature of the peripheral, however. Not all devices support this. Once a peripheral's register has been established by a write, successive reads or writes can occur in auto-increment mode, with the register being incremented with each byte transferred. This results in efficient transfers.

I²C Bus Speed

Unlike the SPI bus, the I²C bus operates at a fixed speed within Raspbian Linux. The SoC document claims I²C operation up to 400 kHz, but the default is 100 kHz.

To use I²C, you must enable it in your /boot/config.txt file by uncommenting it. You can also optionally specify the clock rate by specifying the i2c_arm_baudrate parameter. The following enables I²C and sets the clock to 400 kHz:

```
dtparam=i2c_arm=on,i2c_arm_baudrate=400000
```

The default clock rate is equivalent to:

```
dtparam=i2c_arm=on,i2c_arm_baudrate=100000
```

Save the config.txt file and reboot. You can confirm that the clock rate was accepted as follows:

```
# xxd -g4 /sys/class/i2c-adapter/i2c-1/of_node/clock-frequency
00000000: 00061a80                            ....
# gdb
GNU gdb (Raspbian 7.12-6) 7.12.0.20161007-git
Copyright (C) 2016 Free Software Foundation, Inc.
...
(gdb) p 0x00061a80
$1 = 400000
(gdb) quit
#
```

- The xxd command reports a group of 4 bytes (-g4) as 00061a80.

- The gdb command is used to print (p command) this value in decimal (don't forget to prefix the reported number with 0x to indicate the value is hexadecimal).

I²C Tools

Working with I²C peripherals is made easier with some utilities. These may be preinstalled in your Raspbian Linux but are otherwise easily installed if necessary.

```
$ sudo apt-get install i2c-tools
```

The i2c-tools package includes the following utilities:

i2cdetect: Detects peripherals on the I2C line

i2cdump: Dumps values from an I2C peripheral

i2cset: Sets I2C registers and values

i2cget: Gets I2C registers and values

Each of these utilities has a man page available for additional information.

MCP23017

The MCP23S17 is the I2C chip that provides 16 expansion GPIO ports. At startup, the pins default to inputs, but can be configured as outputs like the native Pi GPIO ports. The MCP23S17 is the companion chip for SPI bus.

The chip allows eight different I2C addresses to be wire configured. Like the native Pi GPIOs, the ports can be configured active high or low. The chip operates from a supply voltage of 1.8 to 5.5 V, making it perfect for Pi 3.3 V operation.

The output mode GPIO can sink up to 8 mA of current and source 3 mA. This should be taken into account when driving loads, even LEDs.

For input GPIOs, it has an interrupt capability, signaling an input change on the INTA (GPIOA0 to GPIOA7) or INTB pins (GPIOB0 to GPIOB7). The chip can be configured to report all changes on INTA, which is the way it will be used here. This is important for inputs because otherwise you would need to continuously poll the device.

Perhaps the best part of all is that a kernel driver is available for it. This makes it very convenient to use.

Driver Setup

The first thing that must be configured is that I²C must be enabled, if you have not done it already. The /boot/config.txt file must have the following line uncommented:

dtparam=i2c_arm=on,i2c_arm_baudrate=100000

Next you must enable the driver in `config.txt`:

```
dtoverlay=mcp23017,gpiopin=4,addr=0x20
```

- Optional parameter `gpiopin=4` specifies that GPIO4 will be used for sensing interrupts in the chip. GPIO4 is the default.

- Optional parameter `addr=0x20` specifies the I²C address for the MCP23017 chip. 0x20 is the default.

After editing these changes, reboot:

```
# sync
# /sbin/shutdown -r now
```

After the Pi boots back up, log in and check for suspicious error messages using the `dmesg` command. You can skip that if you're feeling lucky.

If all went well, you should see something like the following in the `/sys/class/gpio` directory:

```
# ls /sys/class/gpio
export  gpiochip0  gpiochip128  gpiochip496  unexport
```

If you used I2C address 0x20 and you have your MCP23017 wired up to the bus, you should see the subdirectory name `gpiochip496` (higher for other addresses). If you don't see the chip listed, then:

- Scrutinize the `dmesg` log for errors.

- Check the configuration and wiring.

- Make sure that the MCP23017 chip's $\overline{RESET}$ pin is wired to +3.3 V.

Wiring

The wiring used in this example is illustrated in Figure 15-5. A few things are worth noting about the circuit:

- Supply the MCP23017 chip from +3.3 V (not 5 V).

- No resistors are required for the bus since the Raspberry Pi already provides R_1 and R_2.

- Important! Wire the $\overline{RESET}$ line to +3.3 V. Otherwise random or complete failure will occur.

- Wiring the INTA line is not required if you only plan to use *output* mode GPIOs. However, the driver will consume the configured GPIO, whether used or not.

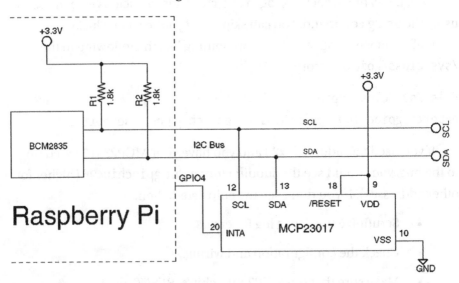

Figure 15-5. *Wiring for the MCP23017 to the Raspberry Pi*

When the $\overline{RESET}$ line is not wired to +3.3 V, the input to the chip will float. Sometimes the CMOS input will float high and sometimes low (causing a chip reset). I ran into this when I initially wired up the circuit. The worst part was that the driver and chip worked for a while but later developed problems.

The purpose of the INTA line (and GPIO4 in Figure 15-5) is to notify the Pi that an input GPIO port has changed state. This informs the mcp23017 driver to send an I²C request to read the inputs. Without this notification, the driver would have to busy the I²C bus with repeated read requests to see if there is new input.

Testing GPIO Output

With the circuit wired up and the configuration set and the system rebooted, you should see the driver report its presence in /sys/class/ gpio as gpiochip496, if you used the I²C address of 0x20.

In the same way that native GPIOs were accessed in Chapter 12, we can export this GPIO. But first we need to determine which GPIO number corresponds to each MCP23017 GPIO port. There are two pseudo files for this purpose:

1. gpiochip496/base lists the starting GPIO number for this device (496).

2. gpiochip496/ngpio lists how many GPIOs are supported (16).

The following shows an example discovery session:

```
# cd /sys/class/gpio
# ls
export    gpio503 gpiochip0 gpiochip128 gpiochip496 unexport
# ls gpiochip496
base device label ngpio power subsystem uevent
# cat gpiochip496/base
496
# cat gpiochip496/ngpio
16
#
```

This information permits the creation of the chart in Table 15-2.

Table 15-2. *GPIO Associations for Gpiochip496 (I²C Address 0x20)*

GPIO	Pin	MCP23017	GPIO	Pin	MCP23017
GPIO496	21	A0	GPIO504	1	B0
GPIO497	22	A1	GPIO505	2	B1
GPIO498	23	A2	GPIO506	3	B2
GPIO499	24	A3	GPIO507	4	B3
GPIO500	25	A4	GPIO508	5	B4
GPIO501	26	A5	GPIO509	6	B5
GPIO502	27	A6	GPIO510	7	B6
GPIO503	28	A7	GPIO511	8	B7

To use the MCP23017 GPIO A7 as an output, we do:

```
# pwd
/sys/class/gpio
# echo out >gpio503/direction
# cat gpio503/direction
out
# echo 1 >gpio503/value
# cat gpio503/value
1
```

If you have an LED wired to A7 in active high configuration, it should be lit. Otherwise measure it with your DMM and you should see +3.3 V on pin 28.

```
# echo 0 >gpio503/value
# cat gpio503/value
0
```

After the above, GPIO A7 should now go low.

Testing GPIO Input

With the GPIO A7 still configured as an output, configure MCP23017 GPIO
A6 as an input:

```
# ls
export     gpio503 gpiochip0 gpiochip128 gpiochip496 unexport
# echo 502 >export
# ls
export
gpio502 gpio503 gpiochip0 gpiochip128 gpiochip496 unexport
# echo in >gpio502/direction
```

Place a jumper wire from A7 (pin 28) to A6 (pin 27). Now let's see if
input A6 agrees with output A7:

```
# cat gpio502/value
0
# cat gpio503/value
0
# cat gpio502/value
0
# echo 1 >gpio503/value
# cat gpio502/value
1
```

As expected, as we changed A7, the input A6 followed.

Test GPIO Input Interrupt

Being able to read a GPIO alone is often not enough. We need to know
when it has changed so that it can be read at that point in time. In
Figure 15-5, the MCP23017 chip has its INTA pin wired to the Pi's GPIO4.
The MCP23017 will activate that line whenever an unread change in inputs

271

occurs, alerting the driver in the Pi. Only then does the driver need to read the chip's current input status.

To test that this is working, we'll reuse that evinput program to monitor gpio502 (GPIO input A6):

```
$ cd ~/RPi/evinput
$ ./evinput -g502 -b
```

Changing to the root terminal session, let's toggle A7 a couple of times:

```
# pwd
/sys/class/gpio
# ls
export
gpio502  gpio503  gpiochip0  gpiochip128  gpiochip496  unexport
# echo 1 >gpio503/value
# echo 0 >gpio503/value
# echo 1 >gpio503/value
# echo 0 >gpio503/value
```

Switch back to the evinput session, and see if we got any edges (the -b option monitors for both rising and falling edges):

```
$ ./evinput -g502 -b
Monitoring for GPIO input changes:

GPIO 502 changed: 1
GPIO 502 changed: 0
GPIO 502 changed: 1
GPIO 502 changed: 0
^C
```

Indeed, this confirms that the interrupt facility works. Note that we monitored GPIO502 (A6) rather than GPIO4. Only the driver needs to monitor GPIO4.

Limitations

The driver support for the MCP23017 provides a very convenient way to add sixteen GPIOs to your Raspberry Pi. As great as this is, here are a few points to consider:

- The extended GPIOs are not as fast as the native Pi GPIOs.

- You may need to do some homework to add more than one MCP23017 chip. While the bus supports up to eight uniquely addressed MCP23017 chips, the device driver might not. It may be possible with added nodes to the device tree.

- I/O performance is directly related to the I²C clock rate.

- The GPIOs are accessed through the sysfs pseudo file system, further impacting performance.

The main thing to keep in mind is that all GPIO interaction occurs over the I²C bus at the clock rate (100 kHz or 400 kHz). Each I/O may require several bytes of transfer because the MCP23017 has a large set of registers. Each byte transferred requires time. At the default of 100 kHz, a one-byte transfer takes:

$$t = \frac{1}{100kHz} \times 8bits$$
$$= 80\,\mu s$$

To read one GPIO input register requires a start bit, three bytes of data, and a stop bit. This results in a minimum transaction time of 260 µs. That limits the number of GPIO reads to approximately 3,800 reads/s. This doesn't account for sharing the bus with other devices.

In the end, the suitability depends upon the application. By shifting the highest rate GPIO transactions to the Pi's native GPIOs and the slower I/Os to the extension GPIOs, you might find that the arrangement works well enough.

I²C API

The bare-metal C language API for the I²C bus transactions will be introduced in this section. Using this API you can program your own interface with another GPIO expander such as the PCF8574, for example. That chip provides eight additional GPIOs but is economical and +3.3 V friendly. It has only one configuration register making it easy to use directly.

Kernel Module Support

Access to the I2C bus is provided through the use of kernel modules. If you have enabled I2C in the config.txt as discussed earlier, you should be able to list the bus controller:

```
# i2cdetect -l
i2c-1 i2c        bcm2835 I2C adapter        I2C adapter
```

Access to the driver is provided by the following nodes:

```
# ls -l /dev/i2c*
crw-rw---- 1 root i2c 89, 1 Jul  7 16:23 /dev/i2c-1
```

Header Files

The following header files should be included in an I²C program:

```
#include <sys/ioctl.h>
#include <linux/i2c.h>
#include <linux/i2c-dev.h>
```

open(2)

Working with I²C devices is much like working with files. You open a file descriptor, do some I/O operations with it, and then close it. The one difference is that the ioctl(2) calls are used instead of the usual read(2) and write(2).

```
#include <sys/types.h>
#include <sys/stat.h>
#include <fcntl.h>

int open(const char *pathname,int flags,mode_t mode);
```

where

> pathname is the name of the file/directory/driver that you need to open/create.

> flags is the list of optional flags (use O_RDWR for reading and writing).

> mode is the permission bits to create a file (omit argument, or supply zero when not creating).

> returns -1 (error code in errno) or open file descriptor >=0.

Error	Description
EACCES	Access to the file is not allowed.
EFAULT	The pathname points outside your accessible address space.
EMFILE	The process already has the maximum number of files open.
ENFILE	The system limit on the total number of open files has been reached.
ENOMEM	Insufficient kernel memory was available.

To work with the I²C bus controller, your application must open the driver, made available at the device node:

```
int fd;

fd = open("/dev/i2c-1",O_RDWR);
if ( fd < 0 ) {
    perror("Opening /dev/i2c-1");
```

Note that the device node (/dev/i2c-1) is owned by root, so you'll need elevated privileges to open it or have your program use setuid(2).

ioctl(2,I2C_FUNC)

In I²C code, a check is normally performed to make sure that the driver has the right support. The I2C_FUNC ioctl(2) call allows the calling program to query the I²C capabilities. The capability flags returned are documented in Table 15-3.

```
long funcs;
int rc;

rc = ioctl(fd,I2C_FUNCS,&funcs);
if ( rc < 0 ) {
    perror("ioctl(2,I2C_FUNCS)");
    abort();
}

/* Check that we have plain I2C support */
assert(funcs & I2C_FUNC_I2C);
```

Table 15-3. *I2C_FUNC Bits*

Bit Mask	Description
I2C_FUNC_I2C	Plain I2C is supported (non SMBus)
I2C_FUNC_10BIT_ADDR	Supports 10-bit addresses
I2C_FUNC_PROTOCOL_MANGLING	*Supports:*
	I2C_M_IGNORE_NAK
	I2C_M_REV_DIR_ADDR
	I2C_M_NOSTART
	I2C_M_NO_RD_ACK

The assert() macro used to check that at least plain I2C support exists. Otherwise, the program aborts.

ioctl(2,I2C_RDWR)

While it is possible to use ioctl(2,I2C_SLAVE) and then use read(2) and write(2) calls, this tends not to be practical. Consequently, the use of the ioctl(2,I2C_RDWR) system call will be promoted instead. This system call allows considerable flexibility in carrying out complex I/O transactions.

The general API for any ioctl(2) call is as follows:

```
#include <sys/ioctl.h>

int ioctl(int fd,int request,argp);
```

where

> fd is the open file descriptor.
>
> request is the I/O command to perform.
>
> argp is an argument related to the command (type varies according to request).

returns -1 (error code in errno), number of msgs completed (when request = I2C_RDWR).

Error	Description
EBADF	fd is not a valid descriptor.
EFAULT	argp references an inaccessible memory area.
EINVAL	request or argp is not valid.

When the request argument is provided as I2C_RDWR, the argp argument is a pointer to struct i2c_rdwr_ioctl_data. This structure points to a list of messages and indicates how many of them are involved.

```
struct i2c_rdwr_ioctl_data {
    struct i2c_msg    *msgs;    /* ptr to array of simple messages */
    int               nmsgs;    /* number of messages to exchange */
};
```

The individual I/O messages referenced by the preceding structure are described by struct i2c_msg:

```
struct i2c_msg {
    __u16    addr;    /* 7/10 bit slave address */
    __u16    flags;   /* Read/Write & options */
    __u16    len;     /* No. of bytes in buf */
    __u8     *buf;    /* Data buffer */
};
```

The members of this structure are as follows:

addr: Normally this is the 7-bit slave address, unless flag I2C_M_TEN and function

I2C_FUNC_10BIT_ADDR are used. Must be provided for each message.

flags: Valid flags are listed in Table 15-4. Flag I2C_M_
RD indicates the operation is a read. Otherwise, a
write operation is assumed when this flag is absent.

buf: The I/O buffer to use for reading/writing this
message component.

len: The number of bytes to read/write in this
message component.

Table 15-4. *I2C Capability Flags*

Flag	Description
I2C_M_TEN	10-bit slave address used
I2C_M_RD	Read into buffer
I2C_M_NOSTART	Suppress (Re)Start bit
I2C_M_REV_DIR_ADDR	Invert R/W bit
I2C_M_IGNORE_NAK	Treat NAK as ACK
I2C_M_NO_RD_ACK	Read will not have ACK
I2C_M_RECV_LEN	Buffer can hold 32 additional bytes

An actual ioctl(2,I2C_RDWR) call would be coded like the following.
In this example, a MCP23017 *register* address of 0x15 is being written out to
peripheral address 0x20, followed by a read of 1 byte:

```
int fd;
struct i2c_rdwr_ioctl_data msgset;
struct i2c_msg iomsgs[2];
static unsigned char reg_addr[] = {0x15};
unsigned char rbuf[1];
int rc;
```

279

```
iomsgs[0].addr   = 0x20;              /* MCP23017-A */
iomsgs[0].flags  = 0;                 /* Write operation. */
iomsgs[0].buf    = reg_addr;
iomsgs[0].len    = 1;

iomsgs[1].addr   = iomsgs[0].addr;    /* Same MCP23017-A */
iomsgs[1].flags  = I2C_M_RD;          /* Read operation */
iomsgs[1].buf    = rbuf;
iomsgs[1].len    = 1;

msgset.msgs      = iomsgs;
msgset.nmsgs     = 2;

rc = ioctl(fd,I2C_RDWR,&msgset);
if ( rc < 0 ) {
    perror("ioctl (2, I2C_RDWR)");
```

The example shown defines iomsgs[0] as a write of 1 byte, containing a register number. The entry iomsgs[1] describes a read of 1 byte from the peripheral. These two messages are performed in one ioctl(2) transaction. The flags member in iomsgs[x] determines whether the operation is a read (I2C_M_RD) or a write (0).

Note   Don't confuse the peripheral's internal register number with the peripheral's I2C address.

Each of the iomsgs[x].addr members must contain a valid I²C peripheral address. Each message can potentially address a different peripheral. The ioctl(2) will return an error with the first message failure. For this reason, you may not always want to combine multiple messages in one ioctl(2) call, especially when different devices are involved.

The returned value, when successful, is the number of struct i2c_msg messages successfully performed.

Summary

From this chapter you saw that adding sixteen GPIOs to your Pi can be realized with the addition of one chip and a little wiring. Considering the cost of add-on boards, this can save your project considerably. With the driver support for the MCP23017, using these extension GPIOs is just as simple as the native ports.

For the developer that wants to interact directly over I^{2}C with his devices, the C API for doing so was presented. Whether though the driver or through direct the C API, no Pi developer is left wanting for access to GPIO ports.

CHAPTER 16

SPI Bus

The Serial Peripheral Interface bus, known affectionately as *spy*, is a synchronous serial interface that was named by Motorola.[18] The SPI protocol operates in full-duplex mode, allowing it to send and receive data simultaneously. Generally speaking, SPI has a speed advantage over the I²C protocol but requires more connections.

SPI Basics

Devices on the SPI bus communicate on a master/slave basis. Multiple slaves coexist on a given SPI bus, with each slave being selected for communication by a slave select signal (also known as chip select). Figure 16-1 shows the Raspberry Pi as the master communicating with one slave device. Additional slaves would be connected as shown with the exception that a different slave select signal would be used.

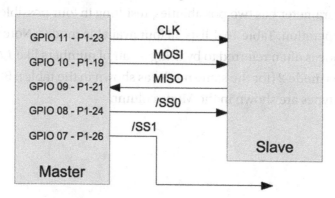

Figure 16-1. *SPI interface*

© Warren Gay 2018
W. Gay, *Advanced Raspberry Pi*, https://doi.org/10.1007/978-1-4842-3948-3_16

Data is transmitted from the master to the slave by using the MOSI line (master out, slave in). As each bit is being sent out by the master, the slave simultaneously sends data on the MISO line (master in, slave out). Bits are shifted out of the master and into the slave, while bits are shifted out of the slave and into the master. Both transfers occur to the beat of the system clock (CLK).

Many SPI devices support only 8-bit transfers, while others are more flexible. The SPI bus is a de facto standard, meaning that there is no standard for data transfer width and SPI mode.[18] The SPI controller can also be configured to transmit the most significant or the least significant bit first. All of this flexibility can result in confusion.

SPI Mode

SPI operates in one of four possible clock signaling modes, based on two parameters:

Parameter	Description
CPOL	Clock polarity
CPHA	Clock phase

Each parameter has two possibilities, resulting in four possible SPI modes of operation. Table 16-1 lists all four available modes. Note that a given mode is often referred to by using a pair of numbers like *1,0* or simply as mode *2* (for the same mode, as shown in the table). Both references types are shown in the Mode column.

Table 16-1. *SPI Modes*

CPOL	CPHA	Mode		Description
0	0	0,0	0	Noninverted clock, sampled on rising edge
0	1	0,1	1	Noninverted clock, sampled on falling edge
1	0	1,0	2	Inverted clock, sampled on rising edge
1	1	1,1	3	Inverted clock, sampled on falling edge
		Clock Sense		Description
		Noninverted		Signal is idle low, active high
		Inverted		Signal is idle high, active low

Peripheral manufacturers did not define a standard signaling convention in the beginning. Consequently SPI controllers often allow configuration of any of the four modes while the remaining only permit two of the modes. However, once a mode has been chosen, all slaves on the same bus must agree.

Signaling

The clock polarity determines the idle clock level, while the phase determines whether the data line is sampled on the rising or falling clock signal. Figure 16-2 shows mode 0,0, which is perhaps the preferred form of SPI signaling. In Figure 16-2, the slave is selected first, by making the $\overline{SS}$ (slave select) active. Only one slave can be selected at a time, since there must be one slave driving the MISO line. Shortly after the slave is selected, the master drives the MOSI line, and the slave simultaneously drives the MISO line with the first data bit. This can be the most or least significant bit, depending on how the controller is configured. The diagram shows the least significant bit first.

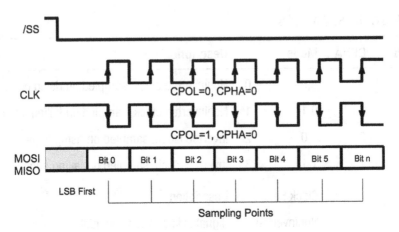

Figure 16-2. *SPI signaling, modes 0 and 2*

In mode 0,0 the first bit is clocked into the master and slave when the clock line falls from high to low. This clock transition is positioned midway in the data bit cell. The remaining bits are successively clocked into master and slave simultaneously as the clock transitions from high to low. The transmission ends when the master deactivates the slave select line. When the clock polarity is reversed (CPOL = 1, CPHA = 0), the clock signal shown in Figure 16-2 is simply inverted. The data is clocked at the same time in the data cell, but on the rising edge of the clock instead.

Figure 16-3 shows the clock signals with the phase set to 1 (CPHA = 1). When the clock is not inverted (CPOL = 0), the data is clocked on the rising edge. The clock must transition to its nonidle state one-half clock cycle earlier than when the phase is 0 (CPHA = 0). When the SPI mode is 1,1, the data is clocked in on the falling edge of the clock.

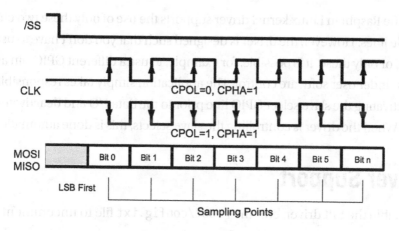

Figure 16-3. *SPI signaling modes 1 and 3*

While the four different modes can be confusing, it is important to realize that the data is sampled at the same times within the data bit cells. The data bit is always sampled at the midpoint of the data cell. When the clock phase is 0 (CPHA = 0), the data is sampled on the trailing edge of the clock, whether falling or rising according to CPOL. When the clock phase is 1 (CPHA = 1), the data is sampled on the leading edge of the clock, whether rising or falling according to CPOL.

Slave Selection

Unlike I²C where slaves are addressed by using a transmitted address, the SPI bus uses a dedicated select line for each. The Raspberry Pi dedicates the GPIO pins listed in Table 16-2 as slave select lines (also known as chip enable lines).

Table 16-2. *Raspberry Pi Built-in Chip Enable Pins*

GPIO	Chip Enable	P1
8	$\overline{CE0}$	P1-24
7	$\overline{CE1}$	P1-26

The Raspbian Linux kernel driver supports the use of only these two chip enable lines. However, the driver is designed such that you don't have to use them, or only these. It is possible, for example, to use a different GPIO pin as a select under user software control. The application simply takes responsibility for activating the slave select GPIO line prior to the data I/O and deactivates it after. When the driver is controlling the slave selects, this is done automatically.

Driver Support

To enable the SPI driver, edit the /boot/config.txt file to uncomment the line as:

```
dtparam=spi=on
```

and then reboot:

```
# sync
# /sbin/shutdown -r now
```

After the reboot, using the lsmod command, you should see the driver spi_bcm2835 listed among the others.

```
$ lsmod
Module              Size   Used by
fuse              106496   3
rfcomm             49152   6
...
spi_bcm2835        16384   0
...
```

Once the kernel module support is present, the device driver nodes should appear:

```
$ ls /dev/spi*
/dev/spidev0.0  /dev/spidev0.1
$
```

These two device nodes are named according to which slave select should be activatd, as shown in Table 16-3.

Table 16-3. *SPI Device Nodes*

Pathname	Bus	Device	GPIO	SS
/dev/spidev0.0	0	0	8	$\overline{CE0}$
/dev/spidev0.1	0	1	7	$\overline{CE1}$

If you open either of these device nodes with the C macro SPI_NO_CS, the node chosen makes no difference. Macro SPI_NO_CS indicates that slave select will be performed by the application instead of the driver, if any select is used at all. When only one slave device is attached, might it be possible to use a permanently hard-wired selected.

SPI API

Like I²C under Linux, the bare-metal API for SPI involves calls to ioctl(2) to configure the interface and for simultaneous read/write. The usual read(2) and write(2) system calls can be used for one-sided transfers.

Header Files

The header files needed for SPI programming are as follows:

```
#include <fcntl.h>
#include <unistd.h>
#include <stdint.h>
#include <sys/ioctl.h>
#include <linux/types.h>
#include <linux/spi/spidev.h>
```

The spidev.h include file defines several macros and the struct spi_ioc_transfer. Table 16-4 lists the main macros that are declared. The macros SPI_CPOL and SPI_CPHA are used in the definitions of the values SPI_MODE_x. If you prefer, it is possible to use SPI_CPOL and SPI_CPHA in place of the mode macros.

Table 16-4. *SPI Macro Definitions*

Macro	Supported	Description
SPI_CPOL	Yes	Clock polarity inverted (CPOL = 1)
SPI_CPHA	Yes	Clock phase is 1 (CPHA = 1)
SPI_MODE_0	Yes	SPI Mode 0,0 (CPOL = 0, CPHA = 0)
SPI_MODE_1	Yes	SPI Mode 0,1 (CPOL = 0, CPHA = 1)
SPI_MODE_2	Yes	SPI Mode 1,0 (CPOL = 1, CPHA = 0)
SPI_MODE_3	Yes	SPI Mode 1,1 (CPOL = 1, CPHA = 1)
SPI_CS_HIGH	Yes	Chip select is active high
SPI_LSB_FIRST	No	LSB is transmitted first
SPI_3WIRE	No	Use 3-Wire data I/O mode
SPI_LOOP	No	Loop the MOSI/MISO data line
SPI_NO_CS	Yes	Do not apply Chip Select
SPI_READY	No	Enable extra Ready signal

Communicating with an SPI device consists of the following system calls:

open(2): Opens the SPI device driver node

read(2): Reads but no transmission

write(2): Writes data while discarding received data

ioctl(2): For configuration and bidirectional I/O

close(2): Closes the SPI device driver node

In SPI communication, the use of read(2) and write(2) is generally unusual. Normally, ioctl(2) is used to facilitate simultaneous read/write transfers.

Open Device

In order to perform SPI communication through the kernel driver, you need to open one of the device nodes by using open(2). The general format of the device pathname is

/dev/spidev<bus>.<device>

The following is a code snippet opening bus 0, device 0.

```
int fd;

fd = open("/dev/spidev0.0",O_RDWR);
if ( fd < 0 ) {
    perror("Unable to open SPI driver");
    exit(1);
}
```

The driver is normally opened for read and write (O_RDWR) because SPI usually involves reading and writing.

SPI Mode Macros

Before SPI communications can be performed, the mode of communication needs to be chosen. Table 16-5 lists the C language macros that can be used to configure the SPI mode to apply.

Table 16-5. *SPI Mode Macros*

Macro	Effect	Comments
SPI_CPOL	CPOL = 1	Or use SPI_MODE_x
SPI_CPHA	CPHA = 1	Or use SPI_MODE_x
SPI_CS_HIGH	SS is active high	Unusual
SPI_NO_CS	Don't assert select	Not used/application controlled

These bit values are simply or-ed together to specify the options that are required. The use of SPI_CPOL implies CPOL = 1. Its absence implies CPOL = 0. Similarly, the use of SPI_CPHA implies CPHA = 1 else CPHA = 0. The macros SPI_MODE_x use the SPI_CPOL and SPI_CPHA macros to define them, so don't use them both in your code. The mode definitions are shown here:

```
#define SPI_MODE_0 (0|0)
#define SPI_MODE_1 (0|SPI_CPHA)
#define SPI_MODE_2 (SPI_CPOL|0)
#define SPI_MODE_3 (SPI_CPOL|SPI_CPHA)
```

The unsupported options are not shown, though one or more of these could be supported in the future.

The following is an example that defines SPI_MODE_0:

```
uint8_t mode = SPI_MODE_0;
int rc;

rc = ioctl(fd,SPI_IOC_WR_MODE,&mode);
if ( rc < 0 ) {
    perror("Can't set SPI write mode.");
```

If you'd like to find out how the SPI driver is currently configured, you can read the SPI mode with ioctl(2) as follows:

```
uint8_t mode;
int rc;

rc = ioctl(fd,SPI_IOC_RD_MODE,&mode);
if ( rc < 0 ) {
    perror("Can't get SPI read mode.");
```

Bits per Word

The SPI driver needs to know how many bits per I/O word are to be transmitted. While the driver will likely default to 8 bits, it is best not to depend on it. Note that the Pi only supports 8 bits or 9 bits in LoSSI mode (low speed serial interface). This is configured with the following ioctl(2) call:

```
uint8_t bits = 8;
int rc;

rc = ioctl(fd, SPI_IOC_WR_BITS_PER_WORD,&bits);
if ( rc < 0 ) {
    perror ("Can't set bits per SPI word.");
```

The currently configured value can be fetched with ioctl(2) as follows:

```
uint8_t bits;
int rc;

rc = ioctl(fd,SPI_IOC_RD_BITS_PER_WORD,&bits);
if ( rc == -1 ) {
    perror("Can't get bits per SPI word.");
```

When the number of bits is not an even multiple of eight, the bits are assumed to be right-justified. For example, if the word length is set to 4 bits, the least significant 4 bits are transmitted. The higher-order bits are ignored.

Likewise, when receiving data, the least significant bits contain the data. All of this is academic on the Pi, however, since the driver supports only byte-wide transfers.

Clock Rate

To configure the data transmission rate, you can set the clock rate with ioctl(2) as follows:

```
uint32_t speed = 500000; /* Hz */
int rc;

rc = ioctl(fd,SPI_IOC_WR_MAX_SPEED_HZ,&speed);
if ( rc < 0 ) {
    perror("Can't configure SPI clock rate.");
```

The clock rate provided in speed should be a multiple of two (it is automatically rounded down). The current configured clock rate can be fetched using the following ioctl(2) call:

```
uint32_t speed; /* Hz */
int rc;

rc = ioctl(fd,SPI_IOC_RD_MAX_SPEED_HZ,&speed);
if ( rc < 0 ) {
    perror("Can't get SPI clock rate.");
```

Data I/O

SPI communication often involves transmitting data while simultaneously receiving data. For this reason, the read(2) and write(2) system calls cannot be used. The ioctl(2) call will, however, perform a simultaneous read and write.

The SPI_IOC_MESSAGE(n) form of the ioctl(2) call uses the following structure as its argument:

```
struct spi_ioc_transfer {
    __u64    tx_buf;         /* Ptr to tx buffer */
    __u64    rx_buf;         /* Ptr to rx buffer */
    __u32    len;            /* # of bytes */
    __u32    speed_hz;       /* Clock rate in Hz */
    __u16    delay_usecs;    /* Delay in microseconds */
    __u8     bits_per_word;  /* Bits per "word" */
    __u8     cs_change;      /* Apply chip select */
    __u32    pad;            /* Reserved */
};
```

The tx_buf and rx_buf structure members are defined as 64-bit unsigned integers (__u64). For this reason, you must cast your buffer pointers when making assignments to them:

```
uint8_t tx[32], rx[32];
struct spi_ioc_transfer tr;

tr.tx_buf = (unsigned long) tx;
tr.rx_buf = (unsigned long ) rx;
```

On the Raspberry Pi, you will see example code that simply casts the pointers to unsigned long. The compiler automatically promotes these 32-bit values to a 64-bit value. This is safe on the Pi because the pointer value is 32 bits in size.

If you don't wish to receive data (maybe because it is "don't care" data), you can null out the receive buffer:

```
uint8_t tx[32];
struct spi_ioc_transfer tr;

tr.tx_buf = (unsigned long) tx;
tr.rx_buf = 0;                          /* ignore received data */
```

Note that to receive data, the master must always transmit data in order to shift data out of the slave peripheral. If any byte transmitted will do, you can omit the transmit buffer. Zero bytes will then be automatically transmitted by the driver to shift the slave data out.

It is also permissible to transmit from the buffer you're receiving into:

```
uint8_t io[32];
struct spi_ioc_transfer tr;

tr.tx_buf = (unsigned long) io;          /* Transmit buffer */
tr.rx_buf = (unsigned long) io;          /* is also recv buffer */
```

The len structure member indicates the number of bytes for the I/O transfer. Receive and transmit buffers (when both used) are expected to transfer the same number of bytes.

The member speed_hz defines the clock rate that you wish to use for this I/O, in Hz. This overrides any value configured in the mode setup, for the duration of the I/O. The value will be automatically rounded down to a supported clock rate when necessary.

When the value speed_hz is 0, the previously configured clock rate is used (SPI_IOC_WR_MAX_SPEED_HZ).

When the delay_usecs member is non-zero, it specifies the number of microseconds to delay between transfers. It is applied at the end of a transfer, rather than at the start. When there are multiple I/O transfers in a single ioctl(2) request, this allows time in between so that the peripheral can process the data.

The bits_per_word member defines how many bits there are in a "word" unit. Often the unit is 1 byte (8 bits), but it need not be (but note that the Raspbian Linux driver supports only 8 bits or 9 in LoSSI mode).

When the bits_per_word value is 0, the previously configured value from SPI_IOC_WR_BITS_PER_WORD is used.

The cs_change member is treated as a Boolean value. When 0, no chip select is performed by the driver. The application is expected to do what is necessary to notify the peripheral that it is selected (usually a GPIO pin is brought low). Once the I/O has completed, the application then must then unselect the slave peripheral.

When the cs_change member is true (non-zero), the slave selected will *depend on the device pathname that was opened*. The bus and the slave address are embedded in the device name:

/dev/spidev<bus>.<device>

When cs_change is true, the driver asserts $\overline{GPIO8}$ for spidev0.0 and asserts $\overline{GPIO7}$ for spidev0.1 prior to I/O and then deactivates the same upon completion. Of course, using these two nodes require two different open(2) calls.

The SPI_IOC_MESSAGE(n) macro is used in the ioctl(2) call to perform one or more SPI I/O operations. This macro is unusual because it requires an argument *n*. (This differs considerably from the I2C approach.) This specifies how many I/O transfers you would like to perform. An array of spi_ioc_transfer structures is declared and configured for each transfer required, as shown in the next example:

```
struct spi_ioc_transfer io[3];     /* Define 3 transfers */
int rc;

io[0].tx_buf = ...;                /* Configure I/O */
...
io[2].bits_per_word = 8;

rc = ioctl(fd,SPI_IOC_MESSAGE(3),& io[0]);
```

The preceding example will perform three I/O transfers. Since the application never gets to perform any GPIO manipulation in between these I/Os, this applies to communicating with one particular slave device.

The following example code brings all of the concepts together, to demonstrate one I/O. The spi_ioc_transfer structure is initialized so that 32 bytes are transmitted and simultaneously 32 are received.

```
uint8_t tx[32], rx[32];
struct spi_ioc_transfer tr;
int rc;

tr.tx_buf        = (unsigned long) tx;
tr.rx_buf        = (unsigned long) rx;
tr.len           = 32;
tr.delay_usecs   = delay;
tr.speed_hz      = speed;
tr.bits_per_word = bits;

rc = ioctl(fd,SPI_IOC_MESSAGE(1),&tr);
if ( rc < 1 ) {
    perror("Can't send spi message");
```

Here a single I/O transmission occurs, with data being sent from array tx and received into array rx. The return value from the ioctl(2) call returns the number of bytes transferred (32 in the example). Otherwise, -1 is returned to indicate that an error has occurred.

Close

Like all Unix I/O operations, the device must be closed when the open file descriptor is no longer required (otherwise it will be done upon process termination):

```
close(fd);
```

Write

The write(2) system call can be used if the received data is unimportant. Note, however, that no delay is possible with this call.

Read

The read(2) system call is actually inappropriate for SPI since the master must transmit data on MOSI in order for the slave to send bits back on the MISO line. However, when read(2) is used, the driver will automatically send out zero bits as necessary to accomplish the read. (Be careful that your peripheral will accept zero bytes without unintended consequences.) Like the write(2) call, no delay is possible.

SPI Testing

When developing your SPI communication software, you can perform a simple loopback test to test your framework. Once the framework checks out, you can then turn your attention to communicating with the actual device.

While the SPI_LOOP mode bit is not supported by the Pi hardware, you can still physically loop your SPI bus by connecting a wire from the MOSI output back to the MISO input pin (connect GPIO 10 to GPIO 9).

A simple program, shown next, demonstrates this type of loopback test. It will write out 4 bytes (0x12, 0x23, 0x45, and 0x67) to the SPI driver. Because you have wired the MOSI pins to the MISO input, anything transmitted will also be received.

When the program executes, it will report the number of bytes received and four hexadecimal values:

```
$ sudo ./spiloop
rc=4 12 23 45 67
$
```

If you remove the wire between MOSI and MISO, and connect the MISO to a high (+3.3 V), you should be able to read 0xFF for all of the received bytes. If you then connect MISO to ground, 0x00 will be received for each byte instead. Be certain to apply to the correct pin to avoid damage (Listing 16-1).

Listing 16-1. The spiloop.c SPI loopback program

```
/*********************************************
 * spiloop.c — Example loop test
 * Connect MOSI (GPIO 10) to MISO (GPIO 9)
 *********************************************/
0005: #include <stdio.h>
0006: #include <errno.h>
0007: #include <stdlib.h>
0008: #include <stdint.h>
0009: #include <fcntl.h>
0010: #include <unistd.h>
0011: #include <sys/ioctl.h>
0012: #include <linux/types.h>
0013: #include <linux/spi/spidev.h>
0014:
0015: static void
0016: errxit(const char *msg) {
0017:    perror(msg);
0018:    exit(1);
0019: }
0020:
0021: int
0022: main(int argc, char ** argv) {
0023:    static uint8_t tx[] = {0x12, 0x23, 0x45, 0x67};
0024:    static uint8_t rx[] = {0xFF, 0xFF, 0xFF, 0xFF};
0025:    struct spi_ioc_transfer ioc = {
```

```
0026:           .tx_buf = (unsigned long) tx,
0027:           .rx_buf = (unsigned long) rx,
0028:           .len = 4,
0029:           .speed_hz = 100000,
0030:           .delay_usecs = 10,
0031:           .bits_per_word = 8,
0032:           .cs_change = 1
0033:       };
0034:   uint8_t mode = SPI_MODE_0;
0035:   int rc, fd=-1;
0036:
0037:   fd = open("/dev/spidev0.0",O_RDWR);
0038:   if ( fd < 0 )
0039:       errxit("Opening SPI device.");
0040:
0041:   rc = ioctl(fd,SPI_IOC_WR_MODE,&mode);
0042:   if ( rc < 0 )
0043:       errxit("ioctl (2) setting SPI mode.");
0044:
0045:   rc = ioctl(fd,SPI_IOC_WR_BITS_PER_WORD,&ioc.bits_per_word);
0046:   if ( rc < 0 )
0047:       errxit("ioctl (2) setting SPI bits perword.");
0048:
0049:   rc = ioctl(fd,SPI_IOC_MESSAGE(1),&ioc);
0050:   if ( rc < 0 )
0051:       errxit("ioctl (2) for SPI I/O");
0052:   close(fd);
0053:
0054:   printf("rc=%d %02X %02X %02X %02X\n",
0055:       rc, rx[0], rx[1], rx[2], rx[3]);
0056:   return 0;
0057: }
```

Summary

The SPI bus and its operation were presented along with the C programming API. The chapter ended with a simple SPI loop test program. No extra hardware was required to run this.

That loop test provides a good coverage of the API being applied. The reader can take this one step further and access an actual slave device on the SPI bus. That last step adds the slave select to the overall picture and any command/response processing required of the device. You are now the SPI master!

CHAPTER 17

Boot

When the power is first applied to the Raspberry Pi, or it has been reset, a *boot sequence* is initiated. It is actually the Pi's GPU that brings up the ARM CPU. Originally, the way that the Raspberry Pi was designed, it *had to* be booted from firmware found on the SD card. RISC code for the GPU is provided by the Raspberry Pi Foundation in the file bootcode.bin. After the second-stage boot loader was executed, it was possible to load other operating systems or boot loaders, such as U-Boot.

Due to public interest, changes have been introduced along the way to allow a direct boot from USB. This chapter covers the process of booting in its various configuratons.

Booting ARM Linux

The modern boot procedure consists of the following sequence of events:

1. At power-up (or reset), the ARM CPU is offline, but the GPU is powered up.

2. A small RISC core in the GPU begins to execute the OTP (one time programmable) ROM code (first-stage boot loader).

© Warren Gay 2018
W. Gay, *Advanced Raspberry Pi*, https://doi.org/10.1007/978-1-4842-3948-3_17

3. By default, it determines booting from the following priority list:

   a. SD card boot

   b. USB device boot

   c. GPIO boot mode

GPIO boot mode is described here:

`https://www.raspberrypi.org/documentation/hardware/raspberrypi/bootmodes/bootflow.md`

There are several warnings described there including:

- OTP settings cannot be undone.

- Do not try to use `program_gpio_bootmode` unless your firmware is dated Oct. 20, 2017 or later.

The `program_gpio_bootmode` is perhaps more applicable to the compute module than the regular Pi.

The boot process continues, according to the media type (SD card, USB, or GPIO):

4. The GPU initializes the SD card/USB/GPIO hardware.

5. The GPU looks at the FAT (file allocation table) partition(s) in the SD card or USB media. The search continues with FAT partitions until the file `bootcode.bin` is found. The sequence changes if the OTP settings are modified. Normally:

   a. The SD card is checked first, which takes up to 5 seconds to fail (when not present).

   b. Then USB mode boot will be tried when enabled by OTP (this requires at least 3 seconds to allow for drive spinup and enumeration).

6. The second-stage boot-loader firmware named bootcode.bin is loaded into the local 128k cache.

7. The GPU control passes to the loaded bootcode.bin firmware and it enables SDRAM.

8. The file start.elf is loaded by the GPU into RAM from the same partition and the GPU gives it control.

9. The file config.txt is examined for configuration parameters that need to be processed.

10. Information found in cmdline.txt is also processed by start.elf.

11. The GPU allows the ARM CPU to execute the program start.elf.

12. The kernel image is loaded into RAM by the GPU running start.elf.

13. Finally, the GPU starts the kernel executing on the ARM CPU.

Boot Files

The FAT partition containing the boot files is normally mounted as /boot when Raspbian Linux has come up. Table 17-1 lists the files that apply to the boot process. The text files can be edited to affect new configurations. The binary files can also be replaced by new revisions of the same.

Table 17-1. */boot Files*

File Name	Purpose	Format
bootcode.bin	Second-stage boot loader	Binary
config.txt	Configuration parameters	Text
cmdline.txt	Command-line parameters for kernel	Text
fixup*.dat	Partitions the SDRAM between ARM CPU and GPU	Binary
start.elf	ARM CPU code to be launched	Binary
kernel.img	Kernel to be loaded	Binary
	Name can be overridden with `kernel=` parameter in config.txt	

config.txt

Unlike many PCs that contain a BIOS system, the Raspberry Pi uses the `config.txt` file. This file is optional, so when it is missing, defaults apply. When Raspbian Linux is booted, this file is found in /boot/config.txt.

What is supported by `vcgencmd` in this file can be displayed with:

```
# vcgencmd get_config int
aphy_params_current=819
arm_freq=1400
audio_pwm_mode=514
config_hdmi_boost=5
core_freq=250
desired_osc_freq=0x33e140
desired_osc_freq_boost=0x3c45b0
disable_commandline_tags=2
disable_l2cache=1
display_hdmi_rotate=-1
display_lcd_rotate=-1
```

```
dphy_params_current=547
enable_uart=1
force_eeprom_read=1
force_pwm_open=1
framebuffer_ignore_alpha=1
framebuffer_swap=1
gpu_freq=300
hdmi_force_cec_address=65535
init_uart_clock=0x2dc6c00
lcd_framerate=60
over_voltage_avs=31250
over_voltage_avs_boost=0x200b2
pause_burst_frames=1
program_serial_random=1
sdram_freq=450
```

For string options use:

```
# vcgencmd get_config str
device_tree=-
```

Additionally, there are additional options including the device tree settings:

```
dtparam=spi=on
```

and

```
dtoverlay=mcp23017,gpiopin=4,addr=0x20
```

Because the support for the original and new options keep changing, with each new model that is released, you can review this resource:

```
https://elinux.org/RPiconfig
```

Composite Aspect Ratio

The sdtv_aspect parameter configures the composite video aspect ratio.

sdtv_aspect	Description
1	4:3 (default)
2	14:9
3	16:9

Color Burst

By default, color burst is enabled. This permits the generation of color out of the composite video jack. Setting the video for monochrome may be desirable for a sharper display in some situations.

sdtv_disable_colourburst	Description
0	Color burst enabled (default)
1	Color burst disabled (monochrome)

High-Definition Video

This section covers config.txt settings that affect HDMI operation.

HDMI Safe Mode

The hdmi_safe parameter enables support of automatic HDMI configuration for optimal compatibility.

hdmi_safe	Description
0	Disabled (default)
1	Enabled

When hdmi_safe=1 (enabled), the following settings are implied:

- hdmi_force_hotplug=1
- config_hdmi_boost=4
- hdmi_group=1
- hdmi_mode=1
- disable_overscan=0

HDMI Force Hot-Plug

This configuration setting allows you to force a hot-plug signal for the HDMI display, whether the display is connected or not. The NOOBS distribution enables this setting by default.

hdmi_force_hotplug	Description
0	Disabled (non-NOOBS default)
1	Use HDMI mode even when no HDMI monitor is detected (NOOBS default)

HDMI Ignore Hot-Plug

Enabling the hdmi_ignore_hotplug setting causes it to appear to the system that no HDMI display is attached, even if there is. This can help force composite video output, while the HDMI display is plugged in.

hdmi_ignore_hotplug	Description
0	Disabled (default)
1	Use composite video even if an HDMI display is detected

HDMI Drive

This mode allows you to choose between DVI (no sound) and HDMI mode (with sound, when supported).

hdmi_drive	Description
1	Normal DVI mode (no sound)
2	Normal HDMI mode (sound will be sent if supported and enabled)

HDMI Ignore EDID

Enabling this option causes the EDID information from the display to be ignored. Normally, this information is helpful and is used.

hdmi_ignore_edid	Description
Unspecified	Read EDID information
0xa5000080	Ignore EDID information

HDMI EDID File

When hdmi_edid_file is enabled, the EDID information is taken from the file named edid.txt. Otherwise, it is taken from the display, when available.

hdmi_edid_file	Description
0	Read EDID data from device (default)
1	Read EDID data from edid.txt file

HDMI Force EDID Audio

Enabling this option forces the support of all audio formats even if the display does not support them. This permits pass-through of DTS/AC3 when reported as unsupported.

hdmi_force_edid_audio	Description
0	Use EDID-provided values (default)
1	Pretend all audio formats are supported

Avoid EDID Fuzzy Match

Avoid fuzzy matching of modes described in the EDID.

avoid_edid_fuzzy_match	Description
0	Use fuzzy matching (default)
1	Avoid fuzzy matching

HDMI Group

The hdmi_group option defines the HDMI type.

hdmi_group	Description
0	Use the preferred group reported by the EDID (default)
1	CEA
2	DMT

HDMI Mode

This option defines the screen resolution to use in CEA or DMT format (see the parameter hdmi_group in the preceding subsection "HDMI Group"). In Table 17-2, the modifiers shown have the following meanings:

H means 16:9 variant of a normally 4:3 mode.

2x means pixel doubled (higher clock rate).

4x means pixel quadrupled (higher clock rate).

R means reduced blanking (fewer bytes are used for blanking within the data stream, resulting in lower clock rates).

Table 17-2. HDMI Mode Settings

Group	CEA			DMT		
Mode	Resolution	Refresh	Modifiers	Resolution	Refresh	Notes
1	VGA			640×350	85 Hz	
2	480 p	60 Hz		640×400	85 Hz	
3	480 p	60 Hz	H	720×400	85 Hz	
4	720 p	60 Hz		640×480	60 Hz	
5	1080 i	60 Hz		640×480	72 Hz	
6	480 i	60 Hz		640×480	75 Hz	
7	480 i	60 Hz	H	640×480	85 Hz	
8	240 p	60 Hz		800×600	56 Hz	
9	240 p	60 Hz	H	800×600	60 Hz	
10	480 i	60 Hz	4x	800×600	72 Hz	
11	480 i	60 Hz	4x H	800×600	75 Hz	
12	240 p	60 Hz	4x	800×600	85 Hz	
13	240 p	60 Hz	4x H	800×600	120 Hz	
14	480 p	60 Hz	2x	848×480	60 Hz	
15	480 p	60 Hz	2x H	1024×768	43 Hz	Don't use
16	1080 p	60 Hz		1024×768	60 Hz	
17	576 p	50 Hz		1024×768	70 Hz	
18	576 p	50 Hz	H	1024×768	75 Hz	
19	720 p	50 Hz		1024×768	85 Hz	
20	1080 i	50 Hz		1024×768	120 Hz	
21	576 i	50 Hz		1152×864	75 Hz	
22	576 i	50 Hz	H	1280×768		R

(*continued*)

Table 17-2. (*continued*)

Group	CEA			DMT		
Mode	Resolution	Refresh	Modifiers	Resolution	Refresh	Notes
23	288 p	50 Hz		1280×768	60 Hz	
24	288 p	50 Hz	H	1280×768	75 Hz	
25	576 i	50 Hz	4x	1280×768	85 Hz	
26	576 i	50 Hz	4x H	1280×768	120 Hz	R
27	288 p	50 Hz	4x	1280×800		R
28	288 p	50 Hz	4x H	1280×800	60 Hz	
29	576 p	50 Hz	2x	1280×800	75 Hz	
30	576 p	50 Hz	2x H	1280×800	85 Hz	
31	1080 p	50 Hz		1280×800	120 Hz	R
32	1080 p	24 Hz		1280×960	60 Hz	
33	1080 p	25 Hz		1280×960	85 Hz	
34	1080 p	30 Hz		1280×960	120 Hz	R
35	480 p	60 Hz	4x	1280×1024	60 Hz	
36	480 p	60 Hz	4x H	1280×1024	75 Hz	
37	576 p	50 Hz	4x	1280×1024	85 Hz	
38	576 p	50 Hz	4x H	1280×1024	120 Hz	R
39	1080 i	50 Hz	R	1360×768	60 Hz	
40	1080 i	100 Hz		1360×768	120 Hz	R
41	720 p	100 Hz		1400×1050		R
42	576 p	100 Hz		1400×1050	60 Hz	
43	576 p	100 Hz	H	1400×1050	75 Hz	
44	576 i	100 Hz		1400×1050	85 Hz	

(*continued*)

Table 17-2. (*continued*)

| Group | | CEA | | DMT | | |
Mode	Resolution	Refresh	Modifiers	Resolution	Refresh	Notes
45	576 i	100 Hz	H	1400×1050	120 Hz	R
46	1080 i	120 Hz		1440×900		R
47	720 p	120 Hz		1440×900	60 Hz	
48	480 p	120 Hz		1440×900	75 Hz	
49	480 p	120 Hz	H	1440×900	85 Hz	
50	480 i	120 Hz		1440×900	120 Hz	R
51	480 i	120 Hz	H	1600×1200	60 Hz	
52	576 p	200 Hz		1600×1200	65 Hz	
53	576 p	200 Hz	H	1600×1200	70 Hz	
54	576 i	200 Hz		1600×1200	75 Hz	
55	576 i	200 Hz	H	1600×1200	85 Hz	
56	480 p	240 Hz		1600×1200	120 Hz	R
57	480 p	240 Hz	H	1680×1050		R
58	480 i	240 Hz		1680×1050	60 Hz	
59	480 i	240 Hz	H	1680×1050	75 Hz	
60				1680×1050	85 Hz	
61				1680×1050	120 Hz	R
62				1792×1344	60 Hz	
63				1792×1344	75 Hz	
64				1792×1344	120 Hz	R
65				1856×1392	60 Hz	
66				1856×1392	75 Hz	

(*continued*)

Table 17-2. (*continued*)

Group	CEA			DMT		
Mode	Resolution	Refresh	Modifiers	Resolution	Refresh	Notes
67				1856×1392	120 Hz	R
68				1920×1200		R
69				1920×1200	60 Hz	
70				1920×1200	75 Hz	
71				1920×1200	85 Hz	
72				1920×1200	120 Hz	R
73				1920×1440	60 Hz	
74				1920×1440	75 Hz	
75				1920×1440	120 Hz	R
76				2560×1600		R
77				2560×1600	60 Hz	
78				2560×1600	75 Hz	
79				2560×1600	85 Hz	
80				2560×1600	120 Hz	R
81				1366×768	60 Hz	
82	1080 p	60 Hz				
83				1600×900		R
84				2048×1152		R
85	720 p	60 Hz				
86				1366×768		R

HDMI Boost

The config_hdmi_boost parameter allows you to tweak the HDMI signal strength.

config_hdmi_boost	Description
0	Non-NOOBS default
1	
2	
3	
4	Use if you have interference issues (NOOBS default setting)
5	
6	
7	Maximum strength

HDMI Ignore CEC Init

When this option is enabled, the CEC initialization is not sent to the device. This avoids bringing the TV out of standby and channel switch when rebooting.

hdmi_ignore_cec_init	Description
0	Normal (default)
1	Don't send initial active source message

HDMI Ignore CEC

When this option is enabled, the assumption made is that CEC is not supported at all by the HDMI device, even if the device does have support. As a result, no CEC functions will be supported.

hdmi_ignore_cec	Description
0	Normal (default)
1	Disable CEC support

Overscan Video

A few options control the overscan support of the composite video output. When overscan is enabled, a certain number of pixels are skipped at the sides of the screen as configured.

Disable Overscan

The disable_overscan option can disable the overscan feature. It is enabled by default:

disable_overscan	Description
0	Overscan enabled (default)
1	Overscan disabled

Overscan Left, Right, Top, and Bottom

These parameters control the number of pixels to skip at the left, right, top, and bottom of the screen.

Parameter	Pixels to Skip
overscan_left=0	At left
overscan_right=0	At right
overscan_top=0	At top
overscan_bottom=0	At bottom

Frame Buffer Settings

The Linux frame buffer support is configured by a few configuration options described in this section.

Frame Buffer Width

The default is to define the width of the frame buffer as the display's width minus the overscan pixels.

framebuffer_width	Description
default	Display width overscan
framebuffer_width=n	Set width to n pixels

Frame Buffer Height

The default is to define the height of the frame buffer as the display's height minus the overscan pixels.

framebuffer_height	Description
default	Display height overscan
framebuffer_height=n	Set height to *n* pixels

Frame Buffer Depth

This parameter defines the number of bits per pixel.

framebuffer_depth	Description
8	Valid, but default RGB palette makes an unreadable screen
16	Default
24	Looks better but has corruption issues as of 6/15/2012
32	No corruption, but requires framebuffer_ignore_alpha=1, and shows wrong colors as of 6/15/2012

Frame Buffer Ignore Alpha

The alpha channel can be disabled with this option. As of this writing, this option must be used when using a frame buffer depth of 32 bits.

framebuffer_ignore_alpha	Description
0	Alpha channel enabled (default)
1	Alpha channel disabled

General Video Options

The display can be flipped or rotated in different ways, according to the display_rotate option. You should be able to do both a flip and a rotate by adding the flip values to the rotate value.

The 90° and 270° rotations require additional memory on the GPU, so these options won't work with a 16 MB GPU split.

display_rotate	Description
0	0° (default)
1	90°
2	180°
3	270°
0x1000	Horizontal flip
0x2000	Vertical flip

While the flip options are documented, I was unable to get them to work. The rotations, however, were confirmed as working.

Licensed Codecs

The following options permit you to configure the purchased license key codes for the codecs they affect.

Option	Notes
decode_MPG2=0x12345678	License key for hardware MPEG-2 decoding
decode_WVC1=0x12345678	License key for hardware VC-1 decoding

Testing

The following test option enables image/sound tests during boot. This is intended for manufacturer testing.

test_mode	Description
0	Disable test mode (default)
1	Enable test mode

Memory

This section summarizes configuration settings pertaining to memory.

Disable GPU L2 Cache

The `disable_l2cache` option allows the ARM CPU access to the GPU L2 cache to be disabled. This needs the corresponding L2 disabled in the kernel.

disable_l2cache	Description
0	Enable GPU L2 cache access
1	Disable GPU L2 cache access

Boot Options

Several options in this section affect the boot process. Many options pertain to the kernel being started, while others affect file systems and devices.

Command Line

The cmdline option allows you to configure the kernel command-line parameters within the config.txt file, instead of the cmdline.txt file.

cmdline	Description
unspecified	Command line is taken from cmdline.txt
cmdline="command"	Command line is taken from parameter

Kernel

By default, start.elf loads the kernel from the file named kernel.img or kernel7.img depending on the Raspberry Pi model. This can be overridden to specify a specific image.

Kernel Address

This parameter determines the memory address where the kernel image is loaded into.

kernel_address	Description
0x00000000	Default

RAM File System File

The ramfsfile parameter names the file for the RAM FS file, to be used with the kernel.

ramfsfile	Description
unspecified	No RAM FS file used
ramfsfile="ramfs.file"	File ramfs.file is used

RAM File System Address

The `ramfsaddr` parameter specifies where the RAM file system image is to be loaded into memory.

ramfsaddr	Description
0x00000000	Default address

Init RAM File System

This option is a convenience option, which combines the options `ramfsfile` and `ramfsaddr`.

initramfs	Arg 1	Arg 2	Description
initramfs	initram.gz	0x00800000	Example

Device Tree Address

The `device_tree_address` option defines where the device tree address is loaded.

device_tree_address	Description
0x00000000	Default

Init UART Baud

The `init_uart_baud` option allows the user to reconfigure the serial console to use a baud rate that is different from the default.

init_uart_baud	Description
115200	Default baud rate

Init UART Clock

The init_uart_clock parameter permits the user to reconfigure the UART to use a different clock rate.

init_uart_clock	Description
3000000	Default

Init EMMC Clock

The init_emmc_clock parameter allows the user to tweak the EMMC clock, which can improve the SD card performance.

init_emmc_clock	Description
100000000	Default

Boot Delay

The boot_delay and boot_delay_ms options allow the user to reconfigure the delay used by start.elf prior to loading the kernel. The actual delay time used is computed from the following:

$$D = 1000 \times b + m$$

where

- D is the computed delay in milliseconds.

- b is the boot_delay value.

- m is the boot_delay_ms value.

boot_delay (b)	Description
1	Default

325

The boot_delay_ms augments the boot_delay parameter.

boot_delay_ms (m)	Description
0	Default

Avoid Safe Mode

A jumper or switch can be placed between pins P1-05 (GPIO 1) and P1-06 (ground) to cause start.elf to initiate a *safe mode* boot. If GPIO 1 is being used for some other I/O function, the safe mode check should be disabled.

avoid_safe_mode	Description
0	Default (check P1-05 for safe mode)
1	Disable safe mode check

cmdline.txt

The cmdline.txt file is used to supply command-line arguments to the kernel. The Raspbian values supplied in the standard image are broken into multiple lines here for easier reading (this sample was for the Raspberry Pi 3 B+):

```
# cat cmdline.txt
dwc_otg.lpm_enable=0 \
console=tty1 \
console=serial0,115200 \
root=PARTUUID=2383b4bd-02 \
rootfstype=ext4 \
elevator=deadline \
fsck.repair=yes \
rootwait \
```

```
quiet \
splash \
plymouth.ignore-serial-consoles
```

This file is provided as a convenience, since the parameters can be configured in the config.txt file, using the cmdline="text" option. When the config.txt option is provided, it supersedes the cmdline.txt file.

Once the Raspbian Linux kernel comes up, you can review the command-line options used as follows (this is the same Raspberry Pi 3 B+):

```
$ cat /proc/cmdline
8250.nr_uarts=1 \
bcm2708_fb.fbwidth=1680 \
bcm2708_fb.fbheight=1050 \
bcm2708_fb.fbswap=1 \
vc_mem.mem_base=0x3ec00000 \
vc_mem.mem_size=0x40000000 \
dwc_otg.lpm_enable=0 \
console=tty1 \
console=ttyS0,115200 \
root=PARTUUID=2383b4bd-02 \
rootfstype=ext4 \
elevator=deadline \
fsck.repair=yes \
rootwait \
quiet \
splash \
plymouth.ignore-serial-consoles
```

This output is interesting because it shows details that are not present in the cmdline.txt file. Options of the format name.option=values are specific to kernel-loadable modules.

Serial console=

The Linux console parameter specifies to Linux what device to use for a console. In this example, it was:

```
console=ttyS0,115200
```

This references the serial device that is made available after boot-up as /dev/ttyS0. The parameter following the device name is the baud rate.

The general form of the serial console option is as follows:

```
console=ttyDevice,bbbbpnf
```

The second parameter is the options field:

Zone	Description	Value	Raspbian Notes
bbbb	Baud rate	115200	Can be more than four digits
p	Parity	n	No parity
		o	Odd parity
		e	Even parity
n	Number of bits	7	7 data bits
		8	8 data bits
f	Flow control	r	RTS
		omitted	No RTS

Virtual console=

Linux supports a virtual console, which is also configurable from the console= parameter. Raspbian Linux specifies the following:

```
console=tty1
```

This device is available from /dev/tty1, after the kernel boots up. The tty parameters used for this virtual console can be listed (edited here for readability):

```
$ sudo -i
# stty -a </dev/tty1
speed 38400 baud ; rows 26; columns 82; line = 0;
intr = ^C; quit = ^\; erase = ^?; kill = ^U; \
eof = ^D; eol = <undef>; eol2 = <undef>; swtch = <undef>;
start = ^Q; stop = ^S ; susp = ^Z; rprnt = ^R; werase = ^W; \
lnext = ^V; flush = ^O; min = 1; time = 0;
-parenb -parodd cs8 hupcl -cstopb cread -clocal -crtscts
-ignbrk brkint -ignpar -parmrk -inpck -istrip -inlcr \
-igncr icrnl ixon -ixoff -iuclc -ixany imaxbel iutf8
opost -o lcuc -ocrnl onlcr -onocr -onlret -ofill -ofdel \
nl0 cr0 tab0 bs0 vt0 ff0
isig icanon iexten echo echoe echok -echonl -noflsh \
-xcase -tostop -echoprt -echoctl echoke
#
```

root=

The Linux kernel needs to know what device holds the root file system. The standard Raspbian image supplies the following:

```
root=PARTUUID=2383b4bd-02
```

This information can be obtained by the blkid command:

```
# blkid
/dev/mmcblk0p1: LABEL="boot" UUID="A75B-DC79" TYPE="vfat"
PARTUUID="2383b4bd-01"
/dev/mmcblk0p2: LABEL="rootfs" UUID="485ec5bf-9c78-45a6-9314-
32be1d0dea38" \
```

```
                    TYPE="ext4"  PARTUUID="2383b4bd-02"
/dev/mmcblk0:  PTUUID="2383b4bd"  PTTYPE="dos"
```

Reviewing that output confirms that the partition named "rootfs" is being used as the root file system. The partition in this example is specified by the partition UUID (a shortened version of a UUID, which is a universally unique identifier).

The general form of the `root=` parameter supports the following forms:

- `root=MMmm`: Boot from major device MM, minor mm (hexadecimal).

- `root=/dev/nfs`: Boot a NFS disk specified by `nfsroot` (see also `nfs-root=` and `ip=`).

- `root=/dev/name`: Boot from a device named `/dev/name`.

- root=PARTUUID=: Boot from a locally unique partition identified by as shortened UUID.

rootfstype=

In addition to specifying the device holding the root file system, the Linux kernel sometimes needs to know the file system type. This is configured through the `rootfstype` parameter. The standard Raspbian image supplies the following:

```
rootfstype=ext4
```

This example indicates that the root file system is the ext4 type.

The Linux kernel can examine the device given in the root parameter to determine the file system type. But there are scenarios where the kernel cannot resolve the type or gets confused. Otherwise, you may need to force a certain file system type.

elevator=

This option selects the I/O scheduler scheme to be used within the kernel. The standard Raspbian image specifies the following:

```
elevator=deadline
```

To find out the I/O scheduler option being used and the other available choices (in your kernel), we can consult the /sys pseudo file system:

```
$ cat /sys/block/mmcblk0/queue/scheduler
noop [deadline] cfq
$
```

The name mmcblk0 is the name of the device that your root file system is on (review the example blkid output earlier). The output shows in square brackets that the deadline I/O scheduler is being used. The other choices are noop and cfq. These I/O schedulers are as follows:

Name	Description	Notes
noop	No special ordering of requests	
cfq	Completely fair scheduler	Older
deadline	Cyclic scheduler, but requests have deadlines	Newest

The deadline I/O scheduler is the newest implementation, designed for greater efficiency and fairness. The deadline scheduler uses a cyclic elevator, except that it additionally logs a deadline for the request. A cyclic elevator is one where the requests are ordered according to sector numbers and head movement (forward and backward). The deadline scheduler will use the cyclic elevator behavior, but if it looks like the request is about to expire, it is given immediate priority.

rootwait=

This option is used when the device used for the root file system is a device that is started asynchronously with other kernel boot functions. This is usually needed for USB and MMC devices, which may take extra time to initialize. The rootwait option forces the kernel to wait until the root device becomes ready.

Given that the root file system is on the SD card (a MMC device), the Raspbian image uses the following:

```
rootwait
```

nfsroot=

The nfsroot option permits you to define a kernel that boots from an NFS mount (assuming that NFS support is compiled into the kernel). The square brackets show placement of optional values:

```
nfsroot=[server-ip:]root-dir[,nfs-options]
```

Field	Description
server-ip	NFS server IP number (default uses ip=)
root-dir	Root dir on NFS server. If there is a %s present, the IP address will be inserted there.
nfs-options	NFS options like ro, separated by commas

When unspecified, the default of /tftpboot/client_ip_address will be used. This requires that root=/dev/nfs be specified and optionally ip= may be added.

To test whether you have NFS support in your kernel, you can query the /proc file system when the system has booted:

```
# cat /proc/filesystems
```

```
nodev   sysfs
nodev   rootfs
nodev   ramfs
nodev   bdev
nodev   proc
nodev   cpuset
nodev   cgroup
nodev   cgroup2
nodev   tmpfs
nodev   devtmpfs
nodev   configfs
nodev   debugfs
nodev   tracefs
nodev   sockfs
nodev   pipefs
nodev   rpc_pipefs
nodev   devpts
        ext3
        ext2
        ext4
        vfat
        msdos
nodev   nfs
nodev   nfs4
nodev   autofs
        f2fs
nodev   mqueue
        fuseblk
nodev   fuse
nodev   fusectl
```

From this example, we see that both the older NFS (nfs) and the newer NFS4 file systems are supported.

ip=

This option permits the user to configure the IP address of a network device, or to specify how the IP number is assigned. See also the `root=` and `nfsroot=` options.

```
ip=client-ip:server-ip:gw-ip:netmask:hostname:device:autoconf
```

Table 17-3 describes the fields within this option. The `autoconf` *value* can appear by itself, without the intervening colons if required. When `ip=off` or `ip=none` is given, no autoconfiguration takes place. The autoconfiguration protocols are listed in Table 17-4.

Table 17-3. *ip= Kernel Parameter*

Field	Description	Default
ip-client	IP address of the client	Autoconfigured
ip-server	IP address of NFS server, required only for NFS root	Autoconfigured
gw-ip	IP address of server if on a separate subnet	Autoconfigured
netmask	Netmask for local IP address	Autoconfigured
hostname	Hostname to provide to DHCP	Client IP address
device	Name of interface to use	When more than one is available, autoconf
autoconf	Autoconfiguration method	Any

Table 17-4. *Autoconfiguration Protocols*

Protocol	Description
off or none	Don't autoconfigure
on or any	Use any protocol available (default)
dhcp	Use DHCP
bootp	Use BOOTP
rarp	Use RARP
both	Use BOOTP or RARP but not DHCP

With the kernel exchanged and the configuration restored to safe options, it should now be possible to boot the emergency kernel. Log in and rescue.

To restore your system back to its normal state, you'll need to follow these steps:

1. Rename kernel.img to kernel_emergency.img (for future rescues).

2. Rename kernel.bak to kernel.img (reinstate your normal kernel).

3. Restore/alter your config.txt configuration, if necessary.

4. Restore/alter your cmdline.txt configuration, if necessary.

At this point, you can reboot with your original kernel and configuration.

CHAPTER 18

vcgencmd

Apart from the usual Linux commands that display status, the Raspberry Pi includes a custom command named vcgencmd, which can report voltages and temperatures among other Pi specific attributes. This chapter documents the known features of the command. The executable file for the command is /usr/bin/vcgencmd.

vcgencmd Commands

There is no man page for this command, but the list of all supported options can be displayed with the commands option. The example command output shown has been broken over several lines for readability:

```
# vcgencmd commands
commands="vcos, ap_output_control, ap_output_post_processing, \
vchi_test_init, vchi_test_exit, vctest_memmap, vctest_start, \
vctest_stop, vctest_set, vctest_get, pm_set_policy, \
pm_get_status, pm_show_stats, pm_start_logging, pm_stop_logging, \
version, commands, set_vll_dir, set_backlight, set_logging, \
get_lcd_info, arbiter, cache_flush, otp_dump, test_result, \
codec_enabled, get_camera, get_mem, measure_clock, measure_volts, \
scaling_kernel, scaling_sharpness, get_hvs_asserts, \
get_throttled, \
measure_temp, get_config, hdmi_ntsc_freqs, hdmi_adjust_clock, \
hdmi_status_show, hvs_update_fields, pwm_speedup, force_audio, \
```

© Warren Gay 2018
W. Gay, *Advanced Raspberry Pi*, https://doi.org/10.1007/978-1-4842-3948-3_18

```
hdmi_stream_channels, hdmi_channel_map, display_power, \
read_ring_osc, memtest, dispmanx_list, get_rsts, schmoo, \
render_bar, disk_notify, inuse_notify, sus_suspend, sus_status, \
sus_is_enabled, sus_stop_test_thread, egl_platform_switch, \
mem_validate, mem_oom, mem_reloc_stats, hdmi_cvt, \
hdmi_timings, file"
#
```

These have been sorted and listed in Table 18-1, summarizing what is known about them.

Table 18-1. *Summary of vcgencmd Command-Line Options*

Command	Arguments	Description
ap_output_control		
ap_output_post_ processing		
arbiter		
cache_flush		Flushes GPU's L1 cache
codec_enabled	codec	Reports status of codec: one of H264 MPG2 WVC1
commands		Lists supported commands
disk_notify		
display_power	0 or 1	Turns the display off or on
dispmanx_list		
egl_platform_switch		
file		
force_audio		
get_camera		

(continued)

Table 18-1. (*continued*)

Command	Arguments	Description
get_config	parameter	Query configuration parameter
get_hvs_asserts		
get_lcd_info		LCD/monitor width, height, and pixel depth of the display framebuffer
get_mem	arm or gpu	Get memory split between CPU (ARM) or GPU
get_rsts		
get_throttled		
hdmi_adjust_clock		
hdmi_channel_map		
hdmi_cvt		
hdmi_ntsc_freqs		
hdmi_status_show		
hdmi_stream_ channels		
hdmi_timings		
hvs_update_fields		
inuse_notify		
measure_clock	clock name	Measure the frequency of various clocks
measure_temp		Measure the temperature of the SoC
measure_volts	device name	Measure the voltage of various devices
mem_oom		Statistics on Out of Memory events
mem_reloc_stats		Relocatable memory statistics

(*continued*)

Table 18-1. (*continued*)

Command	Arguments	Description
memtest		
mem_validate		
otp_dump		Dump OTP settings
pm_get_status		
pm_set_policy		
pm_show_stats		
pm_start_logging		
pm_stop_logging		
pwm_speedup		
read_ring_osc		
render_bar		Debug function
scaling_kernel		
scaling_sharpness		
schmoo		
set_backlight		Reserved for future use
set_logging	level=n	Change the level of the VideoCore logger
set_vll_dir		
sus_is_enabled		
sus_status		
sus_stop_test_ thread		
sus_suspend		
test_result		

(*continued*)

Table 18-1. (*continued*)

Command	Arguments	Description
vchi_test_exit		
vchi_test_init		
vcos	command	Possible commands are log, help, and version
vctest_get		
vctest_memmap		
vctest_set		
vctest_start		
vctest_stop		
version		Display current build version of VideoCore firmware

Option measure_clock

This firmware access option provides the user with clock rate information, according to the argument after measure_clock. Valid values for *<clock>* are listed in Table 18-2.

```
vcgencmd measure_clock <clock>
```

Table 18-2. *Valid Arguments for the*
measure_clock Option

Clock	Description
arm	ARM CPU
core	Core
dpi	Display Pixel Interface
emmc	External MMC device
h264	h.264 encoder
hdmi	HDMI clock
isp	Image Sensor Pipeline
pixel	Pixel clock
pwm	Pulse Width Modulation
uart	UART clock
v3d	Video 3D
vec	

The following shell script fragment can be used to list all available clocks:

```
for src in arm core h264 isp v3d uart pwm emmc pixel vec hdmi
dpi ; do
    echo -e "$src : $(vcgencmd measure_clock $src)" ;
done
```

An example from the Raspberry Pi 3 B+ is shown below:

```
arm : frequency(45)=600000000
core : frequency(1)=250000000
h264 : frequency(28)=250000000
isp : frequency(42)=250000000
```

```
v3d : frequency(43)=250000000
uart : frequency(22)=47999000
pwm : frequency(25)=0
emmc : frequency(47)=200000000
pixel : frequency(29)=146250000
vec : frequency(10)=0
hdmi : frequency(9)=163683000
dpi : frequency(4)=0
```

Option measure_volts

The measure_volts option allows the various subsystem voltages to be reported:

```
# for id in core sdram_c sdram_i sdram_p ; do \
    echo -e "$id: $(vcgencmd measure_volts $id)" ; \
done
core: volt=1.2000V
sdram_c: volt=1.2500V
sdram_i: volt=1.2500V
sdram_p: volt=1.2250V
#
```

Table 18-3 provides a legend for the output report lines.

Table 18-3. *Valid Device Names for* measure_volts

Device	Description
core	Core
sdram_c	SDRAM controller
sdram_i	SDRAM I/O
sdram_p	SDRAM physical

Option measure_temp

The measure_temp option allows the user to retrieve the SoC temperature, in degrees Celsius.

```
$ vcgencmd measure_temp
temp=43.5 °C
```

In this example, the relatively idle core was reported to be 43.5°C.

Option codec_enabled

The codec_enabled option reports the operational status of the codecs supported by the Raspberry Pi. Valid codec names are listed in Table 18-4. The codec support can be summarized with the following command:

```
# for id in H264 MPG2 WCV1 ; do
    echo -e "$id: $(vcgencmd codec_enabled $id)";
done
H264: H264=enabled
MPG2: MPG2=disabled
WCV1: WCV1=disabled
```

Table 18-4. *vcgencmd CODEC Names*

Name	Description
H264	h.264 CODEC
MPG2	MPEG-2 CODEC
WVC1	VC1 CODEC

Option version

The version option reports the GPU firmware version:

```
# vcgencmd version
Apr 16 2018 18:16:56
Copyright (c) 2012 Broadcom
version af8084725947aa2c7314172068f79dad9be1c8b4 (clean)
(release)
```

Option get_lcd_info

The get_lcd_info command provides the LCD/monitor width and height, and pixel depth of the frame buffer:

```
# vcgencmd get_lcd_info
1680 1050 24
```

Option get_config

The get_config option is useful in scripts that need to query the Raspberry Pi's configuration, as found in /boot/config.txt. For example, a script can query whether the uart is enabled:

```
# vcgencmd get_config enable_uart
enable_uart=1
```

otp_dump

The otp_dump command will list your OTP (one time programmable) settings found within your Pi. This session is taken from a Raspberry Pi 3 B+:

```
# vcgencmd otp_dump
08:00000000
09:00000000
10:00000000
11:00000000
12:00000000
13:00000000
14:00000000
15:00000000
16:00280000
17:3020000a
18:3020000a
19:ffffffff
20:ffffffff
21:ffffffff
22:ffffffff
23:ffffffff
24:ffffffff
25:ffffffff
26:ffffffff
27:00001f1f
28:d4b81de4
29:2b47e21b
30:00a020d3
31:00000000
32:00000000
33:00000000
34:00000000
35:00000000
36:00000000
37:00000000
38:00000000
```

```
39:00000000
40:00000000
41:00000000
42:00000000
43:00000000
44:00000000
45:00000000
46:00000000
47:00000000
48:00000000
49:00000000
50:00000000
51:00000000
52:00000000
53:00000000
54:00000000
55:00000000
56:00000000
57:00000000
58:00000000
59:00000000
60:00000000
61:00000000
62:00000000
63:00000000
64:00000000
65:00000000
66:02009eaa
```

CHAPTER 19

Linux Console and Pi Zero

The Raspbian Linux console is configured (or assumed) by the kernel command line at boot time. Before we examine serial console access however, let's step through the challenges of setting up the Pi Zero or Zero W. The main challenge is working with the single USB port and having the correct adapters. Then we'll examine the option of a serial device console.

Pi Zero / Zero W

Starting up a Pi Zero is a problem for two main reasons:

1. The ssh access is disabled on new Raspbian images.

2. There is only one USB port to attach a keyboard and mouse to.

And to see what you're doing, you're going to need a mini HDMI to HDMI adapter.

The reason that ssh is disabled by default is that the Pi's image comes with a default password for the Pi account. Everybody knows it, especially the hackers. The unwitting user could start up a Pi and leave it connected to the network, inviting all kinds of nasty business. So the Raspbian image comes with ssh disabled.

© Warren Gay 2018
W. Gay, *Advanced Raspberry Pi*, https://doi.org/10.1007/978-1-4842-3948-3_19

What you really need is a USB hub that is supported by Raspbian. I tried an old Apple hub with no luck. So I switched to a more recent one. Some keyboards provide an extra USB port or two. That can be useful, provided that Raspbian Linux supports it.

If you're patient, you might be able to get by without a hub at all. Power up the Zero and plug only the mouse into the USB adapter cable. Then mouse around to your system preferences. When you need to type in something, you can unplug the mouse and plug in the keyboard. You may not need the keyboard for much of the initial configuration.

Adapters Needed

The following is a list of adapters you should have on hand, even if you only use them once to set up your Zero. Figure 19-1 illustrates an example.

- Power adapter (black plug plugged into Zero at right).

- USB 2.0 Micro B 5-pin to female USB 2.0 type A adapter cable (white cable in middle).

- HDMI mini adapter (white adapter at Pi left).

- Optional USB to ethernet adapter (far right, white).

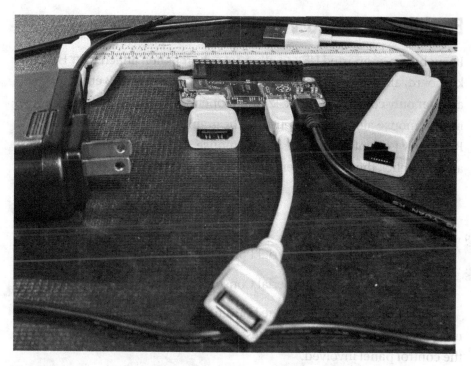

Figure 19-1. *Photo of a Pi Zero with mini HDMI adapter, USB adapter cable, and optional USB Ethernet adapter*

If you use the serial port console later in this chapter, you can get away without the USB and mini HDMI adapters.

Enabling ssh and VNC Access

If you have a supported USB to ethernet adapter, then attach your HDMI, keyboard, and/or mouse and boot Raspbian Linux. My USB ethernet adapter only consumes about 42 mA. If operating without a hub, plug in your mouse alone. Once you have the graphical desktop, open the Raspberry Pi Configuration using the mouse. Click on the Interfaces tab, and then click the following entries to enable them:

- Enable SSH

- Enable VNC

- Optionally enable Serial Port (enabled by default)

- Optionally enable Serial Console (enabled by default)

Don't forget to click OK at the bottom right. Then still using your mouse, click on reboot to apply these new settings. Figure 19-2 illustrates the control panel involved.

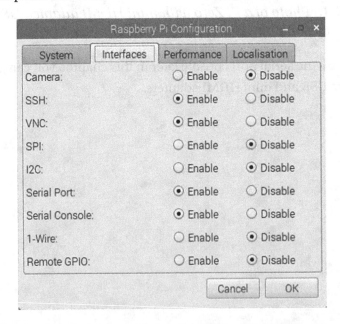

Figure 19-2. *The Raspberry Pi Configuration, Interfaces panel*

Once your Zero reboots, you should be able to:

1. Unplug your mouse (if not using a hub).

2. Plug in your USB to ethernet adapter.

3. Plug in your ethernet cable to a router.

4. Scan your network to discover the assigned IP address.

If you're using a hub, use your keyboard and mouse to open a terminal window and type the ifconfig command to determine the assigned address. The example in Figure 19-3 shows the address as 192.168.1.15.

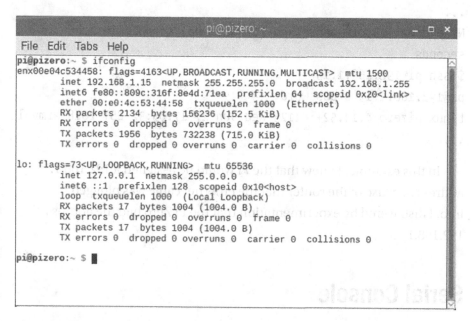

Figure 19-3. *Displaying your USB to ethernet address in the terminal window, using the ifconfig command*

Otherwise, scan for your Pi Zero from the desktop. The following example scans addresses between 192.168.1.2 to 192.168.1.254 on Mac/Linux:

```
$ nmap -sP 192.168.1.2-254

Starting Nmap 7.40 ( https://nmap.org ) at 2018-07-12 20:04 EDT
Nmap scan report for 192.168.1.3
Host is up (0.077s latency).
...
Nmap scan report for 192.168.1.15
Host is up (0.0017s latency).
...
Nmap done: 253 IP addresses (6 hosts up) scanned in 2.86
seconds
$ ssh pi@192.168.1.15
pi@192.168.1.15's password:
Linux pizero 4.14.52+ #1123 Wed Jun 27 17:05:32 BST 2018 armv6l
...
```

In this example, I knew that the Pi would be assigned a 192.168.1.* address because of the router that the ethernet cable was plugged into. I discovered by experimentation that the Pi Zero had the address 192.168.1.15.

Serial Console

If the mouse and HDMI approach isn't suitable, perhaps because you lack the adapters, you might try the serial console approach instead. The Raspbian Linux image has the serial console enabled by default. It uses the baud rate of 115200 baud, without hardware flow control.

It is crucial, however, that you use a serial adapter that works at the 3.3 V level. Do not use 5 V serial adapters because they can cause damage to the Pi. Some adapters can operate at either level, configured by a jumper.

Wire your adapter so that the Pi +3.3 V (P1-01) supplies the serial adapter with power (some USB adapters supply their own power). The connections are summarized below:

- Pi +3.3 V (P1-01) supply to adapter +3.3 V (may be labeled V_{CC}).

- Pi ground (P1-06) to the adapter ground (usually labeled Gnd).

- Pi TX (P1-08) to the adapter TX.

- Pi RX (P1-10) to the adapter RX.

Caution   Do not connect a 5 Volt TTL serial adapter. This can cause damage. Some adapters have a jumper to choose a 3.3 or 5 volt operation.

If you find that this doesn't work, try connecting TX to RX and RX to TX. Some adapters may be labeled according to the DCE (data communication equipment) perspective, while others will use the DTE (data terminal equipment) convention.

Once connected, plug your USB adapter into your desktop, start minicom (or other favorite terminal program), and set your serial parameters for:

- 155200 baud

- 8-Bits, no parity and 1 stop bit (8-N-1)

- Hardware flow control off

Boot your Pi Zero and allow it to come up. Allow extra time, especially when the desktop is coming up. Once it comes up, press Enter to cause the login prompt to show. Then you can log in as usual:

```
Welcome to minicom 2.7

OPTIONS:
Compiled on Sep 17 2016, 05:53:15.
Port /dev/cu.usbserial-A100MX3L, 20:52:57

Press Meta-Z for help on special keys

Raspbian GNU/Linux 9 pizero ttyAMA0
pizero login: pi
Password:
Last login: ...
```

Summary

The serial port console can be very helpful when you lack all of the other devices: keyboard, mouse, and screen. This is often all you need to get a Pi Zero or Pi Zero W initialized for your special project.

The patient user can get by with just one USB adapter cable and a mini HDMI adapter for initial setup. The keyboard and mouse can be swapped in and out as needed. Once ssh or VNC is enabled, you can operate from the comfort of your favorite desktop.

CHAPTER 20

Cross-Compiling

Embedded computers frequently lack the necessary resources for developing and compiling software. The Raspberry Pi is rather special in this regard since it already includes the gcc compiler and the needed linking tools (under Raspbian Linux). But while the code can be developed and built on the Raspberry Pi, it may not always be the most suitable place for software development. One reason is the lower performance of the SD card, while the Pi Zero or Zero W may be underperforming in this regard.

To compile *native* code for the Raspberry Pi, you need a compiler and linker that knows how to generate ARM binary executables. Yet it must run on a host with a different architecture (for example, Mac OS X). Hence the reason it is called a *cross*-compiler. The cross-compiler will take your source code on the local (build) platform and generate ARM binary executables, to be installed on your target Pi.

In this chapter, you'll walk through how to build your own cross-compiler. This will permit you to get the job done using your existing Linux platform.

Terminology

Let's first cover some terminology used in this chapter:

> *build*: Also called the *local* platform, this is the platform that you perform the compiling on (for example, Mac OS X).

> *target*: The destination platform, which is the Raspberry Pi (ARM) for this chapter.

© Warren Gay 2018
W. Gay, *Advanced Raspberry Pi*, https://doi.org/10.1007/978-1-4842-3948-3_20

Let's now consider some of the cross-compiling issues before you take the plunge. There are two main problem areas in cross-compiling:

- All C/C++ include files and libraries for the Raspberry Pi (ARM) must be available on your build platform (when building the kernel, for example).

- The cross-compiler and related tools must generate code suitable for the target platform.

Before you decide that you want to build a cross-compiler environment, are you prepared to

- Provide all matching C/C++ header files from the ARM platform?

- Provide all ARM libraries needed, including libraries for third-party products like sqlite3 that you intend to link with?

- Provide sufficient disk space for the cross-compiler and tools?

The crosstool-NG software will mitigate some of these issues. For example, the correct Linux headers are chosen by the configuration steps shown later in this chapter.

Disk space solves many issues by holding a copy of your Raspberry Pi's root file system on your build platform. Simple programs won't require this (for example, a Hello World program). But software linking to libraries may require this. Even if you're strapped for disk space, you may be able to mount the Raspbian SD card on the build platform, thus gaining access to the Raspberry Pi's root file system.

Operating System

The procedure used for building a cross-compiler environment is somewhat complex and fragile. Using the crosstool-NG software simplifies things considerably. Despite this advantage, it is best to stick with proven cross-compiler platforms and configurations.

You might be tempted to say, "The source code is open, and so it should work on just about any operating system." (You might even say, "I'll fix the problems myself.") The reality is not quite so simple. Unless you are willing to spend time on Internet forums and wait for answers, I suggest you take a more pragmatic approach—build your cross-compiling environment on a recent and stable Ubuntu or Debian/Devuan environment.

This chapter uses a recent install of Devuan, which is Debian based on an older 32-bit computer donated to the lab here. You can use VirtualBox 4.3.12 (www.virtualbox.org) on a Mac OS X MacBook Pro, running an Intel i7 processor instead if you like. Current versions of Debian or Devuan Linux are recommended.

Host, Guest, Build, and Target

At this point, a short note is in order because these terms can get confusing, especially for the first time. Let's list the environment terms, which will be referred to throughout the remainder of this chapter:

- *Host* environment
- *Guest* environment
- *Build/local* environment
- *Target* environment

So many environments! The terms *host* and *guest* environments enter the picture when you are using a virtual machine like VirtualBox. VirtualBox is used to *host* another operating system on top of the one you are using. For example, you might be running Mac OS X on your laptop. In this example, the OS X environment *hosts* Linux instance within VirtualBox. That Linux operating system is thus referred to as the *guest* operating system.

The term *build* (or *local*) environment refers to the Linux environment that is executing the cross-compiler and tools. These Linux tools produce or manipulate code for the *target* environment (the Raspberry Pi's ARM CPU).

Platform Limitations

Many people today are using 64-bit platforms like the MacBook Pro, with an Intel i7 processor or similar. This may present a problem if you want to build a cross-compiler for the Raspberry Pi, which is a 32-bit platform. The 32-bit cross-compiler must be built on a 32-bit processor.

Another item that may be confusing to some is the Raspberry Pi 3 model B+, which runs a 64-bit processor. While it is a 64-bit processor, the current versions of Raspbian Linux run it in a 32-bit mode. Until a 64-bit Linux is available, you need 32-bit tools. Other Linux distributions like SUSE SLES will support a native 64-bit Linux, but then you may have other challenges with firmware blobs, etc. This question was asked in the forum and the following response was added:

> *Re: Can we get an 64bit OS?*
>
> *Sat Dec 23, 2017 3:30 pm*
>
> *AFAIK no there isn't. They don't want to split the OS so they have to support two different OS's, one for PI3 only and another one for all older PI's, and get lots of confused users that complain the 64-bit OS won't work on their older PI.*
> *Also switching to 64-bit CPU's brings almost nothing, not much more speed for example.*

If you are using a 64-bit platform, then you'll probably want to choose a VirtualBox solution or use an older Linux 32-bit server. This gives you a 32-bit operating system to host the cross-compiler on. On the other hand, if you are already running a 32-bit operating system, creating a native cross-compiler should be a slam dunk.

Note   You will need to host the cross-compiler on a 32-bit platform. The cross-compiler does not build on 64-bit platforms.

Without VirtualBox (Native)

If you are already using a Linux development environment like Debian, Devuan or Ubuntu, the term *host* is equivalent to the build (or local) environment. The host and guest environments are likewise equivalent, though it is probably more correct to say there is no guest operating system in this scenario. This simpler scenario leaves us with just two environments:

> *Host/guest/build*: Native environment running the cross-compiler tools

> *Target*: The destination execution environment (Raspberry Pi)

Using VirtualBox (Debian/Linux)

If you do not have a suitable Linux environment, one can be hosted on the platform you have. You can host Linux from Windows, Mac OS X, Solaris, or another distribution of Linux using VirtualBox downloaded from the following:

www.virtualbox.org

When VirtualBox is used, the *host* environment is the environment that is running VirtualBox (for example, Mac OS X). The *guest* operating system will be some flavor of Linux like Debian. This leaves us with three environments in total:

> *Host*: Or native, running VirtualBox (for example, Windows)

> *Guest/build*: Debian/Ubuntu development environment within VirtualBox

> *Target*: The destination execution environment (your Raspberry Pi)

Planning Your Cross-Development Environment

The main consideration at this point is normally disk space. If you are using VirtualBox, limited memory can be another factor. If you are using Linux or Mac OS X, check your mounted disks for available space (or Windows tools as appropriate):

```
$ df -k
Filesystem      1K-blocks      Used  Available Use% Mounted on
/dev/sda1      151903380  15768740  128395300  11% /
udev               10240         0      10240   0% /dev
tmpfs             181080       388     180692   1% /run
tmpfs               5120         4       5116   1% /run/lock
tmpfs             727920         0     727920   0% /run/shm
```

In the preceding example output, we see that the root file system has plenty of space. But your file system is likely to be different. Symlinks can be used when necessary to graft a larger disk area onto your home directory.

If you're using VirtualBox, create virtual disks with enough space for the Linux operating system and your cross-compiler environment. You may want to put your Linux software on one virtual disk with a minimum size of about 10 GB (allow it to grow larger).

Allow a minimum of 10 GB for your cross-compiler environment (and allow it to grow). You must also factor in additional space for the Raspberry Linux kernel, its include files, and all other third-party libraries that you might need to build with (better still, a copy of the Raspberry Pi's root file system).

Within your development Linux build environment, make sure your cross-compiler and build area are using the disk area that has available space. It is easy to glibly create a directory someplace convenient and find out later that the space that you thought you were going to use wasn't available.

Building the Cross-Compiler

At this point, I'll assume that you've set up and installed Linux in VirtualBox, if necessary or using an instance of 32-bit Linux. I'll be using a Devuan Linux, which is based upon Debian.

Download crosstool-NG

The released crosstool-NG downloads are found at:

http://crosstool-ng.org

From the site, find a link to the latest download. As this is written, the following was current:

```
$ wget http://crosstool-ng.org/download/crosstool-ng/crosstool-
ng-1.23.0.tar.bz2
```

Staging Directory

I'll assume that you've symlinked to your disk area with sufficient available disk space. This chapter will use ~/xrpi as the cross-compiler playground.

```
$ mkdir ~/xrpi
$ cd ~/xrpi
```

Next I'll assume that you've created a symlink to your area of disk space, or simply created a subdirectory if the current directory has the space already:

```
$ symlink /some/big/area/of/disk ~/xrpi/devel
```

But if ~/xrpi already has sufficient space, then simply do the following instead:

```
$ mkdir ~/xrpi/devel
```

For convenience, let's now change to that directory:

```
$ cd ~/xrpi/devel
```

In directory ~/xrpi/devel, create a subdirectory named staging (~/devel/staging) and change to it:

```
$ mkdir ./staging
$ cd ./staging          # Dir is ~/xrpi/devel/staging
$ pwd
/home/myuserid/xrpi/devel/staging
$
```

Unpack the Tarball

Assuming the tarball crosstool-ng-1.23.0.tar.bz2 was downloaded to your home directory, you would perform the following (change the option j if the suffix is not .bz2):

```
$ tar xjvf ~/crosstool-ng-1.23.0.tar.bz2
. . .
$
```

After the unpacking completes, you should have a subdirectory named crosstoolng-1.23.0 in your staging directory.

Create /opt/x-tools

You can choose a different location if you like, but for ease of reference, I'm going to assume that the crosstool-NG software is going to install into /opt/x-tools. We'll also assume your user ID is fred (substitute your own).

```
$ sudo mkdir -p /opt/x-tools
$ sudo chown fred /opt/x-tools
```

Optionally, once the installation is complete later, you can change the ownership back to root for protection.

Install Package Dependencies

The crosstool-NG build depends on several packages provided by your Linux distribution as optionally installed software. At a minimum, install the following now:

```
# apt-get install bison
# apt-get install flex
# apt-get install libtool
# apt-get install texinfo
# apt-get install gawk
# apt-get install gperf
# apt-get install automake
# apt-get install subversion
# apt-get install help2man
```

If during the configuration of crosstools-ng you find that you need other packages, they can be installed then and the configuration retried.

Configure crosstools-NG

With the package dependencies installed, you are now in a position to make the crosstool-NG software (substitute the crosstool-ng version as required throughout the remainder of this chapter):

```
$ cd ~/xrpi/devel/staging/crosstool-ng-1.23.0
$ ./configure --prefix=/opt/x-tools
```

If this completes without errors, you are ready to build and install the software. If it reports that you are missing package dependencies, install them now and repeat.

Patch inputbox.c

One *extremely* vexing irritation I have with some modern Linux and tools, is that they don't properly support the *backspace* character (Control-H). This is a standard ASCII character intended precisely for this purpose. Why has it been banished? I'll try to refrain from further ranting about this.

The menu program used by the crosstool-ng suffers from the same problem that the linux kernel menuconfig suffers from: no backspace character (Control-H) support. This can leave you in the curse-worthy situation of not being able to backspace or delete input.

To correct that problem, perform the following:

1. cd ~/xrpi/devel/staging/crosstool-ng-1.23.0/
   kconfig/lxdialog

2. Edit file inputbox.c and go to about line 128, where you should see a line that says:

   ```
   case KEY_BACKSPACE:
   ```

3. Add a line below it that simply reads:

   case 8:

4. Save the file (inputbox.c).

If you already know that your backspace key sends an escape sequence instead of Control-H, then you can safely skip this change. Otherwise, this kind of thing can drive you absolutely batty. With that file saved, some semblance of sanity will follow.

make crosstool-ng

At this point, you should have no trouble building crosstool-NG (including the above fix). Perform the following make command:

```
$ cd ~/devel/staging/crosstool-ng-1.23.0
$ make
  SED    'ct-ng'
  SED    'scripts/scripts.mk'
  SED    'scripts/crosstool-NG.sh'
  SED    'scripts/saveSample.sh'
  SED    'scripts/showConfig.sh'
  GEN    'config/configure.in'
  GEN    'paths.mk'
  GEN    'paths.sh'
  DEP    'nconf.gui.dep'
  DEP    'nconf.dep'
  DEP    'lxdialog/yesno.dep'
  DEP    'lxdialog/util.dep'
  DEP    'lxdialog/textbox.dep'
  DEP    'lxdialog/menubox.dep'
  DEP    'lxdialog/inputbox.dep'
  DEP    'lxdialog/checklist.dep'
```

```
DEP     'mconf.dep'
DEP     'conf.dep'
BISON   'zconf.tab.c'
GPERF   'zconf.hash.c'
LEX     'zconf.lex.c'
DEP     'zconf.tab.dep'
CC      'zconf.tab.o'
CC      'conf.o'
LD      'conf'
CC      'lxdialog/checklist.o'
CC      'lxdialog/inputbox.o'
CC      'lxdialog/menubox.o'
CC      'lxdialog/textbox.o'
CC      'lxdialog/util.o'
CC      'lxdialog/yesno.o'
CC      'mconf.o'
LD      'mconf'
CC      'nconf.o'
CC      'nconf.gui.o'
LD      'nconf'
SED     'docs/ct-ng.1'
GZIP    'docs/ct-ng.1.gz'
$
```

This takes very little time and seems trouble free.

make install

Once the crosstool-NG package has been compiled, it is ready to be installed into /opt/x-tools. From the same directory:

```
$ sudo make install
  GEN     'config/configure.in'
```

```
GEN      'paths.mk'
GEN      'paths.sh'
MKDIR    '/opt/x-tools/bin/'
INST     'ct-ng'
MKDIR    '/opt/x-tools/lib/crosstool-ng-1.23.0/'
INSTDIR 'config/'
INSTDIR 'contrib/'
INSTDIR 'patches/'
INSTDIR 'scripts/'
INST     'steps.mk'
INST     'paths'
INSTDIR 'samples/'
INST     'kconfig/'
MKDIR    '/opt/x-tools/share/doc/crosstool-ng/crosstool-
         ng-1.23.0/'
INST     'docs/manual/*.md'
MKDIR    '/opt/x-tools/share/man/man1/'
INST     'ct-ng.1.gz'
```

For auto-completion, do not forget to install 'ct-ng.comp' into your bash completion directory (usually /etc/bash_completion.d)

If you still own the directory /opt/x-tools from earlier (recall sudo chown fred /opt/x-tools), you won't need to use sudo in the preceding step. After make install is performed, you will have the crosstool-NG command ct-ng installed in the directory /opt/x-tools/bin.

PATH

To use the newly installed ct-ng command, you will need to adjust your PATH environment variable (and every time you log in):

```
$ PATH="/opt/x-tools/bin:$PATH"
```

The website also indicates that you might have to unset environment variable LD_LIBRARY_PATH, if your platform has it defined. If so, then unset it as follows to avoid any unwanted trouble:

```
$ unset LD_LIBRARY_PATH
```

Now you should be able to run ct-ng to get version info (note that there are no hyphens in front of version in the following command). Seeing the version output confirms that your ct-ng command has been installed and is functional:

```
$ ct-ng version
This is crosstool-NG version crosstool-ng-1.23.0

Copyright (C) 2008  Yann E. MORIN <yann.morin.1998@free.fr>
This is free software; see the source for copying conditions.
There is NO warranty; not even for MERCHANTABILITY or FITNESS
FOR A \
   PARTICULAR PURPOSE.
```

Cross-Compiler Configuration

The command ct-ng simplifies the work necessary to configure and build the cross-compiler tool chain. From here, we are concerned with building the cross-compiler tools themselves. When that process is completed, you will have populated the cross-compiler tools into the directory /opt/x-tools/arm-unknown-linux-gnueabi.

Before ct-ng can build your cross-compiler, it must first be configured:

```
$ cd ~/xrpi/devel/staging
$ ct-ng menuconfig
```

If you get a "command not found" error message, check that the PATH variable is set correctly.

Paths and Misc Options

When the ct-ng command starts up, the menu configuration screen is
presented as shown in Figure 20-1. Press Enter to open the Paths and Misc
Options submenu.

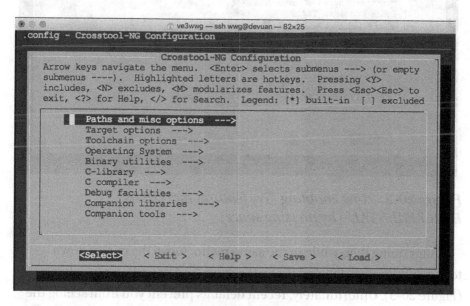

Figure 20-1. ct-ng menuconfig opening dialog

Once in the Paths and Misc Options menu, as shown in Figure 20-2,
use the cursor key to move down to Try Features Marked as Experimental.
Once that line is highlighted, press the spacebar to put an asterisk inside
the square brackets to select the option (pressing space again toggles the
setting).

```
●  ○  ○                    ⓘ ve3wwg — ssh wwg@devuan — 82×25
.config - Crosstool-NG Configuration
> Paths and misc options
                         Paths and misc options
  Arrow keys navigate the menu. <Enter> selects submenus ---> (or empty
  submenus ----). Highlighted letters are hotkeys. Pressing <Y>
  includes, <N> excludes, <M> modularizes features. Press <Esc><Esc> to
  exit, <?> for Help, </> for Search. Legend: [*] built-in [ ] excluded

          *** crosstool-NG behavior ***
      [ ] Use obsolete features
      [ ] Try features marked as EXPERIMENTAL
      [ ]     Allow building as root user (READ HELP!) (NEW)
      [ ] Debug crosstool-NG
          *** Paths ***
      (${HOME}/src) Local tarballs directory
      [*]    Save new tarballs
      (${CT_TOP_DIR}/.build) Working directory
      (${CT_PREFIX:-${HOME}/x-tools}/${CT_HOST:+HOST-${CT_HOST}/}${CT_TAR
      [*]    Remove the prefix dir prior to building


            <Select>     < Exit >    < Help >    < Save >    < Load >
```

Figure 20-2. *ct-ng enabling "Try features marked as EXPERIMENTAL" (by pressing space)*

After doing that, while in the same menu, move the cursor down to the middle entry labeled Prefix Directory and press Enter to select it (Figure 20-3). Unfortunately, recent defaults prevent you from seeing the "Prefix Directory" text at the extreme right of the menu selection.

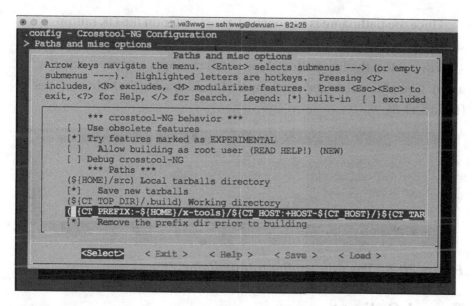

Figure 20-3. *Select the CT_PREFIX line to set the prefix*

For the procedure used in this chapter, modify the path to the following:

```
/opt/x-tools/${CT_TARGET}
```

Figure 20-4 illustrates the input dialog. If you find that you cannot use backspace, then apply the fix discussed in section "Patch inputbox.c".

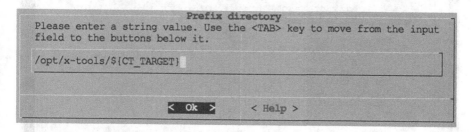

Figure 20-4. *Set the Prefix Directory*

Once the pathname is established, press Enter on the OK button shown. This returns you to the Paths and Misc Options menu.

Then select the Exit button shown at the bottom, and press Enter again. If you have changed anything that needs saving then choose "Yes" (Figure 20-5).

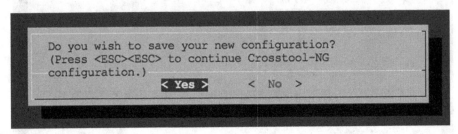

Figure 20-5. *The save configuration dialog*

Target Options

Restart the menu and select Target Options with the cursor and press Enter to open it (Figure 20-6).

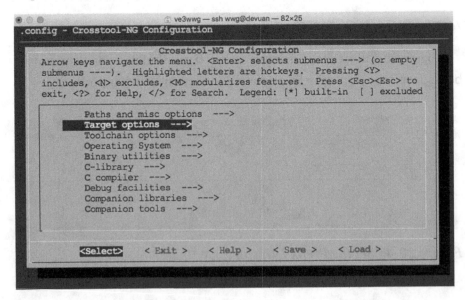

Figure 20-6. *Choose Target options*

Then choose Target Architecture and press Enter (Figure 20-7).

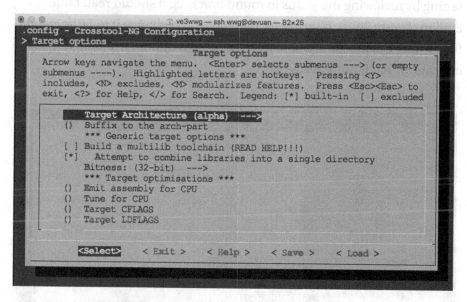

Figure 20-7. *Choose Target Architecture*

In that menu, choose arm and press space (Figure 20-8). Then use the Select button at the bottom. This returns you to the Target Options menu.

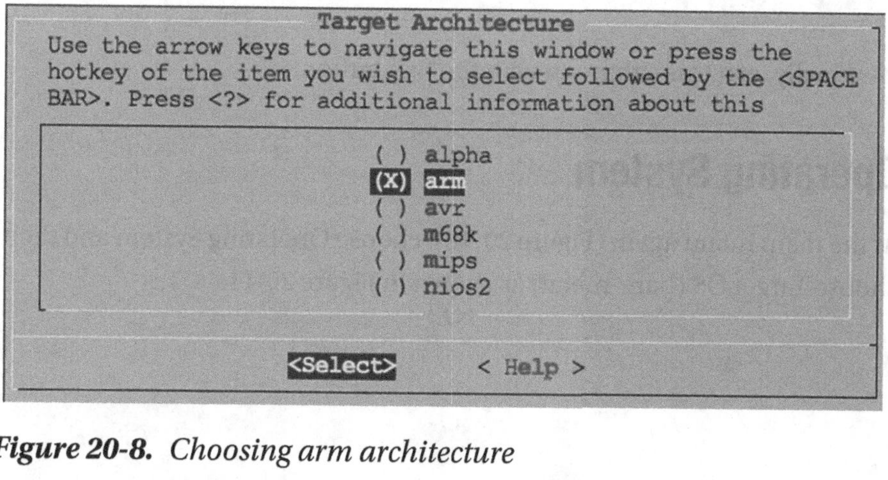

Figure 20-8. *Choosing arm architecture*

While in the Target Options menu (shown next), verify the Endianness setting by reviewing the status in round brackets. It should read Little Endian (Figure 20-9). If not, enter that menu and change it to *Little endian*. Below the Endianness menu item is the Bitness option. It should already indicate 32-bit. If not, change it.

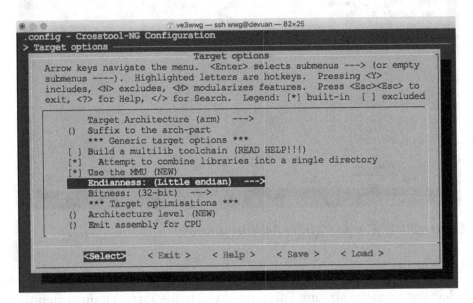

Figure 20-9. *Checking Endianness and Bitness*

Finally, exit this submenu with the Exit button.

Operating System

At the main menu again (Figure 20-10), choose Operating System and then choose Target OS (bare-metal) as shown in Figure 20-11.

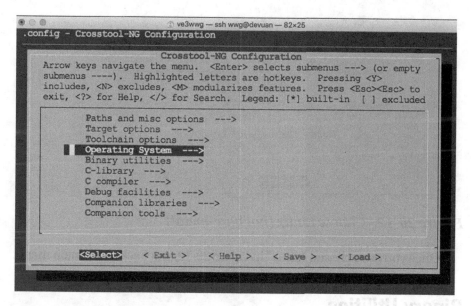

Figure 20-10. *Select Operating System*

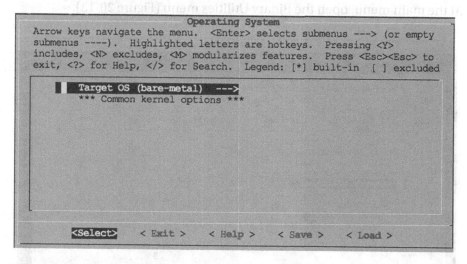

Figure 20-11. *Choose Target OS (bare-metal)*

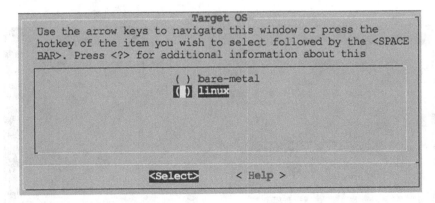

Figure 20-12.   *Choose Linux (not bare-metal)*

Once you have chosen "linux" in Figure 20-12, exit back to the main menu.

Binary Utilities

At the main menu, open the Binary Utilities menu (Figure 20-13).

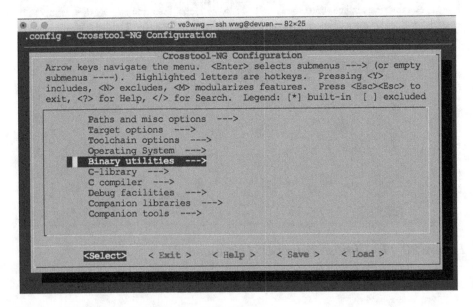

Figure 20-13.   *The Binary utilities menu*

Cursor down to Binutils Version and open it (Figure 20-14).

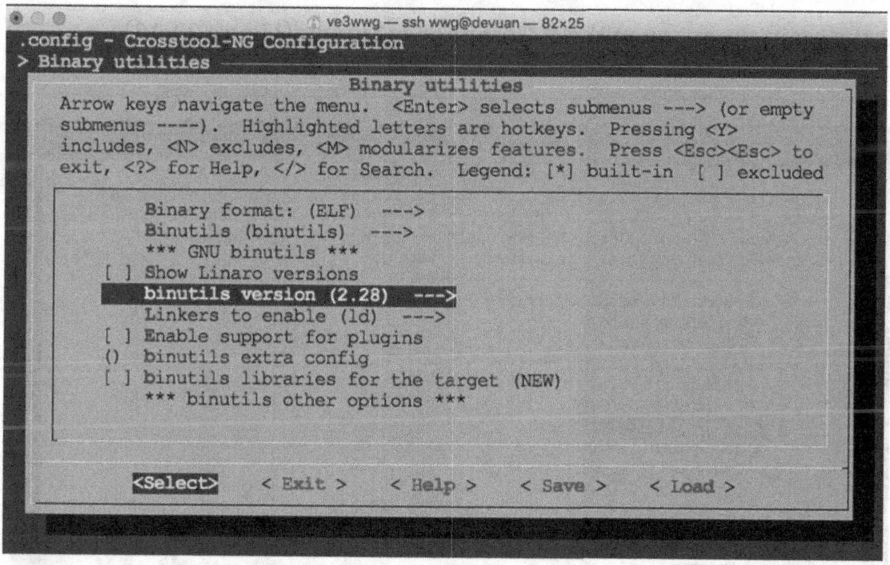

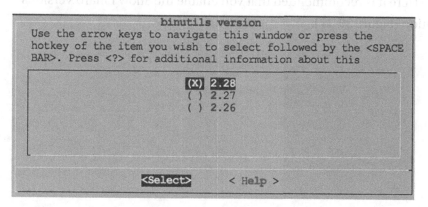

Figure 20-14. *The binutils version menu*

Once into the final binutils version selection menu, pick the most recent version unless you experienced trouble with a prior build attempt (Figure 20-15).

Figure 20-15. *Select the binutils version (normally the most recent)*

Exit back to the main menu.

C Compiler

At the main menu, open the C Compiler submenu (Figure 20-16).

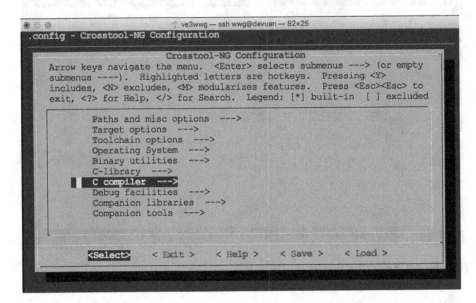

Figure 20-16. *The C compiler submenu of the main menu*

Here it is recommended that you enable the Show Linaro Versions option (Figure 20-17).

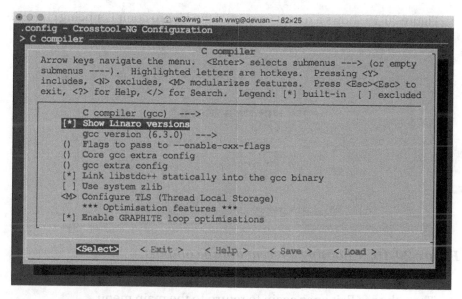

Figure 20-17. *Enable "Show Linaro versions"*

Once that is enabled, you can select the submenu Gcc Version (Figure 20-18).

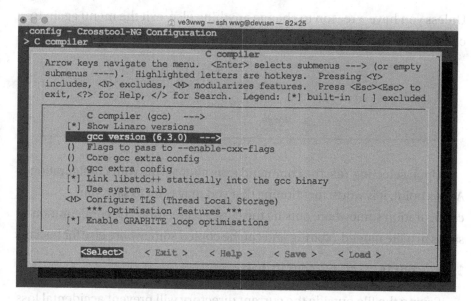

Figure 20-18. *Select menu "gcc version"*

Figure 20-19 shows a recent version of the Linaro compiler being chosen.

```
                        gcc version
    Use the arrow keys to navigate this window or press the
    hotkey of the item you wish to select followed by the <SPACE
    BAR>. Press <?> for additional information about this

                   (X) linaro-6.3-2017.02
                   ( ) 6.3.0
                   ( ) linaro-5.4-2017.01
                   ( ) 5.4.0
                   ( ) linaro-4.9-2017.01
                   ( ) 4.9.4


              <Select>         < Help >
```

Figure 20-19. *Choosing a recent linaro compiler*

Then choose Exit once again to return to the main menu.

Save Configuration

Unless you have a reason to change anything else, exit the menu again to
cause the Save prompt to appear:

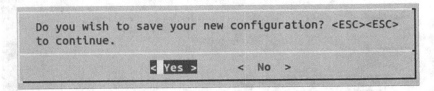

```
    Do you wish to save your new configuration? <ESC><ESC>
    to continue.

                   < Yes >       <  No  >
```

Upon selecting Yes, the command exits after saving your configuration.
At this point, it is worth mentioning that you may want to save your
configuration somewhere outside the current directory. The configuration is
saved in a file named .config and can be copied somewhere else for backup:

```
$ cp .config ~/ct-ng.config.bak
```

Saving the file outside the current directory will prevent accidental loss
if ct-ng distclean is used.

Build Cross-Compiler

Check the ownership of /opt/x-tools. If you don't own this directory, change the ownership now (substitute your userid for fred):

```
$ sudo chown -R fred /opt/x-tools
```

This will save you from having to execute the build process with root privileges. Now you can initiate the building of the cross-compiler. Note that your system needs to be connected to the Internet for downloading, unless the downloads were done on a prior attempt:

```
$ cd ~/xrpi/devel/staging
$ ct-ng build
```

Allow four hours of time for this job, much less if you're repeating it (the first-time downloads files). Ideally, you can just leave the command to run and check for successful completion in the morning. It is not uncommon for different software problems to arise at this stage but if you do, read the next section for some troubleshooting tips. If all goes well, ct-ng compiles and installs tools into /opt/x-tools without any further interaction.

```
$ ct-ng build
[INFO ]   Performing some trivial sanity checks
[INFO ]   Build started 20180713.233346
[INFO ]   Building environment variables
[WARN ]   Directory '/home/wwg/src' does not exist.
[WARN ]   Will not save downloaded tarballs to local storage.
[EXTRA]   Preparing working directories
[EXTRA]   Installing user-supplied crosstool-NG configuration
[EXTRA]   ========================================================
[EXTRA]   Dumping internal crosstool-NG configuration
[EXTRA]   Building a toolchain for:
[EXTRA]     build  = i686-pc-linux-gnu
[EXTRA]     host   = i686-pc-linux-gnu
[EXTRA]     target = arm-unknown-linux-gnueabi
```

```
[EXTRA]  Dumping internal crosstool-NG configuration: done in
         0.20s (at 00:03)
[INFO ]  ==========================================================
[INFO ]  Retrieving needed toolchain components' tarballs
[EXTRA]     Retrieving 'automake-1.15'
[EXTRA]     Retrieving 'libtool-2.4.6'
[EXTRA]     Retrieving 'linux-4.10.8'
...
[INFO ]  Installing C library: done in 1950.45s (at 165:01)
[INFO ]  ==========================================================
[INFO ]  Installing final gcc compiler
[EXTRA]     Configuring final gcc compiler
[EXTRA]     Building final gcc compiler
[EXTRA]     Installing final gcc compiler
[EXTRA]     Housekeeping for final gcc compiler
[EXTRA]        " --> lib (gcc)   lib (os)
[INFO ]  Installing final gcc compiler: done in 3446.75s
         (at 222:28)
[INFO ]  ==========================================================
[INFO ]  Finalizing the toolchain's directory
[INFO ]     Stripping all toolchain executables
[EXTRA]     Installing the populate helper
[EXTRA]     Installing a cross-ldd helper
[EXTRA]     Creating toolchain aliases
[EXTRA]     Removing installed documentation
[INFO ]  Finalizing the toolchain's directory: done in 4.55s
         (at 222:33)
[INFO ]  Build completed at 20180714.031618
[INFO ]  (elapsed: 222:32.13)
[INFO ]  Finishing installation (may take a few seconds)...
[222:33] /
$
```

Based upon the 222:33 figure reported, this download and build took approximately 4 hours and 15 minutes to complete. This build was performed on an older single processor Devuan Linux instance.

Troubleshooting

The session output that you get from this build process is terse. As such, you don't always get a clear idea of what the real failure was. For this reason, you'll often need to check the build.log file:

```
$ less build.log
```

Using less, you can navigate to the end of the build.log file by typing a capital G.

One failure that frequently occurs in the beginning is a *failed download*. While the build process does retry downloads and tries different download methods, it can still fail. All that you need to do is to retry the build. It will download only the remaining files needed. Sometimes it will succeed on the second or third retry attempt.

Sometimes a component will fail in its *configuration phase*. Check the build.log file first to determine precisely which component is involved. Next you will want to examine the config.log file for that particular component. For example, let's say the isl component failed. Dive down into the .build subdirectory until you find its config.log file:

```
$ cd .build/arm-unknown-linux-gnueabi/build/build-isl-host-
i686-build_pc-linux-gnu
$ less config.log
```

Navigate to the end of config.log and work backward a few pages. Eventually, you will see text describing the command that was tried and the error message produced. In one instance, I was able to determine that the custom compiler option that I added (-fpermissive) was causing the failure. The solution then was to remove that option and try again.

Some errors will only occur with certain version choices. At one time, I was receiving errors related to PPL and needed a patch to correct it.

In getting through these issues, you can simply make corrections and then rerun the `ct-ng build` command. It is recommended that you plan for a later rebuild of everything again (after a `clean`), once the problems are solved. This will ensure that you have a good build without dependency issues.

If, after a correction, you run into the same problem, you may need to do a `clean` step first and start over. Depending on how deep you think the problem may be, choose one of the following:

- `ct-ng clean`

- `ct-ng distclean` (Be careful; see the following text.)

The `ct-ng clean` command will usually be enough, forcing the next build to start fresh. Any downloaded files and configuration will remain and will be reused.

The `ct-ng distclean` command is much more drastic, since it removes all of the downloaded content *and your configuration files.* I had copied the `.config` file to `.config.bak` and discovered to my horror that `.config.bak` had also been removed! So if you back up the `.config` file, copy it *outside* the current directory for safety.

Above all, keep your head. It's difficult to troubleshoot these issues if you feel time pressure or get angry over the time invested. When under time pressure, leave it for another day when you can deal with it thoughtfully. Each redo takes considerable time. Wherever possible, eliminate the guesswork.

With each problem, take a deep breath, patiently look for clues, and pay attention to the details in the error messages. Remember that line in the movie *Apollo 13*: "Work the problem, people!"

Summary

In this chapter you have seen how to install a cross-compiler for your Raspberry Pi, whether on an older 32-bit Linux platform or in an instance of VirtualBox. Doing this will provide you with the compiler tools needed to compile your kernel or applications for the lesser powered Raspberry Pis, like the Zero or Zero W.

CHAPTER 21

Cross-Compiling the Kernel

While normally not possible on embedded platforms, it *is* possible to build kernels on your Raspberry Pi with its luxurious root file system. Despite this, cross-compiling on desktop systems is often preferred for faster compile times. This chapter examines the procedure for building your Raspbian kernel outside of the Pi.

It is assumed that you have the cross-compiler tools and environment ready. Either the tool set built in Chapter 20 or an installed prebuilt tool chain will do. In this chapter, I assume that the cross-compiler prefix is as follows (ending in a hyphen):

```
/opt/x-tools/arm-unknown-linux-gnueabi/bin/*
```

Substitute as appropriate, if your tools are installed differently.

The kernel can be built natively on a Pi, with the Raspberry Pi 3 B+ being perhaps the best choice as this is being written. The steps for native builds are also provided in this chapter, since the procedure is very similar to the cross builds.

W. Gay, *Advanced Raspberry Pi*, https://doi.org/10.1007/978-1-4842-3948-3_21

Host Environment Tools

If these tools and library are not yet installed, install them now:

```
$ sudo apt-get install git bc
$ sudo apt-get install libncurses5-dev
```

Kernel Source Code

Fetch the kernel source code, using git unless you've chosen an alternate way:

```
$ cd ~/xrpi/devel/staging
$ git clone --depth=1 https://github.com/raspberrypi/linux
$ cd ./linux
```

Be sure to add the --depth=1 option to the git command to avoid a horribly long download. This avoids downloading history you're not likely to care about.

Note   If you have trouble using git from VirtualBox, there may be networking issues involved (reconfiguration may correct this). The simplest workaround is to simply use git outside VirtualBox and upload the master.tar.gz file with scp.

Fix inputbox.c

Once again, we run into the backspace character support issue. If you care about this, apply the following simple fix:

```
$ nano scripts/kconfig/lxdialog/inputbox.c
```

Around line 128, locate the line:

```
case KEY_BACKSPACE:
```

and add a case statement below it:

```
case 8:
```

and then save it from your editor.

make mrproper

In theory, this step shouldn't be necessary. But the kernel developers want you to do it anyway, in case something was accidentally left out of place. Be warned that this step also removes the .config file (copy it to a backup file if you need to).

```
$ cd ~/xrpi/devel/staging/linux
$ make mrproper
```

Caution   The command make mrproper cleans up everything, including your kernel .config file. Save a copy of .config to ~/.config.bak or some other safe place, outside of the current directory.

Makefile for Pi 1/Zero/Zero W

When *cross-compiling*, edit the Makefile:

```
$ cd ~/xrpi/devel/staging/linux
$ nano Makefile
```

and then add the following two lines to the top of the file:

```
ARCH=arm
CROSS_COMPILE=arm-unknown-linux-gnueabi-
```

The `CROSS_COMPILE` value shown may differ from yours depending upon the content of your /opt/x-tools directory. List it to verify:

```
$ ls /opt/x-tools
arm-unknown-linux-gnueabi  bin  lib  share
```

The value for the macro should exactly agree with the name listed, with one trailing hyphen added to the end of it.

Config for Pi 1/Zero/Zero W

Once the Makefile has been edited, apply the following change to your PATH variable (and again if you have logged out and logged in again):

```
$ PATH="/opt/x-tools/arm-unknown-linux-gnueabi/bin:$PATH"
```

Before building your kernel, you need a configuration. The downloaded kernel source does not include your Pi's kernel settings. To generate a suitable default configuration, perform the following to create a file named .config:

```
$ make bcmrpi_defconfig
```

Once the default configuration file has been generated, you can customize it further using:

```
$ make menuconfig
```

Makefile for Pi 2/3/3+/Compute Module 3

If you're cross-compiling from a non-Raspberry Pi platform, add the following two lines to the Makefile instead:

```
ARCH=arm
CROSS_COMPILE=arm-unknown-linux-gnueabi-
```

Config for Pi 2/3/3+/Compute Module 3

Adjust the PATH variable:

```
$ PATH="/opt/x-tools/arm-unknown-linux-gnueabi/bin:$PATH"
```

And then generate a default configuration followed by customization:

```
$ make bcm2709_defconfig
$ make menuconfig
```

zImage modules dtbs

Now that the configuration has been established, start the build process. If you hadn't planned on making configuration changes, you might still be prompted with some configuration questions. To proceed without configuration changes, simply press Enter to accept the existing value for the parameter.

You can build these components individually, or all at once in order using:

```
$ make zImage modules dtbs
```

The build process takes a fair chunk of time. On an older 32-bit single core Devuan Linux instance, this step took 2 hours and 15 minutes.

Tip   If your /tmp file system is not large enough for the build, you can direct the temporary files to another directory. For example, to use ./tmp in your work area:

```
$ mkdir ./tmp
$ export TMPDIR="$PWD/tmp"
```

Native Install Kernel Image

When building the kernel on a Raspberry Pi 3 B+ or similar, you can install the new kernel with the following steps into your /boot partition:

```
$ sudo make modules_install
$ sudo cp arch/arm/boot/dts/*.dtb /boot/
$ sudo cp arch/arm/boot/dts/overlays/*.dtb* /boot/overlays/
$ sudo cp arch/arm/boot/dts/overlays/README /boot/overlays/
```

The last step depends upon the type of Pi involved. Use the following building for Pi 1/Zero/Zero W:

```
$ sudo cp arch/arm/boot/zImage /boot/kernel.img
```

For the Pi 2/3/3+/Compute Module 3, use the following instead:

```
$ sudo cp arch/arm/boot/zImage /boot/kernel7.img
```

The difference is just the name of the kernel—kernel.img or kernel7.img.

Cross Install

When installing a cross-compiled kernel, you need to get the kernel and related files into the SD card. In the procedure to follow, I assume that you have the SD card mounted on your cross-compile host file system. To figure out where your SD card is under Linux, this is one way using lsblk:

```
$ lsblk
NAME       MAJ:MIN   RM     SIZE   RO   TYPE MOUNTPOINT
sda         8:0       0    149.1G   0   disk
|—sda1      8:1       0    147.3G   0   part /
|—sda2      8:2       0       1K    0   part
|—sda5      8:5       0     1.8G    0   part [SWAP]
sdb         8:16      1     7.2G    0   disk
|—sdb1      8:17      1    43.2M    0   part
|—sdb2      8:18      1     7.2G    0   part
sr0        11:0       1    1024M    0   rom
```

Another command blkid provides more information but must be run as root:

```
$ sudo blkid
/dev/sda1: UUID="51d355c1-2fe1-4f0e-aaae-01d526bb27b5" \
        TYPE="ext4" PARTUUID="61c63d91-01"
/dev/sda5: UUID="83a322e3-11fe-4a25-bd6c-b877ab0321f9"
        TYPE="swap" PARTUUID="61c63d91-05"

/dev/sdb1: LABEL="boot" UUID="6228-7918" \
        TYPE="vfat" PARTUUID="f8dea240-01"
/dev/sdb2: LABEL="rootfs" UUID="6bfc8851-cf63-4362-abf1-
045dda421aad" \
        TYPE="ext4" PARTUUID="f8dea240-02"
```

From the above, it is evident that /dev/sdb1 holds the /boot partition of the inserted SD card. Mount that and the "rootfs" somewhere, for example:

```
# mkdir /mnt/boot
# mkdir /mnt/root
# mount /dev/sdb1 /mnt/boot
# mount /dev/sdb2 /mnt/root
```

With your SD card mounted, you can change out your kernel. It is recommended that you rename the original kernel.img file in case you want to reinstate it later.

```
# cd /mnt/boot
# mv kernel.img kernel.was
```

Cross Modules Install

Once the original kernel is safely renamed on the SD card, you can copy the new kernel onto the SD card's /boot partition. Back to your normal userid, perform:

```
$ cd ~/xrpi/devel/staging/linux
$ sudo make INSTALL_MOD_PATH=/mnt/root modules_install
```

This will install the compiled modules into the mounted root file system. Note how the parameter INSTALL_MOD_PATH specifies where the file system is.

Cross Kernel Files Install

For the smaller Pi's, use the following:

```
$ sudo cp arch/arm/boot/zImage /mnt/boot/kernel.img
```

For the larger Pis, use kernel7.img for the target file name instead:

```
$ sudo cp arch/arm/boot/zImage /mnt/boot/kernel7.img
```

Followed by the following copies:

```
$ sudo cp arch/arm/boot/dts/*.dtb /mnt/boot/
$ sudo cp arch/arm/boot/dts/overlays/*.dtb* /mnt/boot/overlays/
$ sudo cp arch/arm/boot/dts/overlays/README /mnt/boot/overlays/
```

Now you can safely unmount the SD card file systems:

```
$ sudo unmount /mnt/boot
$ sudo unmount /mnt/root
```

The Smoke Test

With all the hard work done, we can now insert the SD card into the target Pi and boot! After inserting the card into the Pi Zero (host named pizero), it was booted up and I logged in to run dmesg. The second line confirms that we were up on the new cross-compiled kernel:

```
[    0.000000] Linux version 4.14.56+ (wwg@devuan) \
   (gcc version 6.3.1 20170109 (crosstool-NG crosstool-
   ng-1.23.0)) \
   #1 Tue Jul 17 23:09:49 EDT 2018
```

Boot Failure

If you see the initial colored flash screen remain on the console, this indicates that the kernel.img file failed to load/start.

Summary

There are several steps in this chapter, but many are related to the differences in the Pi models. Once you distill the steps needed for the target platform, the procedure is straightforward. Having the ability to build new kernels for your Pi means that you can enable and disable components and subsystems of your choice. Even more exciting is the possibility of writing new kernel modules to fully leverage your system.

CHAPTER 22

DHT11 Sensor

The DHT11 humidity and temperature sensor is an economical peripheral manufactured by D-Robotics UK (www.droboticsonline.com). It is capable of measuring relative humidity between 20 and 90% RH within the operating temperature range of 0 to 50°C with an accuracy of ±5% RH. Temperature is also measured in the range of 0 to 50°C with an accuracy of ±2°C. Both values are returned with 8-bit resolution.

This assignment is a challenge for a Linux application because of the signal timing constraints being accommodated. After the Pi initiates the sensor, the first event to be measured occurs within about 12 µs, for example. This requires some special handling. Direct GPIO access is used for this project since the sysfs driver is simply unable to cope with the rate of events involved.

Characteristics

The signaling used by the DHT sensor is *similar* to the 1-Wire protocol but the response times differ. Additionally, there is no device serial number support. These factors make the device incompatible with the 1-Wire drivers within the Linux kernel. Figure 22-1 shows a DHT11 sensor sitting on a breadboard.

© Warren Gay 2018
W. Gay, *Advanced Raspberry Pi*, https://doi.org/10.1007/978-1-4842-3948-3_22

Figure 22-1. *DHT11 sensor front view (left), rear view (right). Pin 1 is the leftmost pin facing the front of the package (left photo).*

The DHT11 sensor requires a power supply unlike many 1-Wire peripherals. The datasheet states that the DHT11 can be powered by a range of 3.3 to 5.5 V (this can also be seen on the back of the device in Figure 22-1). Powering it from the Raspberry Pi's 3.3 V source keeps the signal levels within a safe range for GPIO. The device draws between 0.5 and 2.5 mA. Its standby current is stated as 100 to 150 μA, for those concerned about battery life.

Circuit

Figure 22-2 shows the general circuit connections between the Raspberry
Pi and the DHT11 sensor. Pin 4 connects to the common ground, while pin
1 goes to the 3.3 V supply. Pin 2 is the signal pin, which communicates with
a chosen GPIO pin. The program listing for dht11.c is configured to use
GPIO 22. This can be overridden on the command line.

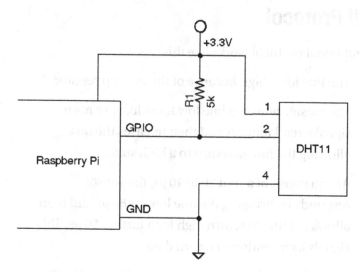

Figure 22-2. *DHT11 circuit*

When the Pi is listening on the GPIO pin and the DHT11 is not sending
data, the line will float. For this reason, R_1 is used to pull the line up to a
level of 3.3 V. The datasheet recommends a 5 kΩ resistor for the purpose
(a more common 4.7 kohm resistor can be substituted safely). This presents
less than 1 mA of load on either the GPIO pin or the sensor when active.
The datasheet also states that the 5 kohm resistor should be suitable for
cable runs of up to 20 meters.

Protocol

The sensor speaks only when prodded by the master (Raspberry Pi). The master must first make a request on the bus and wait for the sensor to respond. The DHT sensor responds with 40 bits of information, 8 of which are a checksum.

Overall Protocol

The overall signal protocol works like this:

1. The line idles high because of the pull-up resistor.

2. The master pulls the line low for at least 18 ms to signal a read request and then releases the bus, allowing the line to return to a high state.

3. After a pause of about 20 to 40 µs, the sensor responds by bringing the line low for 80 µs and then allows the line to return high for a further 80 µs. This signals its intention to return data.

4. Forty bits of information are then written out to the bus by the DHT11: each bit starting with a 50 µs low followed by:

   a. 26 to 28 µs of high to indicate a 0-bit

   b. 70 µs of high to indicate a 1-bit

5. The transmission ends when the sensor drives the line low one more time for 50 µs.

6. The sensor releases the bus, allowing the line to return to a high idle state.

Figure 22-3 illustrates the overall protocol of the sensor. Master control is shown in thick lines, while sensor control is shown in thin lines. Initially, the bus sits idle until the master brings the line low and releases it (labeled Request). The sensor grabs the bus and signals that it is responding (80 µs low, followed by 80 µs high). The sensor finishes with 40 bits of sensor data, ending with one more transition to low (labeled End) to mark the end of the last bit.

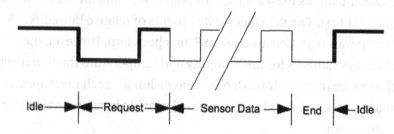

Figure 22-3. *General DHT11 protocol*

Data Bits

Each sensor data bit begins with a transition to low, followed by the transition to high, as shown in Figure 22-4. The end of the bit occurs when the line is brought low again as part of the next bit. The last bit is marked off by one final low-to-high transition.

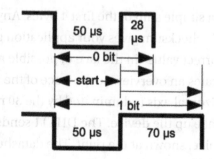

Figure 22-4. *DHT11 data bit*

Each data bit starts with a transition to low, lasting for 50 μs. The final transition to low after the last bit also lasts for 50 μs. After the bit's low-to-high transition, the bit becomes a 0-bit if the high lasts only 26 to 28 μs. A 1-bit stays high for 70 μs instead.

Data Format

Figure 22-5 illustrates the 40-bit sensor response, transmitting the most significant bit first. The datasheet states 16 bits of relative humidity, 16 bits of temperature in Celsius, and an 8-bit checksum. However, the DHT11 always sends 0s for the humidity and temperature fractional bytes. Thus the device really only has 8 bits of precision for each measurement. Presumably, other models (or future ones) provide fractional values for greater precision.

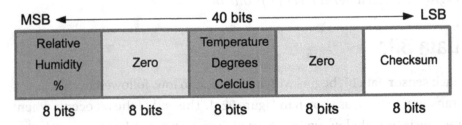

Figure 22-5. DHT11 data format

The checksum is a simple sum of the first 4 bytes. Any carry overflow is simply discarded. This checksum gives your application greater confidence that it has received correct values in the face of possible reception errors.

Figure 22-6 illustrates an overview scope trace of the DHT11 signal. In this figure, the horizontal axis is dominated by the 30 ms of low signal driven by the Pi, to wake up the device. The DHT11 sends its 40 bits of data after the first initial spike, shown at the right. The datasheet indicates that the sensor should be queried no more than once per second.

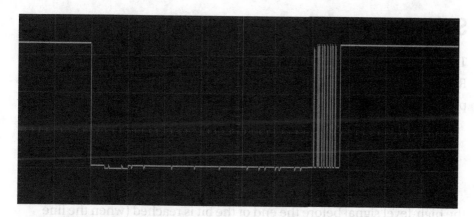

Figure 22-6. *Overview scope trace of the DHT11 signal*

A closeup of the DHT11 response data is shown in Figure 22-7. The first high pulse (at left) is from the Pi releasing the bus and allowing the pull-up resistor to raise the bus voltage. At 12 µs after this, the DHT11 pulls the bus low for 80 µs and then allows the bus to go high for another 80 µs. This marks the beginning of the 40 bits of data that will follow.

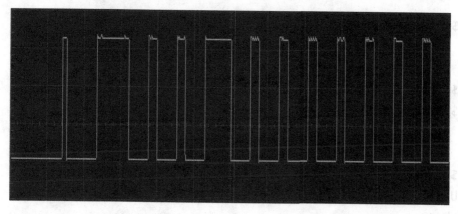

Figure 22-7. *Scope trace of the start of the DHT11 response data bits*

Software

The user space software written to read the DHT11 sensor on the Raspberry Pi uses the direct register access of the GPIO pin. The challenges presented by this approach include the following:

- Short timings: 26 to 70 µs

- Preemptive scheduling delays within the Linux kernel

One approach is to count how many times the program could read the high-level signal before the end of the bit is reached (when the line goes low). Then decide on 0 bits for shorter times and 1s for longer times. After some experimentation, a dividing line could be drawn, where shorter signals mean 0 while the others are 1s.

Source Code

The source code for this project will be found at the following directory:

```
$ cd ~/RPi/dht11
```

To rebuild the application from scratch, perform the following:

```
$ make clobber
$ make
```

There is help available using the -h option:

```
$ ./dht11 -h
Usage: ./dht11 [-g gpio] [-h]
where:
        -g gpio    Specify GPIO pin (22 is default)
        -h         This help
```

Timing

One of the primary challenges of this application is to perform fast and accurate timings. But we can't have accurate timing measurements with the NTP daemon (network time protocol) updating the system clock. So rather than rely on the wall clock sense of time, we use the Linux *monotonic* clock instead. This too can be tweaked by the system slightly, but we are guaranteed that this clock only increments forward in time.

Listing 22-1 illustrates the short inline function used to fetch the monotonic time from Raspbian Linux. The struct timespec is declared by Linux as:

```
struct timespec {
    time_t  tv_sec;    /* seconds */
    long    tv_nsec;   /* and nanoseconds */
}
```

So our timeofday() function will return seconds and nanoseconds.

Listing 22-1. The dht11.c, timeofday() function

```
0042: static inline void
0043: timeofday(struct timespec *t) {
0044:     clock_gettime(CLOCK_MONOTONIC,t);
0045: }
```

The general procedure for computing elapsed time then is to:

1. Capture the initial time (call it t0).

2. Capture the current time after the event (call it t1).

The a function of the form of ns_diff() in Listing 22-2 is used to compute the elapsed time.

407

Listing 22-2. The dht11.c, ns_diff() function to calculate elapsed time in nanoseconds

```
0057: static inline long
0058: ns_diff(struct timespec *t0,struct timespec *t1) {
0059:     int dsec = (int)(t1->tv_sec - t0->tv_sec);
0060:     long dns = t1->tv_nsec - t0->tv_nsec;
0061:
0062:     assert(dsec >= 0);
0063:     dns += dsec * 1000000000L;
0064:     return dns;
0065: }
```

Main Loop

The main loop is found in the main() function. After processing of command-line options, the top of the loop is illustrated in Listing 22-3.

Listing 22-3. The top of the main loop in dht11.c

```
0192: gpio_open();
0193:
0194: gpio_configure_io(gpio_pin,Output);
0195: gpio_write(gpio_pin,1);
0196:
0197: for (;; ++reading) {
0198:     wait_ready();
0199:
0200:     gpio_write(gpio_pin,1);
0201:     gpio_configure_io(gpio_pin,Output);
0202:     wait_ms(3);
```

Line 192 initializes the library for direct GPIO access (see source files libgp.c and libgp.h). Following that, the GPIO pin is configured as Output in line 194 and initially driven high in line 195.

The main loop begins in line 197. The counter variable reading is simply used to provide an incrementing reading counter in the output reports. Line 198 initiates the function wait_ready(), which will be described shortly. Its purpose is to prevent the program from querying the DHT11 device more often than once per second. If it is queried too often, the device simply fails to respond.

After it has been determined that the DHT11 device can be queried, line 200 sets the level of the GPIO output to high. Except for the first time into the loop, the GPIO is configured as an *input* pin. Setting it high before configuring it as an *output* in line 201 means that there is no glitch when transitioning from its current input state to high when the GPIO becomes an output again. Line 202 simply waits for 3 ms to allow the line to stabilize.

wait_ms()

To provide a reasonably accurate millisecond wait function, the poll(2) system call is used (Listing 22-4). This is normally used to monitor open file descriptors. But poll(2) can be used with no descriptors, taking advantage of its timeout argument (argument three in line 92). Notice how argument two indicates zero file descriptor entries.

Listing 22-4. The wait_ms() function in dht11.c

```
0087: static void
0088: wait_ms(int ms) {
0089: struct pollfd p[1];
0090: int rc;
0091:
```

```
0092: rc = poll(&p[0],0,ms);
0093: assert(!rc);
0094: }
```

wait_ready()

This function is used to prevent querying the device too often. Listing 22-5 illustrates the code used.

Listing 22-5. The wait_ready() function in dht11.c

```
0067: static void
0068: wait_ready(void) {
0069: static struct timespec t0 = {0L,0L};
0070: struct timespec t1;
0071:
0072: if ( !t0.tv_sec ) {
0073:         timeofday(&t0);
0074:         --t0.tv_sec;
0075: }
0076:
0077: for (;;) {
0078:         timeofday(&t1);
0079:         if ( ms_diff(&t0,&t1) >= 1000 ) {
0080:                 t0 = t1;
0081:                 return;
0082:         }
0083:         usleep(100);
0084: }
0085: }
```

The static value of variable t0 is established with zeros. When the code is entered for the first time, the date/time is initialized in line 73 and then subtracted by one second (line 74). Subtracting one allows an immediate pass the first time through.

The loop in lines 77 to 84 samples the time every hundred microseconds and returns in line 81 if we have at least one second elapsed, since the last device request.

Reading DHT11

Now comes the fun part—reading the device response. Listing 22-6 illustrates the logic used. Recall that line 206 drives the bus line low, to wake up the device. Then 30 ms is the delay time used before the GPIO is turned into an *input* pin (lines 207 and 208). By configuring the GPIO as an input pin, we now let the pull-up resistor take over and pull the bus voltage up to +3.3 V.

At this point, the DHT11 will eventually grab the bus and respond. We wait for a line change using the function wait_change() (line 210). It returns the current (final) state of the bus line as well as populating the variable nsec with the nanoseconds elapsed.

The first transition sometimes happens so fast (on Raspberry Pi 3 B+) that it sees its own GPIO line go from low to high, *before* the pull-up resistor has done its job. Line 219 tests for this, and if this is indeed true, we wait for one more signal transition—the one we care about, which is the the high to low transition (line 220). If the final state is still a 1-bit, or the time in nsec is too high, we reject the response and start over (lines 221 to 223).

Listing 22-6. Reading the DHT11 response in dht11.c

```
0206:        gpio_write(gpio_pin,0);
0207:        wait_ms(30);
0208:        gpio_configure_io(gpio_pin,Input);
0209:
```

```
0210:          b = wait_change(&nsec);
0211:
0212:          /*
0213:           * If the returned value is 1, it is likely
0214:           * that we were fast enough to catch the
0215:           * pullup resistor action. When that happens
0216:           * look for the next transition (expecting
0217:           * b == 0).
0218:           */
0219:          if ( b == 1 )
0220:              b = wait_change(&nsec);
0221:          if ( b || nsec > 20000 ) { // Expecting about 12 us
0222:              printf("%04d: Fail, b0=%d, %ld nsec\
                      n",reading,b,nsec);
0223:              continue;
0224:          }
0225:
0226:          /*
0227:           * This is the 80 us transition from 0 to 1:
0228:           */
0229:          b = wait_change(&nsec);
0230:          if ( !b || nsec < 40000 || nsec > 90000 ) {
0231:              printf("%04d: Fail, b1=%d, %ld
                      nsec\n",reading,b,nsec);
0232:              continue;
0233:          }
0234:
0235:          /*
0236:           * Wait for the 80 us transition from 1 to 0:
0237:           */
0238:          b = wait_change(&nsec);
```

```
0239:
0240:        if ( b != 0 || nsec < 40000 || nsec > 90000 ) {
0241:            printf("%04d: Fail, b2=%d, %ld
                nsec\n",reading,b,nsec);
0242:            continue;
0243:        }
0244:
0245:        /*
0246:         * Read the 40-bit value from the DHT11. The
0247:         * returned value is distilled into 16-bits:
0248:         */
0249:        unsigned resp = read_40bits();
```

Upon entry to line 229, the line is low. Waiting for the next transition should report that the bus has gone high, with a time near 80 µs. If the final state is not high, or the time is too long, the response is rejected in lines 230 to 232.

If that passes, the next transition from high to low is measured in lines 240 through 243. Again, if the signal measured is not correct, the response is rejected and the program tries again at the top of the loop.

Finally at line 259, the 40-bit response of the DHT11 is ready to be read.

wait_change()

The wait_change() function is used to monitor the GPIO for a signal change. If the signal was low initially, it waits until the signal goes high and returns on. If the signal was originally high, it waits until the signal goes low and returns zero. In addition to waiting for a state change, the number of nanoseconds elapsed is returned. The function is illustrated in Listing 22-7.

Listing 22-7. The wait_change() function from dht11.c

```
0024: static volatile bool timeout = false;
...
0096: static inline int
0097: wait_change(long *nsec) {
0098:   int b1;
0099:   struct timespec t0, t1;
0100:   int b0 = gpio_read(gpio_pin);
0101:
0102:   timeofday(&t0);
0103:
0104:   while ( (b1 = gpio_read(gpio_pin)) == b0 && !timeout )
0105:        ;
0106:   timeofday(&t1);
0107:
0108:   if ( !timeout ) {
0109:        *nsec = ns_diff(&t0,&t1);
0110:        return b1;
0111:   }
0112:   *nsec = 0;
0113:   return 0;
0114: }
```

The program takes a current reading of the GPIO and saves it in variable b0 (line 100). The initial time t0 is captured in line 102. Lines 104 and null statement in line 105 form a tight loop. The current GPIO reading is read and stashed into variable b1. As long as the value of b1 equals the initial value b0, the loop continues. The variable timeout is also tested. As long as the volatile bool timeout remains false, the loop continues. Later on, we'll see how the timeout value gets set.

The loop normally exits once the GPIO has changed from its initial value. The stop time is captured into t1 in line 106. As long as there is no timeout, line 109 computs and returns the number of nanoseconds elapsed. Line 110 returns the current state of the GPIO.

When a timeout has occurred, we simply return zero for the elapsed time and return zero for the current GPIO value. The purpose at this point is to break out of the while loop. Missed events can occur, especially since the Linux operating system can preempt the execution of the program. If it tries to read 40 bits of data but is missing the reading of one or two signal changes, the loop can be hung forever.

Timout Handling

Given the potential for a program hang, an interval timer is used. At the start of a critical section, the timer is started by calling set_timer(), in Listing 22-8. This starts a timer in the Linux kernel that we don't have to manage beyond starting.

The interval timer's configuration is established in the structure timer (line 28 to 31). We don't want the timer to restart, so the timer.it_interval member is initialized to zero (line 29). Lines 34 and 35 establish the time we want to elapse before the timer expires. Once the timer expires, it will not auto renew.

When the timer expires, the Linux kernel will call our timeout handler named sigalrm_handler() declared in lines 145 to 147. All it does is set the Boolean variable timeout to true. Signal handlers are called as asynchronously. Consequently they must never call non-reentrant routines like printf() or malloc() etc. because the call could arrive at any time. You would not want to call malloc() when the signal interrupted malloc() in the middle of doing its thing.

Also because the signal handler is *asynchronous*, its handling is like that of another thread. If the variable timeout were not declared volatile, the looping code might never notice that it was changed to true, because the compiler cached the value in a register.

415

Listing 22-8. The timer and handler in dht11.c

```
0026: static inline void
0027: set_timer(long usec) {
0028:    static struct itimerval timer = {
0029:        { 0, 0 },    // Interval
0030:        { 0, 0 }     // it_value
0031:    };
0032:    int rc;
0033:
0034:    timer.it_value.tv_sec = 0;
0035:    timer.it_value.tv_usec = usec;
0036:
0037:    rc = setitimer(ITIMER_REAL,&timer,NULL);
0038:    assert(!rc);
0039:    timeout = false;
0040: }
...
0144: static void
0145: sigalrm_handler(int signo) {
0146:    timeout = true;
0147: }
```

The initial setup of the timer handler for signal SIGALRM, is performed in the main program as shown in Listing 22-9. Once the timeout handler is established, it merely needs a call to set_timer() to start it "ticking." This is performed at the start of the larger loop that reads the signal on the bus. If the timer gets triggered before the entire response of the DHT11 is read, the loop is exited from line 104, of Listing 22-7.

Listing 22-9. The timer setup in dht11.c

```
0187:    new_action.sa_handler = sigalrm_handler;
0188:    sigemptyset(&new_action.sa_mask);
```

```
0189:   new_action.sa_flags = 0;
0190:   sigaction(SIGALRM,&new_action,NULL);
```

Demonstration

The demonstration program can be started once you have things wired. This example illustrates specifying the GPIO as 22 but this is the default.

```
$ ./dht11 -g22
0000: RH 32% Temperature 25 C
0001: RH 32% Temperature 26 C
0002: RH 32% Temperature 26 C
0003: RH 32% Temperature 26 C
0004: RH 32% Temperature 26 C
0005: RH 32% Temperature 26 C
0006: RH 32% Temperature 26 C
0007: RH 32% Temperature 26 C
0008: RH 32% Temperature 26 C
```

On a fast Pi, like the Pi 3 B+, you should see output like this. If you're not seeing any successful reads, then check your wiring. Don't forget the pull-up resistor.

However, due to missed events, it is possible to see some errors:

```
0040: RH 32% Temperature 26 C
0041: Fail, Checksum error.
0101: RH 32% Temperature 26 C
0102: RH 32% Temperature 26 C
0103: RH 32% Temperature 26 C
0104: RH 32% Temperature 26 C
0105: Fail, Checksum error.
0106: RH 32% Temperature 26 C
```

Don't be surprised by this because we are performing real-time measurement of signals on a non-real-time operating system. The Raspberry Pi Zero and Zero W are likely to see more errors due to the lower performance. The Zero will still return good readings often enough to make the project worthwhile. In a finished project, you will simply modify the code to suppress error reports.

Summary

This chapter has tackled the difficulty of reading the DHT11's real-time signal on a system that does not provide real-time scheduling. Through use of direct GPIO access, we obtained fast enough access to measure signal changes. Applying an interval timer provided recovery safety, if the program got stuck waiting for lost events. These are some of the sneaky things that must be done to solve thorny problems.

CHAPTER 23

Nunchuk-Mouse

You may not have a practical use for the Nintendo Wii Nunchuk as a Raspberry Pi mouse, but it serves as a good example of how LCD touchscreens supply their input events.

The Nunchuk has two buttons: an X-Y joystick; and an X, Y, and Z accelerometer. The sensor data is communicated through the I²C bus. This will give us a practice with the I²C C API as well. Let's have some fun implementing a Nunchuk pointing device for the X Window system desktop.

Project Overview

The challenge before us breaks down into two overall categories:

- The I²C data communication of the Nunchuk device

- Inserting the sensed data into the X Window system desktop event queue

Let's first examine I²C from a Linux API perspective and then complete the chapter inserting received events into the X Window system.

© Warren Gay 2018
W. Gay, *Advanced Raspberry Pi*, https://doi.org/10.1007/978-1-4842-3948-3_23

Nunchuk Features

The basic physical and data characteristics of the Nunchuk are listed in Table 23-1.

Table 23-1. *Nunchuk Controls and Data Characteristics*

User-Interface Features	Bits	Data	Hardware/Chip
C Button	1	Boolean	Membrane switch
Z button	1	Boolean	Membrane switch
X-Y joystick	8x2	Integers	30 *k*ohm potentiometers
X, Y, and Z accelerometer	10x3	Integers	ST LIS3L02 series

For application as a mouse, the C and Z buttons fill in for the left and right mouse buttons. The joystick is used to position the mouse cursor. While the Nunchuk normally operates at a clock rate of 400 kHz, it works just fine at the 100 kHz I^2C rate.

Connector Pin-Out

There are four wires: two of which are power and ground (some units may have two additional wires, one that connects to the shield, and the other to the unused center pin). The remaining two wires are used for I^2C communication (SDA and SCL). The connections looking into the cable-end connector are shown in Table 23-2.

Table 23-2. *Nuncheck Cable Connections*

SCL	Notch	Gnd
+3.3 V	N/C	SDA

The Nunchuk connector is annoyingly nonstandard. Some folks have rolled their own adapters using a double-sided PCB to mate with the inner connections. Others have purchased adapters from eBay. Cheap Nunchuk clones may also be found on eBay. With the growing number of clone adapters becoming available at more-competitive prices, there is less reason to cut off the clone's connector.

Tip   Beware of Nunchuk forgeries.

If you do cut off the connector, you will quickly discover that there is no standard wire color scheme. The only thing you can count on is that the pins are laid out as in Table 23-2. If you have a genuine Wii Nunchuk, the listed wire colors in Table 23-3 might be valid. The column labeled Clone Wire lists the wire colors of my own clone's wires. *Yours will likely differ.*

Table 23-3.   *Nunchuk Connector Wiring*

Pin	Wii Wire	CloneWire[†]	Description	P1
Gnd	White	White	Ground	P1-25
SDA	Green	Blue	Data	P1-03
+3.3 V	Red	Red	Power	P1-01
SCL	Yellow	Green	Clock	P1-05

[†]*Clone wire colors vary!*

Before you cut that connector off that clone, consider that you'll need to trace the connector to a wire color. Cut the cable, leaving about 3 inches of wire for the connector. Then you can cut the insulation off and trace the pins to a wire by using an ohmmeter (or by looking inside the cable-end connector).

Figure 23-1 shows the author's clone Nunchuk with the connector cut off. In place of the connector, solid wire ends were soldered on and a piece of heat shrink applied over the solder joint. The solid wire ends are perfect for plugging into a prototyping breadboard.

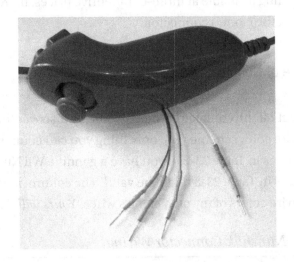

Figure 23-1. *Nunchuk clone with wire ends soldered on*

Enable I2C

You'll need to enable your I2C support. Enter the Raspberry Pi Configuration panel and turn on I2C (Figure 23-2). Then reboot to make it take effect.

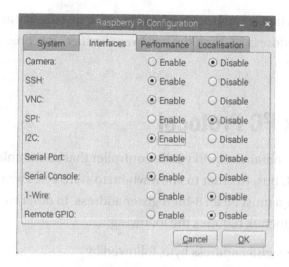

Figure 23-2. *Enabling I2C support in the Raspberry Pi Configuration panel*

Testing the Connection

Plug in the I²C connection to the Pi and probe it with the `i2cdetect` command.

```
$ i2cdetect -y 1
    0  1  2  3  4  5  6  7  8  9  a  b  c  d  e  f
00:          -- -- -- -- -- -- -- -- -- -- -- -- --
10: -- -- -- -- -- -- -- -- -- -- -- -- -- -- -- --
20: -- -- -- -- -- -- -- -- -- -- -- -- -- -- -- --
30: -- -- -- -- -- -- -- -- -- -- -- -- -- -- -- --
40: -- -- -- -- -- -- -- -- -- -- -- -- -- -- -- --
50: -- -- 52 -- -- -- -- -- -- -- -- -- -- -- -- --
60: -- -- -- -- -- -- -- -- -- -- -- -- -- -- -- --
70: -- -- -- -- -- -- -- --
$
```

If the Nunchuk is working, it will show up in this display at hexadecimal address 52. With the hardware verified, it is time to move on to the software.

Nunchuk I²C Protocol

The Nunchuk contains a quirky little controller that communicates through the I²C bus. In order to know where to store bytes written to it, the first byte written must be an 8-bit register address. In other words, each write to the Nunchuk requires the following:

- One *register* address byte, followed by
- Zero or more *data* bytes to be written to sequential locations

Thus for write operations, the first byte sent to the Nunchuk tells it where to begin. Any following write bytes received are written with the register address incremented.

Tip   Don't confuse the register address with the Nunchuk's I²C address of 0x52.

It is also possible to write the register address and then read bytes instead. This procedure specifies the starting location of data bytes to be read.

The quirky aspect of the Nunchuk controller is that there must be a short delay between writing the register address and reading the data. Performing the write followed by an immediate read does not work. Writing data immediately after the register address does succeed, however.

Encryption

The Nunchuk is designed to provide an *encrypted* link. However, that can be disabled by initializing it a certain way. The defeat procedure is as follows:

1. Write 0x55 to Nunchuk register location 0xF0.

2. Pause.

3. Write 0x00 to Nunchuk register location 0xFB.

The following illustrates the message sequence involved. Notice that this is performed as *two* separate I²C write operations:

Write		Pause	Write	
F0	55	-	FB	00

Once this is successfully performed, all future data is returned unencrypted.

Read Sensor Data

The whole point of the Nunchuk is to read its sensor data. When requested, it returns six bytes of data formatted as shown in Table 23-4.

Table 23-4. *Nunchuk Data*

Byte	Bits	Description
1		Analog stick x-axis value
2		Analog stick y-axis value
3		X acceleration bits 9:2
4		Y acceleration bits 9:2
5		Z acceleration bits 9:2
6	0	Z button pressed (active low)
	1	C button pressed (active low)
	3:2	X acceleration bits 1:0
	5:4	Y acceleration bits 1:0
	7:6	Z acceleration bits 1:0

Some of the data is split over multiple bytes. For example, the X acceleration bits 9:2 are obtained from byte 3. The lowest 2 bits are found in byte 6, in bits 3 and 2. These together form the 9-bit X acceleration value.

To retrieve this data, we are always required to tell the Nunchuk where to begin. So the sequence always begins with a write of offset 0x00 followed by a pause:

Write	Pause	Read 6 bytes					
00	-	01	02	03	04	05	06

The Nunchuk doesn't allow us to do this in one ioctl(2) call, as two I/O messages. A write of zero must be followed by a pause. Then the six data bytes can be read as a separate I²C read operation. If the pause is too long, however, the Nunchuk controller times out, resulting in incorrect data being returned. So we must do things the Nunchuk way.

Linux uinput Interface

While reading the Nunchuk is fun, we need to apply it to our desktop as a mouse. We need to insert mouse events based on what we read from it.

The Linux uinput driver allows programmers to develop nonstandard input drivers so that events can be injected into the input stream. This approach allows new input streams to be added without changing application code (like touchscreen input).

Documentation for the uinput API can be found at the following site:

- "1.7. uinput module" https://www.kernel.org/doc/html/v4.12/input/uinput.html

Another source of information is the device driver source code itself:

drivers/input/misc/uinput.c

The example program provided in this chapter can help pull all the necessary details together.

Working with Header Files

The header files required for the uinput API include the following:

```
#include <sys/ioctl.h>
#include <linux/input.h>
#include <linux/uinput.h>
```

To compile code, making use of I²C, you also need to install the libi2c development library, if you have not done so already:

```
$ sudo apt-get install libi2c-dev
```

Opening the Device Node

The connection to the uinput device driver is made by opening the device node:

```
/dev/uinput
```

The following is an example of the required open(2) call:

```
int fd;

fd = open("/dev/uinput",O_WRONLY|O_NONBLOCK);
if ( fd < 0 ) {
    perror("Opening /dev/uinput");
    ...
```

Configuring Events

In order to inject events, the driver must be configured to accept them. Each call to ioctl(2) in the following code enables one class of events based on the argument *event*. The following is a generalized example:

```
int rc;
unsigned long event = EV_KEY;

rc = ioctl(fd,UI_SET_EVBIT,event);
assert(!rc);
```

The list of UI_SET_EVBIT event types is provided in Table 23-5. The most commonly needed event types are EV_SYN, EV_KEY, and EV_REL (or EV_ABS).

Table 23-5. *List of uinput Event Types*

From Header File input.h

Macro	Description
EV_SYN	Event synchronization/separation
EV_KEY	Key/button state changes
EV_REL	Relative axis mouse-like changes
EV_ABS	Absolute axis mouse-like changes
EV_MSC	Miscellaneous events
EV_SW	Binary (switch) state changes
EV_LED	LED on/off changes
EV_SND	Output to sound devices
EV_REP	For use with autorepeating devices
EV_FF	Force feedback commands to input device
EV_PWR	Power button/switch event
EV_FF_STATUS	Receive force feedback device status

Caution   Do not or (|) the event types together. The device driver expects each event type to be registered *separately*.

Configure EV_KEY

Once you have registered your intention to provide EV_KEY events, you need to register all key codes that might be used. While this seems a nuisance, it does guard against garbage being injected by an errant program. The following code registers its intention to inject an Escape key code:

```
int rc;

rc = ioctl(fd,UI_SET_KEYBIT,KEY_ESC);
assert(!rc);
```

To configure all possible keys, a loop can be used. But do not register key code 0 (KEY_RESERVED) nor 255; the include file indicates that code 255 is reserved for the special needs of the AT keyboard driver.

```
int rc;
unsigned long key;

for ( key=1; key<255; ++key ) {
    rc = ioctl(fd,UI_SET_KEYBIT,key);
    assert(!rc);
}
```

Mouse Buttons

In addition to key codes, the same ioctl(2,UI_SET_KEYBIT) call is used to register mouse, joystick, and other button events. This includes touch events from trackpads, tablets, and touchscreens. The long list of button codes is defined in header file linux/input.h. The usual suspects are shown in Table 23-6.

Table 23-6. *Key Event Macros*

Macro	Synonym	Description
BTN_LEFT	BTN_MOUSE	Left mouse button
BTN_RIGHT		Right mouse button
BTN_MIDDLE		Middle mouse button
BTN_SIDE		Side mouse button

The following example shows the application's intention to inject left and right mouse button events:

```
int rc;

rc=ioctl(fd,UI_SET_KEYBIT,BTN_LEFT);
assert(!rc);
rc = ioctl(fd,UI_SET_KEYBIT,BTN_RIGHT);
assert(!rc);
```

Configure EV_REL

In order to inject EV_REL events, the types of relative movements must be registered in advance. The complete list of valid argument codes is shown in Table 23-7. The following example indicates an intention to inject x and y relative axis movements:

```
rc = ioctl(fd,UI_SET_RELBIT,REL_X);
assert(!rc);
rc = ioctl(fd,UI_SET_RELBIT,REL_Y);
assert(!rc);
```

Table 23-7. *UI_SET_RELBIT Options*

Macro	Intention
REL_X	Send relative X changes
REL_Y	Send relative Y changes
REL_Z	Send relative Z changes
REL_RX	x-axis tilt
REL_RY	y-axis tilt
REL_RZ	z-axis tilt
REL_HWHEEL	Horizontal wheel change
REL_DIAL	Dial-turn change
REL_WHEEL	Wheel change
REL_MISC	Miscellaneous

Configure EV_ABS

While this project doesn't use the EV_ABS option, it may be useful to know about this feature. This event represents absolute cursor movements and it too requires registration of intentions. The complete list of EV_ABS codes is defined in linux/input.h. The usual suspects are defined in Table 23-8.

Table 23-8. *Absolute Cursor Movement Event Macros*

Macro	Description
ABS_X	Move X to this absolute X coordinate
ABS_Y	Move Y to this absolute Y coordinate

The following is an example of registering intent for absolute x- and y-axis events:

```
int rc;

rc = ioctl(fd,UI_SET_ABSBIT,ABS_X);
assert(!rc);
rc = ioctl(fd,UI_SET_ABSBIT,ABS_X);
assert(!rc);
```

In addition to registering your intentions to inject these events, you need to define some coordinate parameters. The following is an example:

```
struct uinput_user_dev uinp;

uinp.absmin[ABS_X] = 0;
uinp.absmax[ABS_X] = 1023;

uinp.absfuzz[ABS_X] = 0;
uinp.absflat[ABS_X] = 0;

uinp.absmin[ABS_Y] = 0;
uinp.absmax[ABS_Y] = 767;

uinp.absfuzz[ABS_Y] = 0;
uinp.absflat[ABS_Y] = 0;
```

These values must be established as part of your ioctl(2,UI_DEV_CREATE) operation, which is described next.

Creating the Node

After all registrations with the uinput device driver have been completed, the final step is to create the uinput node. This will be used by the receiving application, in order to read injected events. This involves two programming steps:

1. Write the struct `uinput_user_dev` information to the file descriptor with `write(2)`.

2. Perform an `ioctl(2,UI_DEV_CREATE)` to cause the uinput node to be created.

The first step involves populating the following structures:

```
struct input_id {
    __u16       bustype;
    __u16       vendor;
    __u16       product;
    __u16       version;
};

struct uinput_user_dev {
    char        name[UINPUT_MAX_NAME_SIZE];
    struct input_id id;
    int         ff_effects_max;
    int         absmax[ABS_CNT];
    int         absmin[ABS_CNT];
    int         absfuzz[ABS_CNT];
    int         absflat[ABS_CNT];
};
```

An example populating these structures is provided next. If you plan to inject EV_ABS events, you must also populate the abs members, mentioned in the "Configure EV_ABS" section.

```
struct uinput_user_dev uinp;
int rc;

memset(&uinp,0,sizeof uinp);

strncpy(uinp.name,"nunchuk",UINPUT_MAX_NAME_SIZE);
```

```
uinp.id.bustype = BUS_USB;
uinp.id.vendor = 0x1;
uinp.id.product = 0x1;
uinp.id.version = 1;

//      uinp.absmax[ABS_X] = 1023; /*EV_ABS only */
//      ...

rc = write(fd,&uinp,sizeof(uinp));
assert(rc == sizeof(uinp));
```

The call to write(2) passes all of this important information to the uinput driver. Now all that remains is to request a device node to be created for application use:

```
int rc;
```

```
rc = ioctl(fd,UI_DEV_CREATE);
assert(!rc);
```

This step causes the uinput driver to make a device node appear in the pseudo directory /dev/input. An example is shown here:

```
$ ls -l /dev/input
total 0
crw-rw---- 1 root input 13, 64 Jul 26 06:11 event0
crw-rw---- 1 root input 13, 63 Jul 26 04:50 mice
crw-rw---- 1 root input 13, 32 Jul 26 06:11 mouse0
```

The device /dev/input/event0 was the Nunchuck's created uinput node, when the program was run.

Posting EV_KEY Events

The following code snippet shows how to post a key down event, followed
by a key up event:

```
1 static void
2 uinput_postkey(int fd,unsigned key) {
3     struct input_event ev;
4     int rc;
5
6     memset(&ev,0,sizeof(ev));
7     ev.type = EV_KEY;
8     ev.code = key;
9     ev.value = 1;
10
11    rc = write(fd,&ev,sizeof(ev));
12    assert(rc == sizeof(ev));
13
14    ev.value = 0;
15    rc = write(fd,&ev,sizeof(ev));
16    assert(rc == sizeof(ev));
17 }
```

From this example, you see that each event is posted by writing a
suitably initialized input_event structure. The example illustrates that the
member named type was set to EV_KEY, code was set to the key code, and a
keypress was indicated by setting the member value to 1 (line 9).

To inject a key up event, value is reset to 0 (line 14) and the structure is
written again.

Mouse button events work the same way, except that you supply
mouse button codes for the code member. For example:

```
memset(&ev,0,sizeof(ev));
ev.type = EV_KEY;
ev.code = BTN_RIGHT;            /*Right click */
ev.value = 1;
```

Posting EV_REL Events

To post a relative mouse movement, we populate the input_event as a
type EV_REL. The member code is set to the type of event (REL_X or REL_Y in
this example), with the value for the relative movement established in the
member value:

```
static void
uinput_movement(int fd,int x,inty) {
    struct input_event ev;
    int rc;

    memset(&ev,0,sizeof(ev));
    ev.type = EV_REL;
    ev.code = REL_X;
    ev.value = x;

    rc = write(fd,&ev,sizeof(ev));
    assert(rc == sizeof(ev));

    ev.code = REL_Y;
    ev.value = y;
    rc = write(fd,&ev,sizeof(ev));
    assert (rc == sizeof(ev));
}
```

Notice that the REL_X and REL_Y events are created separately. What if
you want the receiving application to avoid acting on these separately? The
EV_SYN event helps out in this regard (next).

Posting EV_SYN Events

The uinput driver postpones delivery of events until the EV_SYN event has been injected. The SYN_REPORT type of EV_SYN event causes the queued events to be flushed out and reported to the interested application. The following is an example:

```
static void
uinput_syn(int fd) {
    struct input_event ev;
    int rc;

    memset(&ev,0,sizeof(ev));
    ev.type = EV_SYN;
    ev.code = SYN_REPORT;
    ev.value = 0;
    rc = write(fd,&ev,sizeof(ev));
    assert(rc == sizeof(ev));
}
```

For a mouse relative movement event, for example, you can inject a REL_X and REL_Y, followed by a SYN_REPORT event to have them seen by the application as a group.

Closing uinput

There are two steps involved:

1. Destruction of the /dev/input/event%d node

2. Closing of the file descriptor

The following example shows both:

```
int rc;

rc = ioctl(fd,UI_DEV_DESTROY);
assert(!rc);
close(fd);
```

Closing the file descriptor implies the ioctl(2,UI_DEV_DESTROY) operation. The application has the option of destroying the device node while keeping the file descriptor open.

X-Window

The creation of our new uinput device node is useful only if our desktop system is listening to it. Raspbian Linux's X-Window system needs a little configuration help to notice our Frankenstein creation. The following definition can be added to the /usr/share/X11/xorg.conf.d directory. Name the file 20-nunchuk.conf:

```
# Nunchuck event queue

Section "InputClass"
        Identifier "Raspberry Pi Nunchuk"
        Option "Mode" "Relative"
        MatchDevicePath "/dev/input/event0"
        Driver "evdev"
EndSection

# End 20-nunchuk.conf
```

This configuration change works only if your Nunchuk uinput device shows up as /dev/input/event0. If you have other specialized input device creations on your Raspberry Pi, it could well be named event1 or some other number. See the upcoming section "Testing the Nunchuk" for troubleshooting information.

Restart your X-Window server to have the configuration file noticed.

Tip   Normally, your Nunchuk program should be running already. But the X-Window server will notice it when the Nunchuk does start.

Input Utilities

When writing `uinput` event-based code, you will find the package `input-utils` to be extremely helpful. The package can be installed from the command line as follows:

```
$ sudo apt-get install input-utils
```

The following commands are installed:

`lsinput(8)`: List `uinput` devices

`input-events(8)`: Dump selected `uinput` events

`input-kbd(8)`: Keyboard map display

This chapter uses the first two utilities: `lsinput(8)` and `input-events(8)`.

Testing the Nunchuk

Now that the hardware, drivers, and software are ready, it is time to exercise the Nunchuk. Unfortunately, there is no direct way for applications to identify your created `uinput` node. When the Nunchuk program runs, the node may show up as `/dev/input/event0` or some other numbered node if it already exists. If you wanted to start a Nunchuk driver as part of the Linux boot process, you need to create a script to edit the file with the actual device name registered. The affected X-Windows config file is as follows:

```
/usr/share/X11/xord.conf.d/20-nunchuk.conf
```

The script (shown next) determines which node the Nunchuk program created. The following is an example run, while the Nunchuk program was running:

```
$ ./findchuk
/dev/input/event0
```

When the node is not found, the findchuk script exits with a non-zero code and prints a message to stderr:

```
$ ./findchuk
Nunchuk uinput device not found.
$ echo $?
1
```

The findchuk script is shown in Listing 23-1.

Listing 23-1. The findchuk shell script

```
#!/bin/bash
####################################################################
# Find the Nunchuck
####################################################################
#
# This script locates the Nunchuk uinput device by searching the
# /sys/devices/virtual/input pseudo directory for names of the form:
# input[0_9]*. For all subdirectories found, check the ./name
#   pseudo
# file, which will contain "nunchuk". Then we derive the /dev path
# from a sibling entry named event[0_9]*. That will tell use the
# /dev/input/event%d pathname, for the Nunchuk.
```

```
DIR=/sys/devices/virtual/input  # Top level directory
set_eu

cd "$DIR"
find . —type d —name 'input[0—9]*' | (
    set —eu
    while read dirname ; do
            cd "$DIR/$dirname"
            if [—f "name"] ; then
                    set +e
                    name=$(cat name)
                    set —e
                    if [ $(cat name) = nunchuk ] ; then
                            event="/dev/input/$
                            (ls—devent[0—9]*)"
                            echo $event
                            exit 0                    # Found it
                    fi
            fi
    done
    echo "Nunchuk uinput device not found." >&2
    exit 1
)
# End findchuk
```

Testing ./nunchuk

When you want to see what Nunchuk data is being received, you can add
the -d command-line option:

```
$ ./nunchuk —d
Raw nunchuk data: [83] [83] [5C] [89] [A2] [63]
.stick_x = 0083 (131)
```

```
.stick_y = 0083 (131)
.accel_x = 0170 (368)
.accel_y = 0226 (550)
.accel_z = 0289 (649)
.z_button= 0
.c_button= 0
```

The first line reports the raw bytes of data that were received. The remainder of the lines report the data in its decoded form. While the raw data reports the button presses as active low, the Z and C buttons are reported as 1 in the decoded data. The value in the left column is in hexadecimal format, while the value in parentheses is shown in decimal.

Utility lsinputs

When the Nunchuk program is running, you should be able to see the Nunchuk uinput device in the list:

```
$ lsinput
/dev/input/event0
   bustype : BUS_USB
   vendor  : 0x1
   product : 0x1
   version : 1
   name    : "nunchuk"
   bits ev : EV_SYN EV_KEY EV_REL
```

In this example, the Nunchuk shows up as event0.

Utility input-events

When developing uinput-related code, the input-events utility is a great help. Here we run it for event0 (the argument 0 on the command line), where the Nunchuk mouse device is:

```
$ input-events 0
/dev/input/event0
   bustype   : BUS_USB
   vendor    : 0x1
   product   : 0x1
   version   : 1
   name      : "nunchuk"
   bits ev   : EV_SYN EV_KEY EV_REL

waiting for events
23:35:15.345105: EV_KEY BTN_LEFT (0x110) pressed
23:35:15.345190: EV_SYN code=0 value=0
23:35:15.517611: EV_KEY BTN_LEFT (0x110) released
23:35:15.517713: EV_SYN code=0 value=0
23:35:15.833640: EV_KEY BTN_RIGHT (0x111) pressed
23:35:15.833727: EV_SYN code=0 value=0
23:35:16.019363: EV_KEY BTN_RIGHT (0x111) released
23:35:16.019383: EV_SYN code=0 value=0
23:35:16.564129: EV_REL REL_X -1
23:35:16.564213: EV_REL REL_Y 1
23:35:16.564261: EV_SYN code=0 value=0
...
```

The Program

Some of the interesting aspects of the I²C programming are presented as an example for I²C device programming in C. The project directory is:

```
$ cd ~/RPi/nunchuk
```

The source module that will be presented is named nunchuck.c.

To gain access to the I2C bus, we must first open it as it is done in Listing 23-2. Line 44 opens the bus, identified by /dev/i2s-1. This will fail if the I²C bus has not been enabled in the Raspberry Pi control panel.

Listing 23-2. Opening the I2C bus in nunchuk.c

```
0039: static void
0040: i2c_init(const char *node) {
0041:   unsigned long i2c_funcs = 0;     /* Support flags */
0042:   int rc;
0043:
0044:   i2c_fd = open(node,O_RDWR);   /* Open driver /dev/i2s-1 */
0045:   if ( i2c_fd < 0 ) {
0046:         perror("Opening /dev/i2s-1");
0047:         puts("Check that I2C has been enabled in the "
                  "control panel\n");
0048:         abort();
0049:   }
0050:
0051:   /*
0052:    * Make sure the driver supports plain I2C I/O:
0053:    */
0054:   rc = ioctl(i2c_fd,I2C_FUNCS,&i2c_funcs);
0055:   assert(rc >= 0);
0056:   assert(i2c_funcs & I2C_FUNC_I2C);
0057: }
```

Once the bus has been opened successfully, the ioctl(2) call in line 54 returns the functional support available. The assert macro in line 56 tests that normal I²C functions are available using the macro I2C_FUNC_I2C. If no bits remain true after applying the macro, the assertion will abort the program.

The function nunchuk_init() is used to initialize the nunchuk and defeat the encryption for it (Listing 23-3).

Listing 23-3. Initializing the Nunchuk in nunchuk.c

```
0062: static void
0063: nunchuk_init(void) {
0064:   static char init_msg1[] = { 0xF0, 0x55 };
0065:   static char init_msg2[] = { 0xFB, 0x00 };
0066:   struct i2c_rdwr_ioctl_data msgset;
0067:   struct i2c_msg iomsgs[1];
0068:   int rc;
0069:
0070:   iomsgs[0].addr = 0x52;        /* Address of Nunchuk */
0071:   iomsgs[0].flags = 0;          /* Write */
0072:   iomsgs[0].buf = init_msg1;    /* Nunchuk 2 byte
                                          sequence */
0073:   iomsgs[0].len = 2;            /* 2 bytes */
0074:
0075:   msgset.msgs = iomsgs;
0076:   msgset.nmsgs = 1;
0077:
0078:   rc = ioctl(i2c_fd,I2C_RDWR,&msgset);
0079:   assert(rc == 1);
0080:
0081:   timed_wait(0,200,0);          /* Nunchuk needs time */
0082:
0083:   iomsgs[0].addr = 0x52;        /* Address of Nunchuk */
0084:   iomsgs[0].flags = 0;          /* Write */
0085:   iomsgs[0].buf = init_msg2;    /* Nunchuk 2 byte
                                          sequence */
0086:   iomsgs[0].len = 2;            /* 2 bytes */
```

```
0087:
0088:    msgset.msgs = iomsgs;
0089:    msgset.nmsgs = 1;
0090:
0091:    rc = ioctl(i2c_fd,I2C_RDWR,&msgset);
0092:    assert(rc == 1);
0093: }
```

Lines 70 to 76 initialize the structures to send the initial message to the nunchuk. Lines 78 and 79 communicate this information to the device. Line 81 provides the necessary pause for the nunchuk controller. Lines 83 to 92 send the followup message to defeat the encryption.

The last code listing presented is the code used to read the nunchuk (Listing 23-4). Line 106 is a delay to prevent multiple reads from overwhelming the I²C device.

Listing 23-4. The nunchuk_read() function in nunchuk.c

```
0098: static int
0099: nunchuk_read(nunchuk_t *data) {
0100:    struct i2c_rdwr_ioctl_data msgset;
0101:    struct i2c_msg iomsgs[1];
0102:    char zero[1] = { 0x00 };          /* Written byte */
0103:    unsigned t;
0104:    int rc;
0105:
0106:    timed_wait(0,15000,0);
0107:
0108:    /*
0109:     * Write the nunchuk register address of 0x00 :
0110:     */
0111:    iomsgs[0].addr = 0x52;            /* Nunchuk address */
0112:    iomsgs[0].flags = 0;             /* Write */
```

```
0113:    iomsgs[0].buf = zero;              /* Sending buf */
0114:    iomsgs[0].len = 1;                 /* 6 bytes */
0115:
0116:    msgset.msgs = iomsgs;
0117:    msgset.nmsgs = 1;
0118:
0119:    rc = ioctl(i2c_fd,I2C_RDWR,&msgset);
0120:    if ( rc < 0 )
0121:            return -1;                  /* I/O error */
0122:
0123:    timed_wait(0,200,0);                /* Zzzz, nunchuk needs
                                                   time */
0124:
0125:    /*
0126:     * Read 6 bytes starting at 0x00 :
0127:     */
0128:    iomsgs[0].addr = 0x52;                      /* Nunchuk
                                                           address */
0129:    iomsgs[0].flags = I2C_M_RD;                 /* Read */
0130:    iomsgs[0].buf = (char *)data->raw;          /* Receive raw
                                                           bytes here */
0131:    iomsgs[0].len = 6;                          /* 6 bytes */
0132:
0133:    msgset.msgs = iomsgs;
0134:    msgset.nmsgs = 1;
0135:
0136:    rc = ioctl(i2c_fd,I2C_RDWR,&msgset);
0137:    if ( rc < 0 )
0138:            return -1;                          /* Failed */
0139:
0140:    data->stick_x = data->raw[0];
```

```
0141:    data->stick_y = data->raw[1];
0142:    data->accel_x = data->raw[2] << 2;
0143:    data->accel_y = data->raw[3] << 2;
0144:    data->accel_z = data->raw[4] << 2;
0145:
0146:    t = data->raw[5];
0147:    data->z_button = t & 1 ? 0 : 1;
0148:    data->c_button = t & 2 ? 0 : 1;
0149:    t >>= 2;
0150:    data->accel_x |= t & 3;
0151:    t >>= 2;
0152:    data->accel_y |= t & 3;
0153:    t >>= 2;
0154:    data->accel_z |= t & 3;
0155:    return 0;
0156: }
```

Lines 111 to 117 prepare a message to tell the nunchuk that we want to read it starting from register zero for six bytes. The ioctl(2) call in line 199 initiates it. Again, time is given to the quirky nunchuk controller in line 123. After that, it is safe to issue the read command of six bytes (lines 128 to 136).

The remaining lines 140 to 155 extract the relevant information out of the nunchuk register information returned.

Summary

This chapter introduced the uinput mechanism for adding devices to the Raspberry Pi's graphical desktop. Additionally, it served to provide a working example of an I²C C program. With the programming and input utilities provided, you are on your way to build custom interfaces of your own creation.

CHAPTER 24

LCD HDMI Display

Some Pi projects are best served with a simple LCD display. The associated touch control frees you from a keyboard and mouse. This chapter will examine one example of a 5-inch 800x480 pixel LCD touchscreen and describe how to set it up.

The Display Unit

The featured display unit was advertised as "5 Inch 800 x 480 HD TFT LCD Touch Screen For Raspberry PI 2 Model B / B+ / A+ / B" and sold for approximately $42 USD. It features a 4-wire resistive XPT2046 touch controller. Figure 24-1 illustrates what comes in the kit.

© Warren Gay 2018
W. Gay, *Advanced Raspberry Pi*, https://doi.org/10.1007/978-1-4842-3948-3_24

Figure 24-1. *The 5 Inch HDMI Display kit with stylus, DVD, and LCD unit (with plastic covering still attached). USB power cable is not included.*

The backside of the LCD shows an HDMI connector (Figure 24-2, bottom middle), a power USB connector (right of HDMI connector), a backlight switch (upper right), a 13x2 connector (upper center), and a LVDS connector (bottom left).

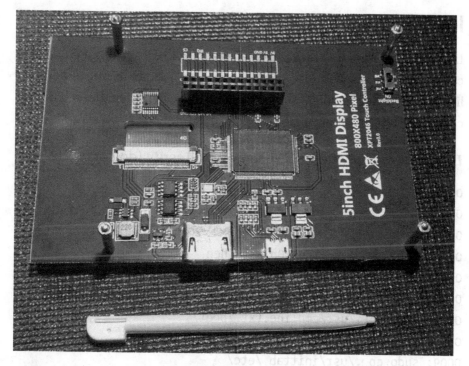

Figure 24-2. *The backside of the 5 Inch HDMI Display with four stand-offs screwed in*

If you read the included DVD instructions, you are expected to run a script named `LCD5-show` but don't run it—it is out of step with the current releases of Raspbian Linux. In fact, the script may leave your Pi unbootable after it is run. This chapter will use the script for a guide, with the corrections applied.

Installation

The first thing to do is to copy the software from DVD or fetch it with git. The following `git` command fetches the software and places it into the ~pi/LCD directory:

```
$ git clone https://github.com/goodtft/LCD-show.git ./LCD
$ cd ./LCD
```

Install Script

Listing 24-1 shows the provided install script that will act as our guide but cannot be used directly. It may render your Pi unbootable. The underlined lines in the listing highlight some problem areas. Let's step through the corrected steps manually in the sections that follow.

Listing 24-1. Provided LCD5-show install script (do not run!)

```
0001: #!/bin/bash
0002: sudo rm -rf /etc/X11/xorg.conf.d/40-libinput.conf
0003: sudo cp -rf ./boot/config-5.txt /boot/config.txt
0004: if [ -b /dev/mmcblk0p7 ]; then
0005: sudo cp ./usr/cmdline.txt-noobs /boot/cmdline.txt
0006: else
0007: sudo cp ./usr/cmdline.txt /boot/
0008: fi
0009: sudo cp ./usr/inittab /etc/
0010: sudo cp -rf ./usr/99-fbturbo.conf-HDMI /usr/share/X11/
       xorg.conf.d/99-fbturbo.conf
0011: sudo mkdir /etc/X11/xorg.conf.d
0012: sudo cp -rf ./usr/99-calibration.conf-5 /etc/X11/xorg.
       conf.d/99-calibration.conf
0013: nodeplatform=`uname -n`
0014: kernel=`uname -r`
0015: version=`uname -v`
0016: if test "$nodeplatform" = "raspberrypi";then
0017: echo "this is raspberrypi kernel"
0018: version=${version%% *}
0019: version=${version#*#}
0020: echo $version
0021: if test $version -lt 970;then
```

```
0022: echo "reboot"
0023: else
0024: echo "need to update touch configuration"
0025: if test $version -ge 1023;then
0026: echo "install xserver-xorg-input-evdev_2.10.5-1"
0027: sudo dpkg -i -B xserver-xorg-input-evdev_2.10.5-1_armhf.deb
0028: else
0029: echo "install xserver-xorg-input-evdev_1%3a2.10.3-1"
0030: sudo dpkg -i -B xserver-xorg-input-evdev_1%3a2.10.3-1_
      armhf.deb
0031: fi
0032: sudo cp -rf /usr/share/X11/xorg.conf.d/10-evdev.conf \
                  /usr/share/X11/xorg.conf.d/45-evdev.conf
0033: echo "reboot"
0034: fi
0035: else
0036: echo "this is not raspberrypi kernel, no need to update
      touch configure, reboot"
0037: fi
0038: sudo reboot
```

Backup

Before changing anything on your system, back up a couple of critical files
in case you want to restore the configuration later. Copy the following two
files to your home directory or a place of your own choosing:

```
# cp /boot/config.txt ~pi/config.txt.bak
# cp /boot/cmdline.txt ~pi/cmdline.txt.bak
```

To restore your original configuration, you merely need to copy these
back and reboot.

File 40-libinput.conf

The install script in Listing 24-1, line 2 attempts to delete a file that does not exist (there is no /etc/X11/xorg.conf.d directory provided by Raspbian Linux). But there is a file in /usr/share/X11/xord.conf.d/40-libinput.conf. You may find that you can leave it there but I recommend that you rename it, to avoid any possible conflict. You'll need to undo this later, if you choose to restore your system to its original state.

To disable it without deleting it, simply rename it with a different suffix (like .was).

```
# mv /usr/share/X11/xorg.conf.d/40-libinput.conf \
    /usr/share/X11/xorg.conf.d/40-libinput.conf.was
```

Now is a good time to change to your LCD software directory, if you are not already at that directory:

```
# cd ~pi/LCD
```

Edit /boot/config.txt

If you ran the install script from Listing 24-1, line 3 would have wiped out any changes that you previously made to your /boot/config.txt file. Worse, the old install file may not be fully applicable to the current version of Raspbian. You are better off to edit the file making the changes you actually need.

```
# nano /boot/config.txt
```

If you think you have messed up badly, you can recover by copying the backup file over it and start over.

When making changes, you can sometimes just uncomment a line. In other cases you will need to add lines (at the end of the file is best). If you have a directive in conflict, you can comment it out with a hash (#) character in the first column and simply add your change at the end of the file.

Make the following changes:

```
dtparam=spi=on
max_usb_current=1
hdmi_force_hotplug=1
config_hdmi_boost=7
hdmi_group=2
hdmi_mode=1
hdmi_mode=87
hdmi_drive=1
hdmi_cvt 800 480 60 6 0 0 0
dtoverlay=ads7846,cs=1,penirq=25,penirq_pull=2,speed=50000,ke
```

Save your changes. This step replaces line 3 of the install script.

Edit /boot/cmdline.txt

The *non-noobs* step that is performed next is line 7 of Listing 24-1. Like the previous step, it clobbers the file with potentially incompatible options (it may affect the path to the root device). It is better to simply edit the file with the changes needed. Add the following text at the end of the line, with a space separating any previous text (for noobs and non-noobs):

```
fbcon=map:10 fbcon=font:ProFont6x11
```

Save the changes.

File 99-fbturbo.conf

Line 9 of the Listing 24-1 install script no longer applies. For better or for worse, Raspbian Linux, like Debian, uses systemd. There is no longer a /etc/inittab file so that step can be skipped.

Line 10 on the other hand instructs us to copy the following:

```
# cp -rf ./usr/99-fbturbo.conf-HDMI /usr/share/X11/xorg.
conf.d/99-fbturbo.conf
```

File 99-calibration.conf-5

Script line 11 does not apply (directory /etc/X11/xorg.conf.d is not searched) and should be skipped.

Perform the following copy, noting the change in the second pathname (underlined):

cp -rf ./usr/99-calibration.conf-5 /usr/share/X11/xorg.
conf.d/99-calibration.conf

The script used target directory /etc/X11, but the correct directory name is /usr/share/X11 in the command above.

Driver Install

The install script attempts to determine if:

1. This is a Raspberry Pi (lines 16–17), and

2. The version of the Raspbian Linux (lines 18–19).

Test #1 depends upon the host name of your Pi being "raspberrypi." If you had already customized the host name and ran that script, it would have installed the wrong driver, thinking it was *not* a Pi. Oops!

There are some tests for the version of Raspbian Linux performed in script lines 21 and 25. These are based upon the results of:

uname -v
#1110 SMP Mon Apr 16 15:18:51 BST 2018

The version number in this example is 1110. Line 21 indicates that no driver install is required *if your Raspbian version is less than 970*. In that case it is time to simply reboot (perform a shutdown and power off instead). On the other hand, a recent version of Raspbian, *version 1023 or later requires that a driver be installed.*

In your ~pi/LCD directory, there should exist the debian driver package you want to install. To see what you're installing, query the package file with -c using the file name shown:

```
# dpkg -c xserver-xorg-input-evdev_2.10.5-1_armhf.deb
drwxr-xr-x root/root        0 2017-01-18 18:26 ./
drwxr-xr-x root/root        0 2017-01-18 18:26 ./usr/
drwxr-xr-x root/root        0 2017-01-18 18:26 ./usr/lib/
drwxr-xr-x root/root        0 2017-01-18 18:26 ./usr/lib/xorg/
drwxr-xr-x root/root        0 2017-01-18 18:26 ./usr/lib/xorg/
                                               modules/
drwxr-xr-x root/root        0 2017-01-18 18:26 ./usr/lib/xorg/
                                               modules/input/
-rw-r--r-- root/root    39292 2017-01-18 18:26 ./usr/lib/xorg/
                                               modules/input/evdev_drv.so
drwxr-xr-x root/root        0 2017-01-18 18:26 ./usr/share/
drwxr-xr-x root/root        0 2017-01-18 18:26 ./usr/share/X11/
drwxr-xr-x root/root        0 2017-01-18 18:26 ./usr/share/
                                               X11/xorg.conf.d/
-rw-r--r-- root/root     1099 2017-01-18 18:26 ./usr/share/X11/
                                               xorg.conf.d/10-evdev.conf
drwxr-xr-x root/root        0 2017-01-18 18:26 ./usr/share/bug/
drwxr-xr-x root/root        0 2017-01-18 18:26 ./usr/share/
                                               bug/xserver-xorg-input-evdev/
drwxr-xr-x root/root        0 2017-01-18 18:26 ./usr/share/doc/
drwxr-xr-x root/root        0 2017-01-18 18:26 ./usr/share/
                                               doc/xserver-xorg-input-evdev/
-rw-r--r-- root/root     6293 2017-01-18 18:26 ./usr/share/doc/\
                                               xserver-xorg-input-evdev/
                                               changelog.Debian.gz
-rw-r--r-- root/root    83217 2017-01-18 07:15 ./usr/share/doc/\
                                               xserver-xorg-input-evdev/
                                               changelog.gz
```

```
-rw-r--r-- root/root        4988 2017-01-18 18:26 ./usr/share/doc/\
                                xserver-xorg-input-evdev/copyright
drwxr-xr-x root/root           0 2017-01-18 18:26 ./usr/share/man/
drwxr-xr-x root/root           0 2017-01-18 18:26 ./usr/share/
                            man/man4/
-rw-r--r-- root/root        4306 2017-01-18 18:26 ./usr/share/man/
                            man4/evdev.4.gz
lrwxrwxrwx root/root           0 2017-01-18 18:26 ./usr/share/
                            bug/xserver-xorg-\
                              input-evdev/script -> ../xserver-
                              xorg-core/script
```

Install the debian package using the following command:

```
# dpkg -i -B xserver-xorg-input-evdev_2.10.5-1_armhf.deb
```

After that install completes, perform the last copy command, from line 32 of the script:

```
# cp -rf /usr/share/X11/xorg.conf.d/10-evdev.conf /usr/share/
X11/xorg.conf.d/45-evdev.conf
```

Shutdown

Now it is time to hook up the hardware with the Pi *powered off.* Perform a system shutdown:

```
# sync
# /sbin/shutdown -h now
```

The shutdown procedure will normally perform the sync command for you, but I like the comfort of knowing it has been done (it flushes out your unwritten disk cache).

Plugging In

At this point the software and configuration is ready. With the power off, plug the LCD unit into the Pi with the 13x2 connector interfacing one end of the Pi's GPIO strip as shown in Figure 24-3. The illustration is from the GPIO side, not fully seated so that you can see the pins being inserted.

Figure 24-3. *The 5 inch LCD 13x2 connector being attached to the GPIO strip, at the end opposite of the USB connectors (Pi 3 B+). The connector is not yet fully seated.*

It is very easy to get this wrong, so check and double-check. A mistake here might ruin your day. If this is mated correctly, the HDMI connectors should line up on the opposite side as shown in Figure 24-4.

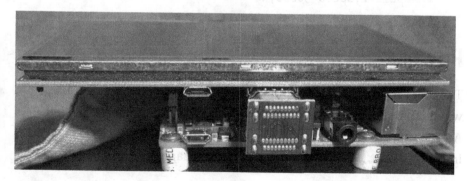

Figure 24-4. *The LCD attached to the Pi using the supplied HDMI to HDMI side adapter*

If the HDMI adapters don't seem to be aligned, recheck that you have the 13x2 connector plugged into the GPIO strip correctly.

With the power cables in inserted, power the unit on. The LCD should display a brief flicker of light as the backlighting starts up. If you see no activity at all, it might be wise to immediately power off and recheck connections.

Boot

Once the Pi is booting up, watch for the desktop to appear. Once your desktop appears and a little mouse arrow is displayed, try tapping the screen to move the arrow. If the touch controls fail to work, check the following:

- Recheck the mating of connections. A bad connection or misplaced connection will affect the touch control.

- Recheck the /boot/config.txt and /boot/cmdline.txt files.

- Check the power usage (next section).

- Check the revision of the LCD panel. Older units used GPIO 22 for the penirq. This is specified in the /boot/config.txt file, underlined below:

    dtoverlay=ads7846,cs=1,penirq=25,penirq_
    pull=2,speed=50000,ke

Power

The unit I have consumes about 242 mA with backlight on and 168 mA when off. Be sure that your Pi and LCD panel are adequately supplied. A 2.5 A supply is recommended for the Pi 3 B+ but with the LCD plugged into a USB port, you might run out of current capacity during peak usage.

Connections

The connections on the 13x2 connector are described in Table 24-1. When wiring the touch controls manually, be careful not to confuse connections "MO" and "MI." These curiously labeled connections indicate MISO (MO) and MOSI (MI) respectively, using the slave device point of view.

Table 24-1. *Connections of the 13x2 LCD Connector*

Description	Pin	#	#	Pin	Description
Power (+5V)	+5V	2	1	+3.3V	
Power (+5V)	+5V	4	3		
Ground	Gnd	6	5		
NC		8	7		
NC		10	9	Gnd	Ground
NC		12	11		
Gnd	Gnd	14	13		
NC		16	15		
NC		18	17	+3.3V	
Gnd	Gnd	20	19	MI	MOSI
Pen IRQ	GPIO 25	22	21	MO	MISO
NC		24	23	SCK	SCK
Pen Chip Select	GPIO-7	26	25	Gnd	Ground

Summary

One problem that often occurs is that hardware gets sale priced when the software becomes stale. This happens as the operating systems are updated and the software remains static. This can work in your favor, if you can work through the details of the install manually, as was done in this chapter.

The LCD screen presented provides you with a flavor of what to expect in similar offerings. One thing to be careful of is to make sure that any necessary driver support exists for your version of Linux before you buy.

A touch-sensitive LCD screen opens many new possibilities for your imagination.

## CHAPTER 25

Real-Time Clock

The DS3231 module sold for the Arduino is perfect for the Raspberry Pi because the IC operates from a range of +2.3 to 5.5 V. This permits the Pi user to power it from the Pi's +3.3 V supply and wire it up to the I²C bus. The module sports a battery backup, allowing it to keep accurate time when the Pi is powered off. The DS3231 includes temperature measurement and adjustment to maintain timekeeping accuracy.

This chapter will exercise the DS3231 with a C program to set and read the date/time. Additionally, there is a 1 Hz output that can be sensed from a GPIO port should you have application for it. The DS3231 RTC (real-time clock) also provides a fairly accurate temperature reading.

DS3231 Overview

A front side photo of the module is provided in Figure 25-1. The module came assembled with right angled pins, which insert nicely into the breadboard. Mine also arrived from eBay with the battery installed but don't count on that. There are often battery shipping restrictions. You may want to purchase a battery separately.

© Warren Gay 2018
W. Gay, *Advanced Raspberry Pi*, https://doi.org/10.1007/978-1-4842-3948-3_25

Figure 25-1. *The front view of the DS3231 module inserted into the breadboard*

From the list of connection labels, it is plain that this is an I²C device. Apart from the power and I²C connections, there is an output labeled SQW, which can be configured to produce a 1 Hz pulse. In this chapter, I suggest you wire it to GPIO 22 for a demonstration. Figure 25-2 illustrates the backside of the pcb.

Figure 25-2. *The backside view of the DS3231 with a battery installed*

Tip Buying a fresh battery ahead of time is recommended, since batteries often arrive exhausted or are not included due to shipping regulations.

Hookup

The DS3231 module also includes an AT24C32 4kx8 I²C EEPROM that can be used, but this will be left as an exercise for the reader. The wiring diagram as it affects the RTC chip is shown in Figure 25-3. The hookup of the SQW output is optional. It can be used to get a 1 Hz pulse at precise intervals.

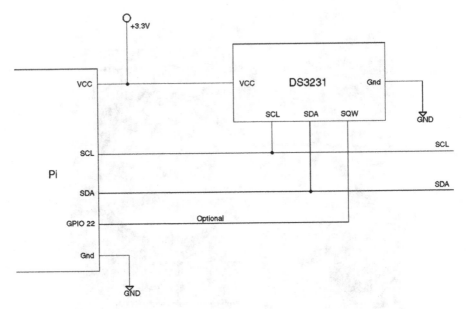

Figure 25-3. *Hookup of the DS3231 to the Raspberry Pi I2C bus*

The module runs at +3.3 V so this is easy to wire up because the Pi and the module share the same power source. Simply wire SDA and SCL connections and the power to the device. Don't forget the ground connection.

With the module hooked up to the Pi's I²C bus, you should be able to detect it.

```
$ i2cdetect -y 1
     0  1  2  3  4  5  6  7  8  9  a  b  c  d  e  f
00:          -- -- -- -- -- -- -- -- -- -- -- -- --
10: -- -- -- -- -- -- -- -- -- -- -- -- -- -- -- --
20: -- -- -- -- -- -- -- -- -- -- -- -- -- -- -- --
30: -- -- -- -- -- -- -- -- -- -- -- -- -- -- -- --
40: -- -- -- -- -- -- -- -- -- -- -- -- -- -- -- --
50: -- -- -- -- -- -- -- 57 -- -- -- -- -- -- -- --
60: -- -- -- -- -- -- -- -- 68 -- -- -- -- -- -- --
70: -- -- -- -- -- -- -- --
```

The numbers shown are hexadecimal addresses of the discovered devices. The 0x68 device is the DS3231, while 0x57 is the AT24C32 EEPROM device. If your devices fail to be discovered, shut down your Pi and recheck your wiring.

Note   The DS3231 RTC uses I2C address 0x68.

Register Map

The DS3231 is compatible with the former 5 V DS1307 chip, but there has been the addition of two alarms among other features. The declaration of the DS3231 registers in C are illustrated in Listing 25-1. Each portion of the register layout is described as a substructure. For example, struct s_00 is the layout for the register at byte offset 0x00.

Listing 25-1. The full C language register map for the DS3231

```
0023: struct s_ds3231_regs {
0024:    struct s_00 {                    /* Seconds */
0025:            uint8_t secs_1s  : 4;    /* Ones digit: seconds */
0026:            uint8_t secs_10s : 3;    /* Tens digit: seconds */
0027:            uint8_t mbz_0    : 1;
0028:    } s00;
0029:    struct s_01 {                    /* Minutes */
0030:            uint8_t mins_1s  : 4;    /* Ones digit: minutes */
0031:            uint8_t mins_10s : 3;    /* Tens digit: minutes */
0032:            uint8_t mbz_1    : 1;
0033:    } s01;
0034:    union u_02 {                     /* Hours */
0035:            struct {
```

```
0036:                      uint8_t hour_1s  : 4;   /* Ones digit:
                           hours */
0037:                      uint8_t hour_10s : 1;   /* Tens digit:
                           hours (24hr mode) */
0038:                      uint8_t ampm     : 1;   /* AM=0/PM=1 */
0039:                      uint8_t mode_1224: 1;   /* Mode bit:
                           12=1/24=0 hour format */
0040:              } hr12;
0041:          struct {
0042:                      uint8_t hour_1s  : 4;   /* Ones digit:
                           hours */
0043:                      uint8_t hour_10s : 3;   /* Tens digit:
                           hours (24hr mode) */
0044:                      uint8_t mode_1224: 1;   /* Mode bit:
                           12=1/24=0 hour format */
0045:              } hr24;
0046:      } u02;
0047:    struct s_03 {                       /* Weekday */
0048:              uint8_t wkday    : 3;     /* Day of week (1-7) */
0049:              uint8_t mbz_2    : 5;
0050:    } s03;
0051:    struct s_04 {                       /* Day of month */
0052:              uint8_t day_1s   : 4;     /* Ones digit: day of
                                                month (1-31) */
0053:              uint8_t day_10s  : 2;     /* Tens digit: day of
                                                month */
0054:              uint8_t mbz_3    : 2;
0055:    } s04;
0056:    struct s_05 {                       /* Month */
0057:              uint8_t month_1s : 4;     /* Ones digit: month
                                                (1-12) */
```

```
0058:            uint8_t month_10s: 1;   /* Tens digit: month */
0059:            uint8_t mbz_4    : 2;
0060:            uint8_t century  : 1;   /* Century */
0061:    } s05;
0062:    struct s_06 {                   /* Year */
0063:            uint8_t year_1s  : 4;   /* Ones digit: BCD year */
0064:            uint8_t year_10s : 4;   /* Tens digit: BCD year */
0065:    } s06;
0066:    struct s_07 {                   /* Alarm Seconds */
0067:            uint8_t alrms01  : 4;   /* Alarm BCD 1s seconds */
0068:            uint8_t alrms10  : 3;   /* Alarm BCD 10s
                                            Seconds */
0069:            uint8_t AxM1     : 1;   /* Alarm Mask 1 */
0070:    } s07;                          /* Alarm Seconds */
0071:    struct s_08 {                   /* Alarm Minutes */
0072:            uint8_t alrmm01  : 4;   /* Alarm BCD 1s Minutes */
0073:            uint8_t alrmm10  : 3;   /* Alarm BCD 10s
                                            Minutes */
0074:            uint8_t AxM2     : 1;   /* Alarm Mask 2 */
0075:    } s08;                          /* Alarm Minutes */
0076:    union u_09 {                    /* Alarm Hours */
0077:            struct {
0078:                    uint8_t alr_hr10 : 1;   /* Alarm 10s
                                                    Hours */
0079:                    uint8_t alr_ampm : 1;   /* Alarm am=0/
                                                    pm=1 */
0080:                    uint8_t alr_1224 : 1;   /* Alarm 12=1 */
0081:                    uint8_t AxM3     : 1;   /* Alarm Mask 3 */
0082:            } ampm;
0083:            struct {
```

```
0084:                        uint8_t alr_hr10 : 2;    /* Alarm 10s
                                                        Hours */

0085:                        uint8_t alr_1224 : 1;    /* Alarm 24=0 */
0086:                        uint8_t AxM3     : 1;    /* Alarm Mask 3 */
0087:              } hrs24;
0088:      } u09;                              /* Alarm 1 Hours */
0089:      union u_0A {                        /* Alarm Date */
0090:              struct {
0091:                        uint8_t day1s    : 4;    /* Alarm 1s
                                                         date */
0092:                        uint8_t day10s   : 2;    /* 10s date */
0093:                        uint8_t dydt     : 1;    /* Alarm dy=1 */
0094:                        uint8_t AxM4     : 1;    /* Alarm Mask 4 */
0095:              } dy;
0096:              struct {
0097:                        uint8_t day1s    : 4;    /* Alarm 1s
                                                         date */
0098:                        uint8_t day10    : 2;    /* Alarm 10s
                                                         date */
0099:                        uint8_t dydt     : 1;    /* Alarm dt=0 */
0100:                        uint8_t AxM4     : 1;    /* Alarm Mask 4 */
0101:              } dt;
0102:      } u0A;
0103:      struct s_08 s0B;                    /* Alarm 2 Minutes */
0104:      union u_09 u0C;                     /* Alarm 2 Hours */
0105:      union u_0A u0D;                     /* Alarm 2 Date */
0106:      struct s_0E {                       /* Control */
0107:              uint8_t A1IE     : 1;       /* Alarm 1 Int enable */
0108:              uint8_t A2IE     : 1;       /* Alarm 2 Int enable */
0109:              uint8_t INTCN    : 1;       /* SQW signal when 1 */
0110:              uint8_t RS1      : 1;       /* Rate select 1 */
```

```
0111:            uint8_t RS2      : 1;   /* Rate select 2 */
0112:            uint8_t CONV     : 1;   /* Temp conversion */
0113:            uint8_t BBSQW    : 1;   /* Enable square wave */
0114:            uint8_t NEOSC    : 1;   /* /EOSC: Enable */
0115:    } sOE;
0116:    struct s_OF {                    /* Control/status */
0117:            uint8_t A1F      : 1;   /* Alarm 1 Flag */
0118:            uint8_t A2F      : 1;   /* Alarm 2 Flag */
0119:            uint8_t bsy      : 1;   /* Busy flag */
0120:            uint8_t en32khz  : 1;   /* Enable 32kHz out */
0121:            uint8_t zeros    : 3;
0122:            uint8_t OSF      : 1;   /* Stop Osc when 1 */
0123:    } sOF;
0124:    struct s_10 {                    /* Aging offset */
0125:            int8_t data      : 8;   /* Data */
0126:    } s10;
0127:    struct s_11 {
0128:            int8_t temp      : 8;   /* Signed int temp */
0129:    } s11;
0130:    struct s_12 {
0131:            uint8_t mbz      : 6;
0132:            uint8_t frac     : 2;   /* Fractional temp bits */
0133:    } s12;
0134: } __attribute__((packed));
```

Register 0x00 (Seconds)

The register at 0x00 consists of two bit fields: s00.secs_1s and s00.secs_10s, repeated below:

```
0024:    struct s_00 {                    /* Seconds */
0025:            uint8_t secs_1s  : 4;   /* Ones digit: seconds */
```

```
0026:                 uint8_t secs_10s : 3;    /* Tens digit: seconds */
0027:                 uint8_t mbz_0    : 1;
0028:    } s00;
```

For students reading this, an explanation about C language bit fields is in order. The colon and the following number specifiy the bit width of the field. The field being divided up is determined by the type, which in this case is an unsigned byte (uint8_t). The fields listed first specify the least significant bits (on the Pi), while the following bit fields represent higher numbered bits. For example, field s00.secs_1s defines bits 3-0 (rightmost), while s00.secs_10s defines for bits 6-4, and s00.mbz_0 declaring bits 7-6 (leftmost two bits). Specifying bit fields saves us from having to use bitwise and shift operations to move values in and out.

The members secs_1s and secs_10s represent BCD (binary coded decimal) digits, for the time in seconds. So a value of 0x23 (in the uint8_t) byte represents the decimal value 23. These and the other time values are automatically incremented by the RTC (real-time clock) as the DS3231 IC keeps time.

Register 0x01 (Minutes)

The minutes reading is provided at byte offset 0x01, in a format similar to the seconds component. Again, members mins_10s and mins_1s are the BCD digits of the minutes time component.

```
0029:    struct s_01 {                     /* Minutes */
0030:                 uint8_t mins_1s  : 4;    /* Ones digit: minutes */
0031:                 uint8_t mins_10s : 3;    /* Tens digit: minutes */
0032:                 uint8_t mbz_1    : 1;
0033:    } s01;
```

Fields with names like mbz_1, are "must be zero" fields and can otherwise be ignored.

Register 0x02 (Hours)

The hours component at byte offset 0x02 is a little more interesting because it can exist in two *views*. The component u03.hr12 selects a 12-hour format while union member u02.hr24 selects a 24-hour format. The view that is used is determined by the member mode_1224. When member mode_1224 is a 1-bit, then the correct view to be used is u02.hr12, otherwise u02.hr24 should be used instead.

```
0034:    union u_02 {                              /* Hours */
0035:          struct {
0036:                  uint8_t hour_1s  : 4;    /* Ones digit:
                                                    hours */
0037:                  uint8_t hour_10s : 1;    /* Tens digit:
                                                    hours (24hr
                                                    mode) */
0038:                  uint8_t ampm     : 1;    /* AM=0/PM=1 */
0039:                  uint8_t mode_1224: 1;    /* Mode bit:
                                                    12=1/24=0
                                                    hour format */
0040:          } hr12;
0041:          struct {
0042:                  uint8_t hour_1s  : 4;    /* Ones digit:
                                                    hours */
0043:                  uint8_t hour_10s : 3;    /* Tens digit:
                                                    hours (24hr
                                                    mode) */
0044:                  uint8_t mode_1224: 1;    /* Mode bit:
                                                    12=1/24=0
                                                    hour format */
0045:          } hr24;
0046:    } u02;
```

The member values hours_10s and hours_1s are again BCD values representing the hourly time as decimal digits. In the 24-hour format, there is one additional bit to describe the larger hourly 10s digit.

In the 12-hour format, the value of u02.hr12.ampm represents AM when the bit is a 0-bit, otherwise PM.

Register 0x03 (Weekday)

The weekday value is found at offset 0x03 in the field s03.wkday.

```
0047:    struct s_03 {                    /* Weekday */
0048:            uint8_t wkday    : 3;    /* Day of week (1-7) */
0049:            uint8_t mbz_2    : 5;
0050:    } s03;
```

Note that valid values range from 1 for Sunday to 7 for Saturday. Unix/Linux uses the value range of 0–6 for weekday instead.

Register 0x04 (Day of Month)

Register offset 0x04 contains the day of the month.

```
0051:    struct s_04 {                    /* Day of month */
0052:            uint8_t day_1s   : 4;    /* Ones digit: day of
                                             month (1-31) */
0053:            uint8_t day_10s  : 2;    /* Tens digit: day of
                                             month */
0054:            uint8_t mbz_3    : 2;
0055:    } s04;
```

Members day_10s and day_1s are BCD values for the day of the month with a range of 1 to 31.

Register 0x05 (Month)

Register offset 0x05 holds the month of the year.

```
0056:    struct s_05 {                     /* Month */
0057:            uint8_t month_1s  : 4;     /* Ones digit: month */
0058:            uint8_t month_10s : 1;     /* Tens digit: month */
0059:            uint8_t mbz_4     : 2;
0060:            uint8_t century   : 1;     /* Century */
0061:    } s05;
```

The values month_10s and months_1s are the month's BCD digits with
a range of 1 to 12. The member century is provided to indicate a century
rollover, from 1999 to 2000.

Register 0x06 (Year)

The year is provided at register offset 0x06.

```
0062:    struct s_06 {                     /* Year */
0063:            uint8_t year_1s   : 4;     /* Ones digit: BCD year */
0064:            uint8_t year_10s  : 4;     /* Tens digit: BCD year */
0065:    } s06;
```

The year_10s and year_1s member pair provide the BCD digits for
the year.

Register 0x07 (Alarm1 Seconds)

The DS3231 chip supports two alarms. This register provides the Alarm 1
seconds value.

```
0066:    struct s_07 {                     /* Alarm Seconds */
0067:            uint8_t alrms01   : 4;     /* Alarm BCD 1s seconds */
```

```
0068:                  uint8_t alrms10   : 3;   /* Alarm BCD 10s Seconds */
0069:                  uint8_t AxM1      : 1;   /* Alarm Mask 1 */
0070:     } s07;
```

Members alrms01 and alrms10 form the pair of seconds digits in BCD form for Alarm 1. Bit field AxM1 is a bit, determines that the seconds must match for the alarm (AxM1=0), or that the alarm is triggered for every second (AxM1=1).

Register 0x08 (Alarm1 Minutes)

The minutes for Alarm 1 are specified by the register at offset 0x08.

```
0071:   struct s_08 {                          /* Alarm Minutes */
0072:                  uint8_t alrmm01   : 4;   /* Alarm BCD 1s Minutes */
0073:                  uint8_t alrmm10   : 3;   /* Alarm BCD 10s Minutes */
0074:                  uint8_t AxM2      : 1;   /* Alarm Mask 2 */
0075:   } s08;
```

The members alrmm10 and alrmm01 specify the BCD pair defining the minutes for the alarm, according to the mask bit AxM2.

Register 0x09 (Alarm 1 Hours)

Register offset 0x09 holds the hour time of the alarm.

```
0076:   union u_09 {                           /* Alarm Hours */
0077:             struct {
0078:                     uint8_t alr_hr10 : 1;   /* Alarm 10s
                                                     Hours */
0079:                     uint8_t alr_ampm : 1;   /* Alarm am=0/
                                                     pm=1 */
0080:                     uint8_t alr_1224 : 1;   /* Alarm 12=1 */
```

```
0081:                        uint8_t AxM3     : 1;   /* Alarm Mask 3 */
0082:              } ampm;
0083:              struct {
0084:                        uint8_t alr_hr10 : 2;   /* Alarm 10s
                                                        Hours */
0085:                        uint8_t alr_1224 : 1;   /* Alarm 24=0 */
0086:                        uint8_t AxM3     : 1;   /* Alarm Mask 3 */
0087:              } hrs24;
```

Like the union u_02 described earlier, there are two views depending upon whether 12 or 24 hour format is used. The hours apply according to the mask bit AxM3.

Register 0x0A (Alarm 1 Date)

The date of the alarm to be applied is given by the offset 0x0A in the DS1332 register file.

```
0089:    union u_0A {                          /* Alarm Date */
0090:           struct {
0091:                    uint8_t day1s    : 4;   /* Alarm 1s
                                                    date */
0092:                    uint8_t day10s   : 2;   /* 10s date */
0093:                    uint8_t dydt     : 1;   /* Alarm dy=1 */
0094:                    uint8_t AxM4     : 1;   /* Alarm Mask 4 */
0095:           } dy;
0096:           struct {
0097:                    uint8_t day1s    : 4;   /* Alarm 1s
                                                    date */
0098:                    uint8_t day10    : 3;   /* Alarm 10s
                                                    date */
0099:                    uint8_t dydt     : 1;   /* Alarm dt=0 */
```

```
0100:                        uint8_t AxM4    : 1;   /* Alarm Mask 4 */
0101:            } dt;
0102:    } uOA;
```

This is a union of two views according to whether a weekday (dydt=1) or a day of the month is used (dydt=0). The pair day10s and day1s is the BCD pair specifying the date. The mask AxM4 determines how the date factors into the alarm.

Alarm 2

Alarm 2 is like Alarm 1, except that it lacks the seconds specifier.

```
0103:    struct s_08 sOB;           /* Alarm 2 Minutes */
0104:    union u_09 uOC;            /* Alarm 2 Hours */
0105:    union u_OA uOD;            /* Alarm 2 Date */
```

It otherwise is used the same way.

Register 0x0E (Control)

Register offset 0x0E offers some control options.

```
0106:    struct s_OE {              /* Control */
0107:            uint8_t A1IE    : 1;   /* Alarm 1 Int enable */
0108:            uint8_t A2IE    : 1;   /* Alarm 2 Int enable */
0109:            uint8_t INTCN   : 1;   /* SQW signal when 1 */
0110:            uint8_t RS1     : 1;   /* Rate select 1 */
0111:            uint8_t RS2     : 1;   /* Rate select 2 */
0112:            uint8_t CONV    : 1;   /* Temp conversion */
0113:            uint8_t BBSQW   : 1;   /* Enable square wave */
0114:            uint8_t NEOSC   : 1;   /* /EOSC: Enable */
0115:    } sOE;
```

Member bits A1IE and A2IE enable alarm interrupts when set to a 1-bit. INTCN determines whether the chip emits an interrupt signal (active low) or a square wave output (INTCN=1). Option BBSQW must also be set to a 1-bit to enable the square wave output. Bits RS1 and RS2 when both set to zero choose a 1 Hz rate for the square wave output. CONV is used to enable the reading of the chip temperature. Finally, bit NEOSC (*not* EOSC) enables the oscillator when a 0-bit and otherwise stops the oscillator when true.

Reading Temperature

The DS3231 keeps accurate time in part because it monitors its own temperature and applies compensation. The temperature can be read by performing the following:

1. Check that the BSY flag and CONV flag is not set.

2. Set the CONV flag to begin the conversion.

3. When the CONV flag resets to zero, read the register value at offsets 0x11 and 0x12.

Register 0x0F (Control/Status)

More control and status bits are available at register offset 0x0F.

```
0116:    struct s_OF {                        /* Control/status */
0117:            uint8_t A1F      : 1;    /* Alarm 1 Flag */
0118:            uint8_t A2F      : 1;    /* Alarm 2 Flag */
0119:            uint8_t bsy      : 1;    /* Busy flag */
0120:            uint8_t en32khz  : 1;    /* Enable 32kHz out */
0121:            uint8_t zeros    : 3;
0122:            uint8_t OSF      : 1;    /* Stop Osc when 1 */
0123:    } sOF;
```

Flags A1F and A2F indicate when the respective alarm has been triggered. The member bsy is the device's busy flag. Member en32khz enables a 32 kHz signal output, when combined with other options. The oscillator is stopped when flag OSF is set to a 1-bit.

Register 0x10 (Aging)

The aging value used internally by the DS3231 to adjust the timekeeping according to temperature and can be read from this register. It is a signed 8-bit number.

```
0124:   struct s_10 {                      /* Aging offset */
0125:          int8_t data    : 8;   /* Data */
0126:   } s10;
```

Register 0x11 and 0x12 (Temperature)

This pair of registers is used to read the internal temperature of the DS3231, to a quarter of a Celsius degree.

```
0127:   struct s_11 {
0128:          int8_t temp     : 8;   /* Signed int temp */
0129:   } s11;
0130:   struct s_12 {
0131:          uint8_t mbz    : 6;
0132:          uint8_t frac   : 2;    /* Fractional temp bits */
0133:   } s12;
```

The value of s11.temp contains the integer component in degrees Celsius. The s12.frac contains a pair of bits specifying a value of 0 to 3. The formation of the temperature can be determined by:

```
s11.temp + (float) s12.frac * 0.25;
```

Reading from DS3231

The full source code for the program ds3231.c is provided in the directory:

```
$ cd ~/RPi/ds3231
```

Build or force rebuilt it as follows:

```
$ make clobber
rm -f *.o core errs.t
rm -f ds3231
$ make
gcc -c -Wall -OO -g ds3231.c -o ds3231.o
gcc ds3231.o -o ds3231
sudo chown root ./ds3231
sudo chmod u+s ./ds3231
```

The function that performs the read from the DS3231 device is illustrated in Listing 25-2.

Listing 25-2. The i2c_rd_rtc() function for the DS3231

```
0136: static const char *node = "/dev/i2c-1";
0137: static int i2c_fd = -1;              /* Device node:
                                               /dev/i2c-1 */
...
0175: static bool
0176: i2c_rd_rtc(ds3231_regs_t *rtc) {
0177:    struct i2c_rdwr_ioctl_data msgset;
0178:    struct i2c_msg iomsgs[2];
0179:    char zero = 0x00;                  /* Register 0x00 */
0180:
0181:    iomsgs[0].addr = 0x68;             /* DS3231 */
0182:    iomsgs[0].flags = 0;               /* Write */
```

```
0183:    iomsgs[0].buf = &zero;           /* Register 0x00 */
0184:    iomsgs[0].len = 1;
0185:
0186:    iomsgs[1].addr = 0x68;           /* DS3231 */
0187:    iomsgs[1].flags = I2C_M_RD;      /* Read */
0188:    iomsgs[1].buf = (char *)rtc;
0189:    iomsgs[1].len = sizeof *rtc;
0190:
0191:    msgset.msgs = iomsgs;
0192:    msgset.nmsgs = 2;
0193:
0194:    return ioctl(i2c_fd,I2C_RDWR,&msgset) == 2;
0195: }
```

This code assumes that the I²C bus has already been opened and the file descriptor saved in i2c_fd (line 137). Two messages are assembled into array iomsgs in line 178. Lines 181 through 184 prepare a write of one byte to indicate that we are addressing starting with register offset 0x00 in the DS3231. Lines 186 to 189 prepare a message to read all of the device's register into buffer structure rtc. The read is a success when ioctl(2) returns 2, indicating that two messages were carried out successfully.

Writing to DS3231

Listing 25-3 lists the function used to write to the DS3231 device.

Listing 25-3. The function i2c_wr_rtc() for writing to the DS3231

```
0198: static bool
0199: i2c_wr_rtc(ds3231_regs_t *rtc) {
0200:    struct i2c_rdwr_ioctl_data msgset;
0201:    struct i2c_msg iomsgs[1];
```

```
0202:   char buf[sizeof *rtc + 1];        /* Work buffer */
0203:
0204:   buf[0] = 0x00;                     /* Register 0x00 */
0205:   memcpy(buf+1,rtc,sizeof *rtc);     /* Copy RTC info */
0206:
0207:   iomsgs[0].addr = 0x68;             /* DS3231 Address */
0208:   iomsgs[0].flags = 0;               /* Write */
0209:   iomsgs[0].buf = buf;               /* Register + data */
0210:   iomsgs[0].len = sizeof *rtc + 1; /* Total msg len */
0211:
0212:   msgset.msgs = &iomsgs[0];
0213:   msgset.nmsgs = 1;
0214:
0215:   return ioctl(i2c_fd,I2C_RDWR,&msgset) == 1;
0216: }
```

This function is similar to the reading function except that only one ioctl(2) message is required. The RTC values to be written are copied to buf in line 205. The first byte is set to 0x00 to indicate the register number that we want to start writing to. The message is prepared in lines 207 to 210, and the actual write is performed in line 215. The operation is a success when ioctl(2) returns the value 1, indicating one successful message was executed.

Reading Temperature

For those that like to know the temperature, the function that reads the temperature is provided in Listing 25-4.

Listing 25-4. Reading the DS3231 temperature

```
0221: static float
0222: read_temp(void) {
```

```
0223:    ds3231_regs_t rtc;
0224:
0225:    do      {
0226:            if ( !i2c_rd_rtc(&rtc) ) {
0227:                    perror("Reading RTC for temp.");
0228:                    exit(2);
0229:            }
0230:    } while ( rtc.sOF.bsy || rtc.sOF.CONV ); /* Until not busy */
0231:
0232:    rtc.sOE.CONV = 1;                    /* Start conversion */
0233:
0234:    if ( !i2c_wr_rtc(&rtc) ) {
0235:            perror("Writing RTC to read temp.");
0236:            exit(2);
0237:    }
0238:
0239:    do      {
0240:            if ( !i2c_rd_rtc(&rtc) ) {
0241:                    perror("Reading RTC for conversion.");
0242:                    exit(2);
0243:            }
0244:    } while ( rtc.sOE.CONV );            /* Until converted */
0245:
0246:    return rtc.s11.temp + (float)rtc.s12.frac * 0.25;
0247: }
```

The function first loops while the sOF.bsy or sOF.CONV flag is true, indicating that the device is busy. The sOE.CONV flag is set in line 232 and then written out in line 234 to the device. After that, the DS3231 is polled to see when the sOE.CONV flag returns to zero. Once sOE.CONV is reset, we can safely read the temperature from the s11 and s12 registers (line 246).

Demo Time

Once the demonstration has been compiled and wired up according to Figure 25-3, we can exercise the C program. The -h option reports usage information:

```
$ ./ds3231 -h
Usage:  /ds3231 [-S time] [-f format] [-d] [-e] [-v] [-h]
where:
        -s      Set RTC clock based upon system date
        -f fmt  Set date format
        -e      Enable 1 Hz output on SQW
        -d      Disable 1 Hz output on SQW
        -t      Display temperature
        -S time Set DS3231 time from given
        -v      Verbose, show SQW register settings
        -h      This help
```

Read Date/Time

To read the device's current date/time, just run the program:

```
$ ./ds3231
RTC time is 2018-08-05 00:54:55 (Sunday)
```

If you get an error, run the i2c-detect again and make sure that the device is wired correctly.

Read Temperature

To read the temperature, use the -t option:

```
$ ./ds3231 -t
RTC time is 2018-08-05 01:23:06 (Sunday)
Temperature is 26.75 C
```

The accuracy of the temperature reading is fairly decent and this fact is instrumental in its timekeeping stability.

Setting RTC

You can set the RTC time using the -S option:

```
$ ./ds3231 -S '2018-08-04 12:00:00'
Set RTC to 2018-08-04 12:00:00 (Saturday)
RTC time is 2018-08-04 12:00:00 (Saturday)
```

The second printed line is the value read back from the RTC device. If you need to use a different format for date/time, supply the -f option.

1 Hz Square Wave

To test the 1 Hz SQW output, use the -e (enable) command. The -v (verbose) option just confirms with some values displayed:

```
$ ./ds3231 -ev
RTC time is 2018-08-05 01:24:34 (Sunday)
 BBSQW=1 INTCN=0 RS2=0 RS1=0
```

Now run the evinput program that was used earlier in the book to monitor the GPIO 22 pin (assuming you wired it as per Figure 25-3). Substitute the GPIO you used, if you chose another:

```
$ ../evinput/evinput -g22
Monitoring for GPIO input changes:

GPIO 22 changed: 0
GPIO 22 changed: 1
GPIO 22 changed: 0
GPIO 22 changed: 1
```

```
GPIO 22 changed: 0
GPIO 22 changed: 1
GPIO 22 changed: 0
```

From the output, you can see that the input changes at a rate of about one half second (a full cycle requires one second).

Kernel Support

Up until now, we have played with the DS3231 device using a C program. But you might already know that Raspbian Linux has kernel module support for the DS3231. Before setting it up, you need to disable ntp (at least temporarily):

```
# systemctl disable systemd-timesyncd.service
```

To configure ds3231 module support in the kernel, perform the following:

1. `sudo -i`

2. Edit /boot/config.txt and add line "dtoverlay=i2c-rtc,ds3231" to the file at the end.

3. Uncomment or add "dtparam=i2c_arm=on" to the same file.

4. Edit file /lib/udev/hwclock-set and comment out the following three lines, by placing a hash (#) in front:

   ```
   #if [ -e /run/systemd/system ] ; then
   #    exit 0
   #fi
   ```

5. Reboot

After rebooting, try the following:

```
# hwclock -r
2018-08-04 08:13:18.719447-0400
```

You can check it against the ds3231 program:

```
# ~pi/RPi/ds3231/ds3231
RTC time is 2018-08-04 12:14:23 (Saturday)
```

There is a difference of four hours here but this is the difference in timezone and daylight savings time. As my Pi is configured, it keeps the time in UTC. To get the DS3231, the kernel module, and the system date all on the same page, you can perform the following:

```
# ~pi/RPi/ds3231/ds3231 -S '2018-08-05 02:22:00'
Set RTC to 2018-08-05 02:22:00 (Sunday)
RTC time is 2018-08-05 02:22:00 (Sunday)
root@rpi3bplus:~# hwclock -s
root@rpi3bplus:~# date
Sat Aug  4 22:22:26 EDT 2018
root@rpi3bplus:~#
```

This can be confusing when there is a timezone offset involved. In the ds3231 -S command, I set the date/time to the UTC date/time required. Then the command hwclock -s causes it to reset the system sense of time from the DS3231 chip. Following that, the date command reports the local time with my timezone offset.

Summary

The ds3231 is the perfect mate for the Raspberry Pi, particularly when they are not network connected. With its battery backup, the ds3231 will keep accurate time to within a few seconds every month.

The program presented gave you insight into the operation of the chip as well as practice communicating with it from C. Within the C program, a demonstration of the bit fields language feature was applied. This is something often only seen in system or device programming.

Finally, the Raspbian kernel support for the ds3231 was demonstrated so that you can use it in future Pi projects. If you're looking for an I²C project, why not try communicating with that onboard EEPROM?

CHAPTER 26

Pi Camera

Some applications require a camera, like a birdie-cam, for example. Giving your Pi an eye can be done fairly inexpensively and is fun. This chapter examines the Pi camera, its installation, and its use.

Hookup

You'll normally get the camera with a flat ribbon cable included. Most instructions will just say "plug in the camera" as part of the setup. But how do you plug in this type of cable? Which way does it go? Mine won't go in, what gives?

With the power off, locate the connector labeled "CAMERA" on the Pi. Figure 26-1 illustrates what the connector looks like. Your Pi may still have a protective plastic adhesive strip on top of that connector (mine was red). This is presumably to keep the dust out. Peel it off, and then you should see a connector like the figure. Without peeling off the protective strip, you might be left scratching your head as to how a cable is to fit in there.

© Warren Gay 2018

W. Gay, *Advanced Raspberry Pi*, https://doi.org/10.1007/978-1-4842-3948-3_26

Figure 26-1. *The camera connector on the Pi, with the protective adhesive strip removed (Pi 3 B+)*

In the figure you can see a black C-shaped part of the connector that can be lifted up by gently pulling up the sides (Figure 26-2). This exposes a slot for cable insertion.

Figure 26-2. *Camera connector with the black locking part lifted to receive the ribbon cable (Pi 3 B+)*

With the power off, gently insert the ribbon cable with the contacts facing away from the black part of the connector. In other words, face the contacts toward the label shown in Figure 26-2.

You may or may not still be able to see some contact surface showing after the cable is inserted (Figure 26-3 exposes some contact area above the connector). Don't use too much force but use enough to fully insert. While holding the cable, push down on the shoulders of the connector to bind that C-shaped black part into the socket.

Figure 26-3. *Insertion of the camera cable, with the contacts facing away from the black binding part of the connector*

Figure 26-4 illustrates what the backside of the cable should look like in the connector. The blue strip of the cable will be facing that black binding part of the socket. After pushing the binding component down on the inserted cable, gently pull on the cable to see if it is firmly installed. If it comes out, then try again.

Figure 26-4. *The backside of the cable (blue) should face the black binding C-shapped part of the socket*

Camera

The camera may come with a protective covering, which should be removed. Figure 26-5 illustrates.

Figure 26-5. *Camera with protective lens cover (left) and covering removed (right)*

With the camera hardware ready to go, the Pi can be powered up and configured for the camera.

Configuration

Boot up into the Pi desktop and open the Raspberry Pi Configuration. Choose the Interfaces tab and then enable the camera (Figure 26-6). After enabling the camera, don't forget to click OK and then reboot.

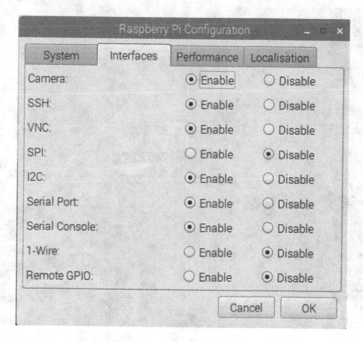

Figure 26-6. *Enabling the camera in the Raspberry Pi Configuration, Interfaces tab. Click OK and then reboot.*

Commands

The Raspbian Linux distribution is convenient because aside from configuration conveniences, it also provides tools for working with the camera among other things. The command `raspistill` can be used to capture an image after a five-second preview period.

```
$ raspistill -o itworks.jpg
```

Figure 26-7 was a capture from the Pi camera using the `raspistill` command. The camera preview only displays on the graphical desktop, which must be running. The preview will also not display in a VNC session but will appear on your monitor.

Figure 26-7. *The author running the raspistill command, exclaiming "it worked!"*

There are currently three commands supporting the camera:

- raspistill for still captures.

- raspivid for recording video.

- raspistillyuv for still captures with no encoding (records YUV/RGB information to the file).

Documentation for these commands can be found here:

```
https://www.raspberrypi.org/app/uploads/2013/07/RaspiCam-
Documentation.pdf
```

Python

If you have an interest in Python, you can try using the supplied Python package picamera. For example, create a Python file with the following statements in it:

```
from picamera import PiCamera
from time import sleep

camera = PiCamera()

camera.start_preview()
sleep(10)
camera.stop_preview()
```

Save that as pieye.py (do *not* name it picamera.py). Then run the program:

```
$ py pieye.py
```

The camera preview will be shown on the graphical desktop, which must be running.

Summary

This chapter gets you up and running with your Pi camera. Raspbian Linux supports it well with bult-in drivers and Raspbian Linux commands like raspistill. With the Raspbian supplied tools, you are well equipped for camera-related projects. Advanced developers can pursue the use of projects like OpenCV (opencv.org).

This chapter also brings this book to a close. I hope the content has inspired you to do more with your Pi. Thank you for allowing me to be your guide.

Power Standards

The following table references the standard ATX power supply voltages, regulation (tolerance), and voltage ranges. This has no direct bearing on the Raspberry Pi but does provide for comparison of power tolerances.

Supply Volts	Tolerance		Minimum	Maximum	Ripple (Peak)
+5 V	±5%	± 0.25 V	+4.75 V	+5.25 V	50 mV
-5 V	±10%	±0.50 V	−4.50 V	−5.50 V	50 mV
+12 V	±5%	±0.60 V	+11.40 V	+12.60 V	120 mV
-12 V	±10%	±1.2 V	−10.8 V	−13.2 V	120 mV
+3.3 V	±5%	±0.165 V	+3.135 V	+3.465 V	50 mV
+5 VSB	±5%	±0.25 V	+4.75 V	+5.25 V	50 mV

© Warren Gay 2018
W. Gay, *Advanced Raspberry Pi*, https://doi.org/10.1007/978-1-4842-3948-3

APPENDIX B

Electronics Reference

The experienced electronic hobbyist or engineer will already know these formulas and units. This reference material is provided as a convenience for the student or beginning hobbyist.

Ohm's Law

Using the following triangle, cover the unknown property to determine the formula needed. For example, if current (I) is unknown, cover the I in the diagram and the formula $\frac{V}{R}$ remains.

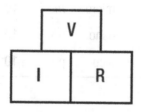

© Warren Gay 2018
W. Gay, *Advanced Raspberry Pi*, https://doi.org/10.1007/978-1-4842-3948-3

Power

Power can be computed from these formulas:

$$P = I \times V$$

$$P = I^2 \times V$$

$$P = \frac{V^2}{R}$$

Units

The following chart summarizes the main metric prefixes used in electronics.

Category	Name	Prefix	Factor
Multiples	mega	M	10^6
	kilo	k	10^3
Fraction	milli	m	10^{-3}
	micro	m	10^{-6}
	nano	n	10^{-9}
	pico	p	10^{-12}

Bibliography

1. Kabade, Rajat. "Intel's Raspberry Pi Competitor Comes with Sky-High Price Tag." Open Source For You. January 23, 2017. Accessed May 31, 2018. `https://opensourceforu.com/2016/12/intel-raspberry-pi-competitor-sky-high-price/`.

2. "Raspberry Pi." Wikipedia. May 29, 2018. Accessed May 31, 2018. `https://en.wikipedia.org/wiki/Raspberry_Pi`.

3. "Coloured Splash Screen," R-Pi Troubleshooting. `<http://elinux.org/R-Pi_Troubleshooting#Coloured_splash_screen>`

4. "Ethernet Connection Is Lost When a USB Device Is Plugged In," R-Pi Troubleshooting. `<http://elinux.org/R-Pi_Troubleshooting#Ethernet_connection_is_lost_when_a_USB_device_is_plugged_in>`

5. Matt. "Raspberry Pi Status LEDs Explained." Raspberry Pi Spy. November 10, 2016. Accessed June 04, 2018. `https://www.raspberrypi-spy.co.uk/2013/02/raspberry-pi-status-leds-explained/`.

6. "RPI Safe Mode." RPi-Cam-Web-Interface - ELinux. org. Accessed June 05, 2018. `https://elinux.org/RPI_safe_mode`.

7. "meminfo:," "The /proc Filesystem." <http://www.kernel.org/doc/Documentation/filesystems/proc.txt>

8. Ascierto, Jerry. "Cypress Acquires Anchor Chips." EDN. Accessed June 08, 2018. https://www.edn.com/electronics-news/4356714/Cypress-Acquires-Anchor-Chips.

9. "Wear Leveling Methodology," White Paper, SanDisk Flash Memory Cards Wear Leveling. <http://ugweb.cs.ualberta.ca/~c274/resources/hardware/SDcards/WPaperWearLevelv1.0.pdf>

10. "Chapter 3, SD Bus Topology," SD Card Interface Description, SD Card Product Manual. <http://www.convict.lu/pdf/ProdManualSDCardv1.9.pdf>

11. "Baudot Code," Baudo Code, From Wikipedia, the free encyclopedia. <http://en.wikipedia.org/wiki/Baudot_code>

12. "Microchip 3V Tips 'n Tricks." <http://www.newark.com/pdfs/techarticles/microchip/3_3vto5vAnalogTipsnTricksBrchr.pdf>

13. "Interfacing 3V and 5V applications AN240," Application Note, Phillips Semiconductors. <https://datasheetspdf.com/pdf/501591/Philips/AN240/1>

14. Gay, Warren. *Custom Raspberry Pi Interfaces: Design and Build Hardware Interfaces for the Raspberry Pi*. United States: Apress, 2017.

15. "1-Wire," From Wikipedia, the free encyclopedia.
    `<http://en.wikipedia.org/wiki/1-Wire>`

16. "1-Wire® (Protocol)," Company: Dallas
    Semiconductor/Maxim, Linus Wong. `<coecsl.ece.`
    `illinois.edu/ge423/sensorprojects/1-wire_`
    `full.doc>`

17. "I²C," I²C, From Wikipedia, the free encyclopedia.
    `<http://en.wikipedia.org/wiki/I%C2%B2C>`

18. "Serial Peripheral Interface Bus," From Wikipedia,
    the free encyclopedia. `<http://en.wikipedia.org/`
    `wiki/Serial_Peripheral_Interface_Bus>`

Index

Printed in the United States
By Bookmasters